The Reformation

Other Books in the Turning Points Series:

Turning | Points
IN WORLD HISTORY

The Reformation

Stephen P. Thompson, *Book Editor*

David L. Bender, *Publisher*
Bruno Leone, *Executive Editor*
Bonnie Szumski, *Editorial Director*

Greenhaven Press, Inc., San Diego, California

Every effort has been made to trace the owners of copyrighted material. The articles in this volume may have been edited for content, length, and/or reading level. The titles have been changed to enhance the editorial purpose.

No part of this book may be reproduced or used in any form or by any means, electrical, mechanical, or otherwise, including, but not limited to, photocopy, recording, or any information storage and retrieval system, without prior written permission from the publisher.

Library of Congress Cataloging-in-Publication Data

The Reformation / Stephen P. Thompson, book editor.
    p.   cm. — (Turning points in world history)
    Includes bibliographical references and index.
    ISBN 1-56510-961-9 (lib. bdg. : alk. paper). —
ISBN 1-56510-960-0 (pbk. : alk. paper)
    1. Reformation. 2. History, Modern—16th century.
I. Thompson, Stephen P. 1953– . II. Series: Turning points in
world history (Greenhaven Press)
D228.R44 1999
909.5—dc21   98-38941
                                        CIP

Cover photo: AKG, London

©1999 by Greenhaven Press, Inc.
P.O. Box 289009, San Diego, CA 92198-9009

Printed in the U.S.A.

Contents

Chapter 1: The Origins of the Protestant Reformation

1. The Church and Society Before the Reformation
by Karl H. Dannenfeldt   27

The Christian church was the most extensive and powerful institution in medieval Europe, and the rituals and sacraments of the Church were an integral part of life before the Reformation. Profound economic changes, corruption, and the development of the secular state led to the Church's declining power and influence.

2. Religion and Social Conditions During the Early Sixteenth Century *by James M. Kittelson*   36

Poverty, disease, violence, and high infant mortality made life in Luther's time especially hard. Ordinary people sought comfort and relief from these conditions in church rituals, and they believed that various acts of penance, such as pilgrimages or the purchase of indulgences, would help secure their salvation.

3. Problems in the Catholic Church Prior to the Reformation *by Lewis W. Spitz*   43

In the years just before the Reformation, Catholic popes all too often behaved like Renaissance princes, while immorality and ignorance among the lower clergy also undermined confidence in the Church. These abuses, along with excessive taxation and other monetary abuses, led to widespread calls for reform, even though the Catholic Church was healthy in other respects.

4. Martin Luther and the Appeal of Protestantism
by E. Harris Harbison   52

The origins of the Reformation movement can be traced to the spiritual convictions and actions of the German professor Martin Luther. Out of his study of the Bible and his abhorrence over the sale of indulgences, Luther posted his ninety-five theses and took an unwavering, highly publicized stand against church abuses.

concepts of individualism and tolerance, were unforeseen consequences of Protestant values.

Foreword

Certain past events stand out as pivotal, as having effects and outcomes that change the course of history. These events are often referred to as turning points. Historian Louis L. Snyder provides this useful definition:

> A turning point in history is an event, happening, or stage which thrusts the course of historical development into a different direction. By definition a turning point is a great event, but it is even more—a great event with the explosive impact of altering the trend of man's life on the planet.

History's turning points have taken many forms. Some were single, brief, and shattering events with immediate and obvious impact. The invasion of Britain by William the Conqueror in 1066, for example, swiftly transformed that land's political and social institutions and paved the way for the rise of the modern English nation. By contrast, other single events were deemed of minor significance when they occurred, only later recognized as turning points. The assassination of a little-known European nobleman, Archduke Franz Ferdinand, on June 28, 1914, in the Bosnian town of Sarajevo was such an event; only after it touched off a chain reaction of political-military crises that escalated into the global conflict known as World War I did the murder's true significance become evident.

Other crucial turning points occurred not in terms of a few hours, days, months, or even years, but instead as evolutionary developments spanning decades or even centuries. One of the most pivotal turning points in human history, for instance—the development of agriculture, which replaced nomadic hunter-gatherer societies with more permanent settlements—occurred over the course of many generations. Still other great turning points were neither events nor developments, but rather revolutionary new inventions and innovations that significantly altered social customs and ideas, military tactics, home life, the spread of knowledge, and the human condition in general. The developments of writing, gunpowder, the printing press, antibiotics, the electric light, atomic energy, television, and the computer, the last two of which have recently ushered in the world-altering information age, represent only some of these innovative turning points.

Each anthology in the Greenhaven Turning Points in World History series presents a group of essays chosen for their accessibility. The anthology's structure also enhances this accessibility. First, an introductory essay provides a general overview of the principal events and figures involved, placing the topic in its historical context. The essays that follow explore various aspects in more detail, some targeting political trends and consequences, others social, literary, cultural, and/or technological ramifications, and still others pivotal leaders and other influential figures. To aid the reader in choosing the material of immediate interest or need, each essay is introduced by a concise summary of the contributing writer's main themes and insights.

In addition, each volume contains extensive research tools, including a collection of excerpts from primary source documents pertaining to the historical events and figures under discussion. In the anthology on the French Revolution, for example, readers can examine the works of Rousseau, Voltaire, and other writers and thinkers whose championing of human rights helped fuel the French people's growing desire for liberty; the French *Declaration of the Rights of Man and Citizen*, presented to King Louis XVI by the French National Assembly on October 2, 1789; and eyewitness accounts of the attack on the royal palace and the horrors of the Reign of Terror. To guide students interested in pursuing further research on the subject, each volume features an extensive bibliography, which for easy access has been divided into separate sections by topic. Finally, a comprehensive index allows readers to scan and locate content efficiently. Each of the anthologies in the Greenhaven Turning Points in World History series provides students with a complete, detailed, and enlightening examination of a crucial historical watershed.

Introduction: Intimations of the Modern World

The beginning of the sixteenth century was a time of momentous change in Europe, and the Reformation played a seminal role in reshaping the political and social life of European society. Because so many modern ideas and institutions first took shape in the sixteenth century, historians call this the "early modern" period. The three leading figures of the Reformation were Martin Luther from Germany; Ulrich Zwingli from Zurich, Switzerland; and the Frenchman John Calvin, who spent the second half of his life in exile in Geneva, Switzerland. Luther and Calvin were undoubtedly the most prolific and most published writers in Europe in the sixteenth century. Over eighty editions of Calvin's various works, for example, were published between 1560 and 1600 in England alone. These Reformation writers radically changed the way Europeans—and later, Americans—looked at their religion, their society, and themselves.

Between 1517, the year Martin Luther posted his ninety-five theses on indulgences, and 1559, the year the English church was settled in its Protestant form, the religious beliefs and habits of millions of Europeans changed dramatically. Within those forty years, the power of the Catholic Church was diminished in many European countries and supplanted entirely in others by powerful national princes. Many practices that had been under the control of the Catholic Church now came under state control. As scholar Charles G. Nauert Jr. explains,

> Heretofore, all society had been based on the acceptance of the one "true religion" by all people, and the other institutions—marriage, property, education, the state—derived their sanction from the religious ideology acknowledged by all. The Church, the institution that embodied, created, and applied the prevailing ideology, controlled many matters that modern man regards as concerns of the secular state: educa-

tion, censorship of books, and regulation of marriage and of many other types of legal relationships. The practical effect of the Reformation was to demolish, or at least decisively to weaken, the control of religious officials over life.[1]

In addition to the shift of powers to the state, Christianity itself had fragmented into five main branches: the Catholic Church and the four major branches of Protestantism. These branches were: Lutheran, Reformed (based primarily on the theology of Calvin), Anabaptist (the radical groups, emphasizing complete separation of church and state), and Anglican (the compromise solution in England). Some of these churches were in bitter conflict with each other as well as with the Catholic Church well into the next century.

The Reformation of the sixteenth century was an age of turmoil and repression, civil wars between Protestant and Catholic groups, and persecution of dissidents by Protestants and Catholics alike. Yet it was also the breeding ground for modern ideas of freedom of speech, freedom of religion, and social equality. As Harvard historian Steven Ozment suggests, "To the people of all nationalities the first Protestants bequeathed in spite of themselves a heritage of spiritual freedom and equality, the consequences of which are still working themselves out in the world today."[2]

Abuses in the Church

Of the social and intellectual conditions that contributed to the spread of the Reformation, corruption in the Catholic Church deserves prominent mention. Though some modern scholars question the extent of corruption, they concede that the popular perception in Luther's day was that corruption was widespread and profound. Many people believed that Christianity had steadily decayed through the centuries, as in the following analysis from the Italian writer Niccolo Machiavelli 1513:

> If the Christian religion had from the beginning been maintained according to the principles of the founder, the Christian states and republics would have been much more united and happy than what they are. Nor can there be a greater

proof of its decadence than to witness the fact that the nearer people are to the Church of Rome, which is the head of our religion, the less religious they are. And whoever examines the principles upon which that religion is founded, and sees how widely different from those principles its present practice and application are, will judge that her ruin or chastisement is near at hand.[3]

This widespread perception of corruption is reinforced by a 1510 sermon by Johann Geiler preached in front of the Emperor Maximilian. Geiler predicted that "since neither pope, nor emperor, kings nor bishops, will reform our life, God will send a man for the purpose. I hope to see that day . . . but I am too old. Many of you will see it; think, then, I pray you of these words."[4] The corruption alluded to by both Machiavelli and Geiler was of two basic kinds: corruption and immorality among the clergy and corruption and abuse within the structure of the church itself.

The morals of the Catholic clergy at the beginning of the Reformation were frequently lax, as they had been for centuries. Though priests were supposed to be celibate, as many as half of all priests had unofficial wives and children, according to some scholarly estimates. This was a serious social problem. The famous scholar Erasmus, for example, was the illegitimate son of a priest and a washerwoman who lived together for a time but separated during Erasmus's childhood. Like many others in the same situation, Erasmus's career choices would be severely limited due to the stigma placed on illegitimacy. Because they could not find employment elsewhere, the church offered these illegitimate children careers in the church. Erasmus always resented his illegitimacy, and he felt restricted in the church career forced upon him. But the failure rates of clerical celibacy introduced a widespread distrust of the clergy and a popular perception of hypocrisy among the clergy. This issue of clerical celibacy may have contributed more than any other abuse to the readiness of the people to listen to the message of reform.

Also at this time, many Catholic clergy were failing to fulfill their pastoral duties, absenteeism being one of the main causes. As Alister McGrath notes,

> In Germany, it is reported that only one parish in fourteen
> had its pastor in residence. The Frenchman Antoine du Prat,
> archbishop of Sens, turned up for only one service at his
> cathedral: moreover, his presence and role at this service was
> somewhat passive, since it was his funeral.[5]

A related problem that often interfered with the dedication
of clergy is the problem of nepotism, through which church
appointments were made on the basis of family or other connections rather than on the basis of spiritual qualifications.
McGrath supplies examples of this practice:

> Duke Amadeus VIII of Savoy secured the appointment of his
> son to the senior position of bishop of Geneva in 1451; if
> anyone had misgivings about the fact that the new bishop
> had never been ordained and was only eight years of age,
> they were wise enough to keep quiet about them. Pope
> Alexander VI, a member of the Borgia family (famous for its
> lethal dinner parties), secured his election to the papacy in
> 1492 despite having several mistresses and seven children,
> largely because he bought the papacy outright over the heads
> of his nearest rivals.[6]

These abuses were widely known and discussed, rivalled in
terms of popular resentment only by the financial practices
of the Catholic Church, including various forms of taxation
and the sale of indulgences.

The Problem of Indulgences

The abuse that most ignited the fervor of Luther and other
reformers was the Catholic doctrine of indulgences. Indulgences were conceived as a way for repentant sinners to gain
release from the temporal penalties their sins called down on
them. In the Catholic tradition, confession to priests provided absolution for the spiritual guilt and punishment each
sinner ought to have received. But the church taught that
genuine repentance must be demonstrated through acts of
devotion and penitence, such as pilgrimages. This temporal
penalty, as it was called, could also be satisfied by writs of in-

dulgence, which excused the recipient from further action. Indulgences gradually became substitutions for various acts of penitence and devotion, such as prayers for the dead. For a sum of money, an indulgence could be acquired by any sinner. The money involved was to be used to further some church cause, such as a crusade against infidels or heretics.

Though in Catholic theory indulgences were never "sold," and though they were never conceived as a substitute for the remorse and contrition that were the essence of repentance, in the popular mind, the purchase of indulgences became a common substitution for acts of devotion and a central part of the process of repentance. The indulgence that became the object of Luther's scorn was the Mainz Indulgence of 1515, initiated as a fund-raiser in order to build St. Peter's Cathedral in Rome. One well-known Dominican friar was selling indulgences in Germany in 1517 with the notorious slogan "so soon as coin in coffer rings, the soul from Purgatory springs."[7] To Luther and many others, this was a monstrous corruption of the concepts of repentance and devotion. So Luther posted his ninety-five theses attacking the doctrine of indulgences, and with the help of the printing press and zealous friends, he became an overnight sensation in Europe for his stance. When Luther refused to recant his criticisms under papal pressure a few years later, he was excommunicated from the Catholic Church and the Reformation was irreversibly underway.

The Role of Martin Luther

Certainly rapid changes in religion and society may have taken place had Martin Luther never been born. But as it is, the events and ideas of the early Reformation bear the undeniable imprint of Luther's spiritual insights and his forceful personality. As scholar Lewis Spitz says,

> Luther, the first reformer, an Augustinian monk, embodied in his own person all the driving forces and reformatory impulses of his generation. He cried out from the depths of his soul, he was pressed into becoming a spokesman of the German nation, and he served as the conscience of Christendom,

for his call corresponded to a widely felt need for reform and spiritual renewal. . . . So many of the subsequent religious and political developments were conditioned and even determined by the nature of Luther's evangelical breakthrough and by the events of the period from 1517 to 1521.[8]

Much evidence shows that Luther was known—and either loved or hated—throughout Europe within several years of posting his ninety-five theses about indulgences in 1517. Within just a few years, this professor at a small German university was carrying on debates in print with such luminaries as king of England Henry VIII and Catholic writer Erasmus.

The basis for Luther's remarkable self-confidence was his insight in 1515 concerning the idea of justification by faith alone. If Christians are saved by their faith and not by their actions, then not only are indulgences unnecessary for salvation, they actually inhibit faith by providing a false confidence to those who buy them. Further, the doctrine of justification by faith led to Luther's second insight that what Christians need to know about faith is to be found in the Bible; it does not require the mediation of priests, the church, or the pope. The logical outcome of this viewpoint was the "priesthood of all believers, a precursor of modern ideas of equality." As scholar Bruce Shelley puts it, "Luther brushed aside the traditional view of the church as a sacred hierarchy headed by the pope and returned to the early Christian view of a community of believers in which all believers are priests called to offer spiritual sacrifices to God."[9] In 1520 Luther published three books in which he expounded these views: *Appeal to the German Nobility*, *The Babylonian Captivity of the Church*, and *The Freedom of the Christian*. Through these books, Luther became the voice of Protestantism throughout Europe.

When the Reformation began, it could be described fairly enough as an attempt to improve the Catholic Church, but within just a few years of Luther's theses, under Luther's guidance, the Reformation had evolved into a full-fledged attempt to transform the face of European society. According to scholar Eugene F. Rice Jr.,

> The Reformation was a passionate debate on the proper
> conditions of salvation. It concerned the very foundation of
> faith and doctrine. Protestants reproached the clergy not so
> much for living badly as for believing badly, for teaching
> false and dangerous things. Luther attacked not the corrup-
> tion of institutions but what he believed to be the corruption
> of faith itself. The Protestant Reformation was not strictly a
> "reformation" at all. In the intention of its leaders it was a
> restoration of biblical Christianity. In practice it was a revo-
> lution, a full-scale attack on the traditional doctrines and
> sacramental structure of the Roman Church.[10]

Given the passionate response to Luther, it would be fair to
say that many Europeans were ready and willing to explore
the promise of a restructured church and society.

Conditions Favorable to Protestantism

Though Luther was extremely industrious and outspoken, it
is also true that conditions in Europe in 1517 were congenial
to the spread of the Protestant message. Princes of the various territories of Germany, for example, were in frequent
conflict with the pope in Rome, particularly over tax collection and other money-making enterprises, which they
sought to control. Ordinary Germans also resented the
amount of money leaving Germany for Rome, never to be
seen again. To an extent, Protestantism provided these
princes a wedge with which to loosen the grip of Rome over
affairs in Germany. Luther appealed directly to this kind of
nationalistic sentiment in his 1520 treatise *Appeal to the German Nobility*, in which Luther tries to persuade the nobility
to stand up to the pope and to undertake measures of church
reform in their territories. From the start, Luther received
the sympathetic protection of Frederick, the elector of Saxony, and it is doubtful whether Luther's protest over indulgences would have survived to become the movement it did
without this protection. As scholar Hans J. Hillerbrand
writes, "Had Luther taught fifty miles to the south at
Leipzig and been a subject of the rabidly Catholic Duke

George of Saxony, he would not have seen the success of his Reformation or the establishment of a new Christian tradition."[11] But political protection is only one factor contributing to the rapid spread and success of Protestantism.

In addition, economic conditions contributed to the embrace of Protestantism, at least in Germany in its early years. The economic system of feudalism, which had dominated the Middle Ages, was being steadily replaced in Germany by a system involving such capitalist innovations as competition, the growth of international markets, and the use of paper money. The instability created by these new economic arrangements resulted in widespread confusion and intermittent unemployment, mainly among the lesser nobility and the large peasant class, which felt dissatisfaction and resentment for the new system. Both of these groups were attracted to Lutheranism, which they saw as an opportunity to reject the status quo and rearrange society to their advantage. Of course, this was not what Luther had in mind, and it led to Luther's direct denunciation of the peasants when large numbers of them took up arms in rebellion in 1524–1525, sometimes referring to Luther as their inspiration. But economic discontent, too, was only one of many reasons why the early Reformation flourished.

The Influence of Renaissance Humanism

The Renaissance intellectual movement called humanism—present in universities throughout Europe—also paved the way for the success of Protestantism. In the decade before Luther became a household name, leading Christian humanists published popular satires of abuses within the Catholic church, thus contributing to the widespread mood of dissatisfaction with the status quo. The best known of these texts was Erasmus's satire *The Praise of Folly*, which criticized both the immorality and the lack of education of the clergy.

The basic principles of humanist scholarship were *ad fontes*, or a return to the original sources, and *bonae litterae*, or eloquence in writing. This latter principle entailed a heavy emphasis on educational reform, including the learn-

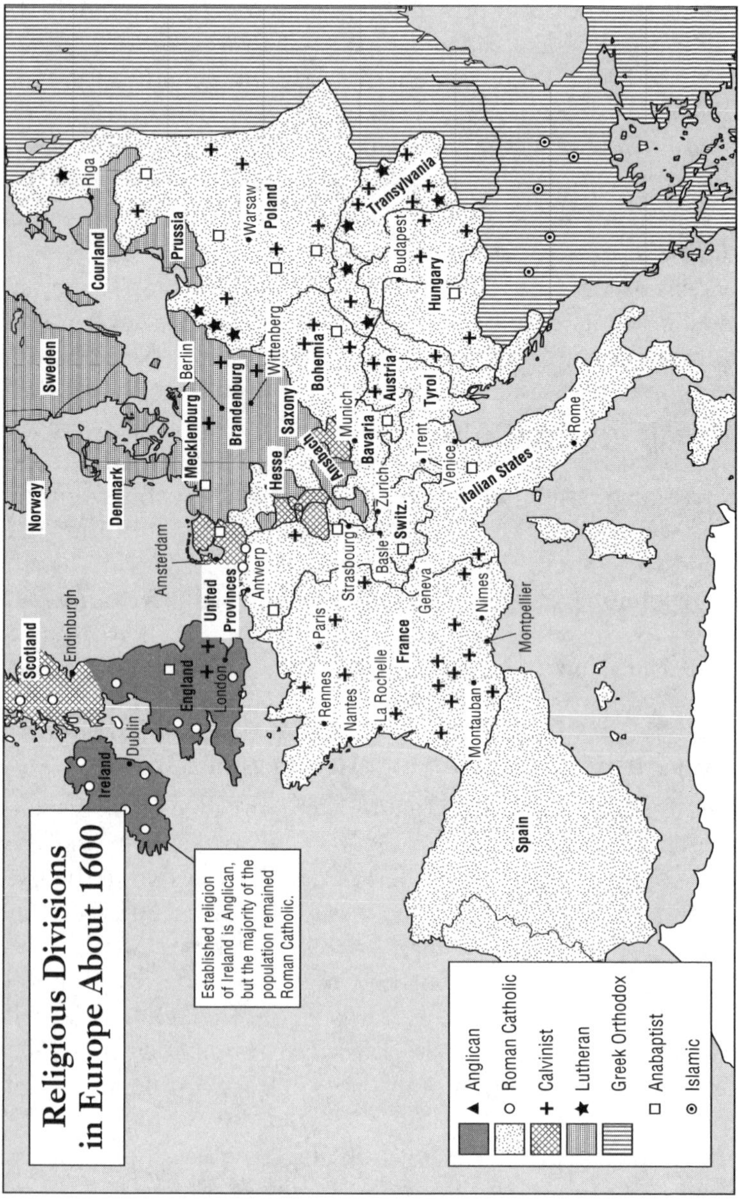
Religious Divisions in Europe About 1600
Established religion of Ireland is Anglican, but the majority of the population remained Roman Catholic.
Anglican
Roman Catholic
Calvinist
Lutheran
Greek Orthodox
Anabaptist
Islamic
Scotland
Endinburgh
Ireland
Dublin
England
London
Norway
Sweden
Denmark
Amsterdam
United Provinces
Antwerp
Courland
Riga
Prussia
Mecklenburg
Berlin
Brandenburg
Wittenberg
Saxony
Hesse
Ansbach
Poland
Warsaw
Bohemia
Transylvania
Budapest
Hungary
Austria
Tyrol
Munich
Bavaria
Zurich
Trent
Venice
Basle
Switz.
Strasbourg
Geneva
Paris
Rennes
Nantes
La Rochelle
France
Nimes
Montpellier
Montauban
Italian States
Rome
Spain

ing of ancient languages like Greek, Latin, and Hebrew, to enable the reading of ancient writings in the language in which they were written. As part of this project, Erasmus published in 1516 a Greek text of the New Testament, making it available for the first time for scholars to compare to the Vulgate Latin translation of the Bible used by the Catholic Church for centuries. In his Latin translation of that Greek text, Erasmus pointed out over six hundred inaccuracies of the Vulgate Bible, and some of these passages cast into doubt doctrines and practices of the Church. These discoveries were grist for the Protestant mills. Through the combination of his scholarship and his well-known critique of Catholic abuses, Erasmus was said, even during his lifetime, to have "laid the egg that Luther hatched."

Some leading Protestants, such as Zwingli and Calvin, began their scholarly careers as Christian humanists. Influenced by the humanist emphasis on the study of Greek and Hebrew, Protestant scholars sought a more accurate understanding of Christian beliefs and practices by reading the Bible firsthand rather than dictated by tradition and the Catholic Church.

The Role of the Printing Press

Another important factor in the success and spread of the Protestant message was the availability and use of the printing press, which coincided with an increasingly literate general public. Under the influence of Renaissance humanism, schools at all levels were being founded, and the literacy rate across Europe was increasing steadily. The number of universities in Europe also expanded phenomenally during this period, with twenty-five new universities opening between 1450 and 1517, including the university at Wittenberg in 1501. Thus, the audience for Protestant views, an audience with humanist sympathies, was immense. In addition, the control of many printing presses, including the very productive press at Basel, Switzerland, was in the hands of those sympathetic to the Protestant message. The explosion in printing, especially during the Reformation period, is described by scholar Steven Ozment:

> More books were printed in the . . . years between 1460 and
> 1540 than had been produced by scribes and monks through-
> out the entire Middle Ages. . . . Between 1518 and 1524, the
> crucial years of the Reformation, the publication of books in
> Germany alone increased sevenfold. . . . Between 1517 and
> 1520, Luther wrote approximately thirty tracts, which were
> distributed in 300,000 copies. . . . The famous Reformation
> pamphlets of 1520, the *Address to the German Nobility* and the
> *Freedom of a Christian*, reached sixteen and nineteen editions
> respectively within the space of a year.[12]

Clearly, if the German people were willing to buy that many
tracts, there was a definite readiness to hear the Protestant
message. In any case, Protestantism was the first popular
movement in history fueled by the power of the printing
press.

The Counter-Reformation

Obviously, not all Europeans who heard the Protestant message were convinced by it. Notable among those who stayed
firmly with the Catholic Church, in spite of its flaws, was
Erasmus. Protestants appealed to him to change sides, but
he remained staunchly Catholic, and he wrote pamphlets on
reconciliation of the two sides. By mid-century, though,
Erasmus's earlier reform-oriented writing had earned him
the title "leader of all heretics" by Pope Paul IV, who called
for the burning of Erasmus's books. Though there were frequent calls for reform from within the Catholic Church in
the early sixteenth century, there were too many in the
church hierarchy who benefited from the current system.
Reformers within the Church pushed for a church council to
address abuses and formulate a Catholic response to Protestantism. But the popes in the early years of the Reformation
were preoccupied by such concerns as the war against the
Muslims in Spain and various artistic and cultural projects in
Rome. In addition, popes had to take into account the resistance to reform by members of the church hierarchy who
had something to lose. Due primarily to this sense of self-
interest, a council that could effectively deal with the

Lutheran heresy was delayed for more than twenty-five years. One of the most remarkable internal reform efforts came in 1537, when a commission of nine cardinals wrote a critical report condemning the widespread abuses and corruption in the Catholic Church and urging reform. This report was published inadvertently to the glee of Protestants, and it was later repudiated by the Catholic Church.

After Protestantism had become firmly entrenched, some promising countermeasures were initiated, including the commission of the militant order of the Society of Jesus in 1540, which sought to combat Protestantism through extensive educational and missionary efforts. Through the founding of Jesuit schools and the vigorous assertion of the Catholic theology, the Jesuits were a very successful organization. In 1542 the pope established the Roman Inquisition, which used persecution in all forms to eliminate overt Protestant sympathy in Italy, as it had been eliminated in Spain. As scholar E. Harris Harbison writes,

> Faced by the defection of almost half Europe, the Catholic Church developed spiritual resources which hardly seemed to exist when Luther first appeared on the scene, strengthened its organization, and rolled back the tide of heresy until by the end of the century Protestantism was limited roughly to the northern third of Europe, as it is today.[13]

The bulwark of this Counter-Reformation was the Council of Trent, which was initiated in 1545 to formulate and reaffirm the Catholic theology and repudiate that of the reformers. The Council of Trent resulted in a point-by-point rejection of the premises of Protestantism, especially that of justification by faith alone. It also affirmed basically all the doctrines that had been challenged, including papal infallibility and the use of indulgences.

Legacies of the Reformation

The Reformation bequeathed to the modern world what has proven to be a permanent division of churches within Christianity. And much of the modern world continues to find these competing allegiances and worldviews deeply meaningful. Most of the distinctions between Catholics and Protestants that endure today can be traced to the Reformation. In terms of theology, Protestants continue to emphasize the doctrine of justification by faith alone, through which good works are seen as inevitably following faith but are not a factor in salvation. Catholics affirm faith along with human cooperation with God's will, cooperation that means performing good works. Protestants today emphasize the primacy of the Bible as the authority for Christian life and faith, and they stress the reading of the Bible by individuals as the central activity of Christians. Catholics continue to affirm the necessary mediation of the church hierarchy—the pope and bishops, in particular—to make Christian doctrine meaningful to Christians. Protestants believe in the priesthood of all believers, that all Christians are equal in the sight of God. Thus, any one Christian, for example, is qualified to hear a confession from any other Christian. The Catholic position affirms the special status of priests as intermediaries between ordinary Christians and God. Priests alone may hear confessions, handle the sacraments of the Eucharist (the communion with God), or conduct last rites, for example. Priests are set apart from ordinary Christians and may not marry, while Protestant ministers usually do. In terms of the sacraments, the rituals endorsed as sacred by Christ, Catholics hold to seven while Protestants believe in only two, baptism and the Eucharist. These constitute the essential differences between the two main modern branches of Christianity.

But the legacy of the Reformation extends beyond the church itself and into the life of modern society. The Reformation established a new model for the relationship between church and state in Europe, and it offered a less authoritarian view of the way individuals relate to both their church and their state. Protestantism also promoted a new, more positive view of marriage and of family life. Moreover, the Protestant ideals of popular education and the primacy of individual conscience, along with the rejection of unjust authority, laid the foundation for the development of modern democratic values and the concept of individual rights.

Notes

1. Charles G. Nauert Jr., *The Age of Renaissance and Reformation*. Lanham, MD: University Press of America, 1981, p. 133.

2. Steven Ozment, *Protestants: The Birth of a Revolution*. New York: Doubleday, 1991, p. 217.

3. Quoted in Karl H. Dannenfeldt, *The Church of the Renaissance and Reformation*. St. Louis: Concordia, 1970, p. 30.

4. Quoted in Paul Johnson, *A History of Christianity*. New York: Atheneum, 1976, p. 267.

5. Alister McGrath, *Reformation Thought: An Introduction*. 2nd ed. Oxford: Blackwell, 1993, p. 2.

6. McGrath, *Reformation Thought*, pp. 2–3.

7. Quoted in E. Harris Harbison, *The Age of Reformation*. Ithaca, NY: Cornell University Press, 1955, p. 51.

8. Lewis Spitz, *The Protestant Reformation: 1517–1559*. New York: Harper & Row, 1985, p. 59.

9. Bruce Shelley, *Church History in Plain Language*. Dallas: Word, 1995, p. 241

10. Eugene F. Rice Jr., *The Foundations of Early Modern Europe: 1460–1559*. New York: W.W. Norton, 1970, p. 125.

11. Hans J. Hillerbrand, *Men and Ideas in the Sixteenth Century*. Chicago: Rand McNally, 1969, p. 18.

12. Steven Ozment, *The Age of Reform: 1250–1550*. New Haven, CT: Yale University Press, 1980. p. 199.

13. Harbison, *The Age of Reformation*, p. 82.

The Origins of the Protestant Reformation

Turning Points

IN WORLD HISTORY

The Church and Society Before the Reformation

Karl H. Dannenfeldt

From the cradle to the grave, from infant baptism to last rites, from event to event on the church calendar, the lives of ordinary Christians were pervasively influenced by the rituals and traditions of the medieval Christian church. This extensive power was somewhat disrupted in the decades before the Reformation by rapid economic and social changes outside the control of the church, including erosion of the feudal system and the rising power of European kings. Further, growing abuses within the medieval church led to calls for reform from many quarters, even before the advent of the Reformation. The following overview of the church in medieval society is excerpted from Karl H. Dannenfeldt's book *The Church of the Renaissance and Reformation*. A scholar of both the Renaissance and the Reformation, Dannenfeldt was a longtime academic vice-president of Arizona State University.

It is difficult for anyone today to comprehend how the life of the late medieval Christian, lived in a world largely devoid of distracting and competing interests, was so completely influenced and governed by his religion. His daily activities and behavior, his visual arts and songs, his amusements and social life, and his entire reason for being, living, and dying revolved around the religious teachings of the Christian church which represented to him the divine order of things in a confusing world. The medieval Christian lived the whole year according to the church's calendar. He joyously celebrated the mysteries of nature and of human redemption together during the various seasons, as well as the innumerable saints' days that crowded the ecclesiastical calendar. As the situation demanded, he prayed to the patron saint of his occupation, town, illness, or hazard; but especially he fervently called upon Mary, the kind mother of God. While the line between right and wrong in his everyday code of ethics was primarily that drawn by the authoritative church, this was reinforced by established practice, common agreement, and the interpretation through reason of what was "natural."

The medieval Christian sinned, confessed, and in weakness sinned again; yet the hope of salvation was always there—a future blessed release from the trials and tribulations that were his lot on earth. Yet this very hope was fraught with fear and tension, for death would lead to a confrontation with Christ, who was often viewed as a stern judge who readily condemned despairing sinners to everlasting torments among the devils and flames of hell. The terrors of this evil abode were mitigated for the dying Christian by the teachings of the church which made possible an alternate fate in purgatory, where the punishment was severe yet temporal and where the time of suffering could be shortened by the prayers of friends still living and by endowed masses offered in his name.

The Organization of the Church

That an all-pervading religious atmosphere was present and effective was in part due to the organization of the powerful medieval Christian church. From the small group of the original disciples, the followers of Christ had by the late medieval period grown into a vast "Christian body," an international community of the faithful to which almost everyone in Europe belonged. Basic to this unity was a complex hierarchy, rationally organized and modeled after the Roman imperial system, headed in the West by the pope in Rome. By accident of history and geography, the Roman successors of Peter had developed the claims of primacy, along with a firm tradition of orthodoxy, into a position of strength and leadership.

Assisting the pope was a varying number of cardinals organized into a "college." From their number the cardinals selected the next pope. In the secular hierarchy the archbishops came next. These administrative officials governed archdioceses made up of a number of bishoprics, that is, dioceses of varying size administered by bishops. The bishop had spiritual duties, like ordination and confirmation, and also exercised temporal management and supervision of the clergy and properties in his diocese. In each diocese it was the parish priests who performed the spiritual duties of saying or singing mass, administering most of the sacraments, visiting the sick and dying, burying the dead in consecrated ground, hearing the confessions of the penitent, and in general exercising the care of souls. All too frequently, like his parishioners, the parish priest was barely literate. He usually did not preach, at least not until the reforms in church life in the 15th century.

It was this secular and celibate hierarchy, centered on the pope at Rome, that provided the unity of doctrine, liturgy, language, law, education, and control that was so important in establishing and maintaining an international medieval civilization. Because of its influence and control, the church as an institution became synonymous with Christianity. Eternal salvation, the goal of every Christian, was obtainable only through the church, for it alone was the absolute custodian of the Scriptures, the creeds, and the sacraments.

The Central Beliefs

The sacraments, the indispensable "channels of grace," were seven in number, that number having been established in the late 12th century but not made official until 1439. Covering the crucial stages of human life, the sacramental system led to an exaltation of the power of the clergy who held such exclusive and awesome control in their hands.

The sacrament prerequisite to all the others was *Baptism*. This rite washed away original sin and mystically united the baptized infant with Christ. This sacrament was normally administered by the parish priest, and the use of water was required. The sacrament of *confirmation* was administered by a bishop to children. Due to difficulties of travel and the slackness of some bishops, the sacrament was rather frequently bypassed. It was not a prerequisite for first Communion. Next in importance to Baptism was the sacrament of the *Eucharist*, or Holy Communion, the essential part of the Mass. The Mass, with its elaborate and complicated ceremonies, its costly vestments and vessels, varied with time and purpose, but all Masses were essentially the same—sacrificial rites in which the officiating priest (celebrant) mystically offered up Christ once again. By the late medieval period, the Mass had become primarily a spectacle, with much of the Latin liturgy being recited by the priest in an inaudible voice. The most dramatic and central moment of the service was the elevation of the host (sacramental bread) at the time of consecration. Originally the congregation had joined in the services by singing hymns, but this vocal participation had become restricted to choristers during the medieval period.

The Fourth Lateran Council (1215) approved the doctrine of *transubstantiation*, according to which the consecrated bread and wine of the Eucharist were miraculously changed by God through the power of the words of institution ("This is My body"), spoken by the officiating priest, into the body and blood of Christ. In the 13th century of Western Christendom, because of the fear of spilling the precious blood of Christ, the practice developed for the laity to receive only the unleavened bread, which, however, was taught to be actually the entire Christ, with body and blood. Although the sacrament of the Eucharist was the fruit of the Mass, the laity usually did not commune at Mass. Indeed, the average medieval Christian, afraid of being unworthy of Communion, communed very infrequently, generally only at Eastertime.

The fourth sacrament was that of *penance*, which consisted of three phases: contrition, confession and absolution, and satisfaction (penance). The sacrament of *ordination* was administered by a bishop, empowering a priest or deacon to fulfill certain spiritual tasks. A priest, once ordained, obtained an indelible spiritual character, or mark, and a power which never deteriorated or became inefficacious. The sacrament of *matrimony*, appropriately solemnized by the clergy, was in the West for the laity alone, since the Latin church regarded celibacy as a superior condition for its clergy. The final sacrament was *extreme unction*, in which the gravely ill Christian confessed to the priest and was anointed with consecrated oil.

The Use of Indulgences

Associated with the sacrament of penance was the indulgence. The origin of the use of indulgences was simple and harmless enough, as originally it was a remission of a part or all of the temporal punishment imposed by the church on a confessing sinner. During the Crusades a plenary, or full, indulgence was granted to those who died fighting the infidel—a good recruiting device. This was then extended to all who participated in a crusade and then to those who contributed a certain amount to send a soldier in their place. After the Crusades the use of indulgences was extended in various ways. While originally indulgences were granted for virtuous deeds, they soon were sold for money. Then agents spread the highly marketable wares throughout Europe. By drawing on the treasury of "surplus merits" accumulated by Christ and the saints, the popes could issue indulgence letters and release the purchaser from temporal punishment both on earth and in purgatory. In 1476 Sixtus IV promised the purchaser the immediate release from purgatory of someone already dead. Although this papal power was questioned by some and although canon law did not legalize such indulgences, the sale of indulgences among the simple people increased rapidly. Gone was the initial emphasis on contrition and confession; the monetary aspect of the traffic became uppermost.

Besides the "secular" clergy who played an active role in medieval society, there were the monastic or "regular" clergy (*regula*, "rule") and the lay brothers who, to a certain extent, withdrew from the world and the problems of life facing the average Christian. Originally the monks led ascetic lives of self-denial, rigorous discipline, and solitary contemplation. The vocation of a monk or nun came to be regarded by most men as a more perfect way of following Christ. The ascetic life was seen as the truly apostolic one. Most monastic orders were under direct supervision of the pope in Rome, where the generals of the orders also resided.

Changes in Monasticism

As the needs of medieval Christianity changed, monasticism of the old type was no longer of great use to society. To meet the changing needs, a new kind of brotherhood was brought into being; the friars ("brothers"), originally laymen, wandered about preaching and teaching, hearing confessions, and ministering to the poor, the sick, and the ignorant. Early in the 13th century, St. Francis of Assisi organized the Franciscan Brothers (Friars Minor or Grey Friars), the original mendicant, or begging, order. Another such order, the Dominican (Black Friars), was founded in the same period (1216).

All monks and their female counterparts, the nuns, took the oaths of poverty, chastity, and obedience. However, the orders usually became rich and powerful, and with wealth frequently came arrogance, sloth, immorality, general moral decline, and the loss of original ideals. This was especially so in the late medieval period as the monastic communities and the friars freed themselves from the supervision and discipline of the local bishops. Yet, it must be remembered that evil, as always, attracted the most attention and the good work done by the monks and nuns was often overlooked and unpraised.

The monasteries had figured very strongly in the intellectual life of the early Middle Ages, for the intellectual realm was especially dominated by Christian theology. However, in the monasteries of the 12th and later centuries the atmosphere was often such as to foster little advance in intellectual inquiry and study. It was rather the schools, usually associated with the urban cathedrals, that showed increased activity as centers of learning. From some of these schools there gradually developed the organizations of students and masters known as universities.

In the schools of the 13th century, philosophy, the "handmaiden" of Christian theology, developed into a system of inquiry called scholasticism. This was an attempt to use the deductive logic of Aristotelian philosophy to arrive by debate at new Christian insights and also to harmonize pagan philosophy with Christian revelation. It was Thomas Aquinas (1225–74) who especially developed the use of reason in support and in defense of the revealed truth.

Some of the scholastic reasoning bordered on heresy; indeed, intellectual and philosophical speculations in theology had always been a source of heterodoxy in Christianity. Others had been labeled heretics for criticizing the church's practices and clergy—which they had often done with good reason. The authoritarian church could not countenance the growth of opposition to its monopolistic dogmas and ecclesiastical practices. Obstinate individuals were excommunicated as dissenters and deviates. By the formula of excommunication, the unrepentant sinner was expelled from the church's communions, accursed of God and the saints, and assured of eternal damnation unless he repented and rendered satisfaction. Should a king or region resist the authority of the church or break its laws, the entire kingdom or area could be placed under a papal interdict until submission or correction was gained. An interdict (prohibition) meant the closing of the churches and the suspension of the usual rites and ceremonies, thus creating a dangerous situation that threatened the salvation of all in the area under the interdict.

The formulas of excommunication and the interdict were fearsome enough to hold most Christians in line, but frequently more drastic means were considered necessary. Obdurate heretics were burned at the stake as subversives whose presence in the Christian community could not be tolerated. As heresy increased in frequency and variety in the late Middle Ages, the aged Gregory IX (1227–41) introduced the Inquisition, a papal tribunal whose agents were directed to detect and try heretics by due process of law. . . .

Feudalism and Abuses in the Church

At the end of the 13th century, Western Christendom stood on the threshold of a period of dramatic changes. The two institutions most important in late medieval civilization were about to be radically altered. These institutions were feudalism and the Christian church, both conservative yet creative forces that molded medieval man and society.

By 1300, alien elements, in the forms of money economy and town population, had entered into the feudal system. New forms of wealth, based on a revival of commerce that originated in the northern Italian cities, were disrupting the traditional political, economic, and social pattern of the medieval and primarily rural and agrarian economy. Towns, peopled by burghers becoming increasingly wealthy, were slowly achieving political independence from their feudal lords and were affecting an economic revolution. Feudal society was being transformed, with the urban centers exerting more and more influence beyond the city walls. The new forms of wealth in a money economy opened up great possibilities of taxation to the rulers of Europe, who were thus increasingly freed from the limitations imposed by a natural, or moneyless, economy with its barter and services. The monarchs of France and England led the way in exerting royal authority, royal law, and royal taxation—erecting nonfeudal systems more in line with the economic and social changes occurring in their realms.

The Christian church was very much involved in the medieval feudal system. Bishops and abbots, the heads of monasteries, were holders of fiefs and manors, and the church's economic structure was closely tied to that of feudalism. Anything that affected a change in this basic and traditional pattern of behavior was sure to cause a change in the church. While the practices and dogmas of medieval Christianity were not immediately altered by the economic and social changes, the growing secularism, especially that of the urban population, had a decidedly adverse effect on medieval asceticism, otherworldliness, and religiosity. The love of money pervaded both laity and clergy despite the church's attempts to limit profiteering with the theories of "no usury" and a "just price." The papal claim of international authority and control, dependent as it had been on the political weakness of the state due to feudal decentralization, was directly challenged both by the rising monarchs and by the influential towns and cities. In general, the church failed to maintain the loyalty and devotion of the upper and middle classes, who gradually turned to the state for leadership. . . .

Calls for Reform

The secularized Renaissance papacy had lost touch with popular piety and with Christian ideals. The ecclesiastical hierarchy, reflecting the worldliness of the times only too well, was frequently mercenary, covetous of wealth, and immoral. To be sure, the officials of civil governments of the time exhibited the same sins and weaknesses of mankind, but Christians have always demanded and hoped for a higher morality among those who represented the church. It was natural, therefore, that complaints and demands for reform were common among Christians everywhere.

All the denunciations and complaints occasioned by the varied abuses, corruption, wealth, and immorality among the clergy, as well as their commanding secular power and offices, are summed up by the word *anticlericalism*. With the rise of national states and strong monarchs, anticlericalism was often motivated by feelings of nationalism and resentment at the great tax-free wealth of the church, the loss of money to Rome, and papal interference in the politics and economy of the national state. With the increase of a humanistically educated laity, frequent attacks were made on the ignorance of the clergy. Humanists from Italy and later from northern Europe called for a reform from within the church and used their training and knowledge to pen bitter satires and other works of condemnation. Preachers of reform thundered dire warnings from their pulpits, and everywhere shocked Christians prayed for reform and sought to live pious lives despite the poor example of the clergy.

Religion and Social Conditions During the Early Sixteenth Century

James M. Kittelson

According to scholar James M. Kittelson, life at the time of the Reformation was hard for most Europeans. Infant mortality, the plague, poverty, violence all affected ordinary people. These calamities were also the factors that caused people to seek comfort and security in the church and its rituals. Relief from the problems of this life and assurance of salvation could be secured through active participation in what Kittelson calls the "cycle of sin, confession, and penance." A professor of history at Ohio State University, Kittelson is best known for his book *Luther: The Reformer*, from which this excerpt is taken.

In the early 16th century, security of any sort was a very elusive thing to come by. Life in Luther's time was tenuous in ways that are nearly impossible for people living in the modern world to appreciate. To be sure, these were the years that historians refer to as the Renaissance, and Luther was a contemporary of truly extraordinary people—Machiavelli, Michelangelo, Raphael, Erasmus, and Thomas More, among many others. Copernicus's revolutionary book on the solar system was published before Luther died. Christopher Columbus set sail when Luther was halfway through grammar school, and Luther was aware of the discovery of the new world. He remarked that if Europeans did not respond to the gospel, they would likely lose it to these new people.

Luther lived in exciting times. Even today, the magnificent achievements of his 16th-century contemporaries and the splendor of life at a Renaissance court excite the imagination. But these images also obscure the realities of everyday life for ordinary people. Luther lived in hard times. For example, in Florence at the height of the Renaissance, 61 percent of the infants were either stillborn or died within six months. At least one of Luther's younger brothers died in this way. Luther's mother, Margaretta, was convinced that the death of her child was the work of the woman next door, who, she was certain, was a witch.

These were the years when the Plague ravaged Europe. The territory of Alsace, to the southwest, illustrates what could happen when sickness stalked the countryside. In the city of Strasbourg, which normally had about 25,000 inhabitants, some 16,000 fell to the scourge in one year. In the region around this large city, 300 villages were left deserted and the total land under cultivation did not climb back to normal levels until two centuries later.

Nor was the Plague the only new and horrifying disease with which Europeans had to contend. During these same years syphilis (which the Germans called the "French disease") arrived on the continent to torment European lovers. All were agreed on the name for another dread disease, the "English Sweats," which featured a high fever that permanently shattered the victims' nervous systems and left them with long lesions on their bodies.

About a century later, the English philosopher Thomas Hobbes aptly depicted life in Luther's time as being "nasty, brutish, and short." Even those tough enough to surmount the hazards of disease commonly struggled just to find enough to eat. Transportation networks were primitive, so each area had to be self-sufficient. When food production failed to meet the local need, territories removed from the major waterways were especially vulnerable. A local drought, a terribly wet spring, or an early frost could force grain prices up as much as 150% over the previous year.

Speculators, whose numbers included the heads of great churches and monasteries, were therefore in a position to make enormous profits. Ordinary people simply suffered.

Many who had once been employed were reduced to begging for their food and clothing. They could be seen on every street of every village and city. The sheer number of beggars was so overwhelming that the authorities on the west bank of the Rhine would annually combine forces, round up all the undesirables, and force them over to the east bank. On that side of the river the procession of beggars and homeless, maimed, insane, and mentally retarded people would be met by another group of princes with their armies, who marched them through the Black Forest and into central Germany. But the constant flow of society's outcasts never stopped. A year later the authorities would start the whole process over again.

A Violent Time

In one respect, life at the turn of the 16th century must be painted in even darker hues than these. It was not just the times that were hard. The people were hardened by the world in which they lived. Many were also exceedingly violent. German peasants were far from being placid workers of the land. They quickly exercised the right of feud, and they continued to do so for another 150 years. When they had real or imagined grievances, they sought recourse not in the courts but with their fists, knives, or clubs.

While a peace-loving, respectable family such as Luther's might not have engaged in such random violence, they could not entirely escape it. Hans Luder had a younger brother by virtually the same name who must have been a constant source of embarrassment. Young Hans, as he was called, lived in Mansfeld for 14 years. During that time he was charged with assault and battery on 11 separate occasions. But people in Mansfeld were fortunate in that Young Hans was repeatedly brought to justice. In the early 16th century the arms of the law had not yet grown very long, and they were often simply unable to remove criminals from the midst of law-abiding citizens. One of Luther's later followers recalled that his own first professor at the University of Freiburg was struck dead on the street by a wandering soldier. There is no record that the murderer ever had to answer for his crime. . . .

The Search for Spiritual Security

The religion practiced by people of the 16th century was much like the world in which they lived. They struggled to gain spiritual security, just as in their daily lives they struggled to achieve material security. Salvation was something to be earned, and so theirs was a religion of work.

It was an age of pilgrimages. People were exhorted to travel in groups to this or that shrine in order to work off the penalties for the sins they had committed. Frequently enough, they temporarily took up the life of apostolic poverty and begged for their sustenance as they traveled.

It was also an age of saints and relics. The faithful were taught that praying to the saints or venerating their relics would atone for individual sins of both omission and commission. To assist them in this work, the major churches and shrines collected pieces of bone and hair that were alleged to have come from the body of one saint or another. Some boasted of drops of milk from the Virgin's breast or splinters from the cross of Christ.

It was an age of death. Painters, sculptors, and wood carvers seized on this theme and the "Dance of Death" became one of the most common motifs in late medieval art. Like the Pied Piper, the skeletal Grim Reaper with scythe in hand led representatives of every social group twirling off to their own inevitable end.

Above all, it was an age of fire and brimstone. No one could escape knowing that there was a judgment to come. Christ himself was commonly pictured not just on the cross, but seated on his throne. Coming from one side of his head was a lily, symbolizing the resurrection. From the other side came a sword. The burning question was, How can I avoid the sword and earn the lily?

The church had an answer to this question. By the time Luther was born it had been sharpened into one short command: "Do what is in your power!" "Use well your natural capacities and whatever special gifts have been granted you." Then, through the power of the church, God would add his grace and smile. Although they by no means understood (nor were they intended to understand) just how this happened, people like the Schalbes and Luther's parents did what they were told.

Others did far more. Luther never forgot seeing Prince William of Anhalt, who had renounced his noble estate to become a Franciscan monk and to spend his life as a beggar. "He had fasted so often, kept so many vigils, and so mortified his flesh," Luther later wrote, "that he was the picture of death, just skin and bones." Prince William was certainly exceptional, but there were so many people zealously working out their salvation that the city of Marseilles passed a law forbidding religious beggars from passing its walls. Nearly every city sought at least to control them.

Sin, Confession, Penance

Most people were not so zealous in their efforts to guarantee their salvation. Leaders of the church therefore tried to make sure that everyone at least *thought* about the status of their souls. Chief among their methods was the obligation to confess one's sins to a priest. At least once a year (commonly at the beginning of Lent, but the more often the better), every man, woman, and child admitted to Communion was obligated to go to their priest and confess all the sins they had committed since their previous visit.

It is impossible to know exactly what happened inside the confessional in Luther's day (even as it is impossible to know exactly what happens in it today), but if the confessors followed the manuals that were written for them, it was a very rigorous examination. A priest would begin by asking what sins a penitent wished to confess to almighty God. When the response was insufficiently detailed or when the penitent, now on his or her knees on the stone floor, could not remember any particular sins, the confessor would begin asking questions. "Have you ever become angry with your spouse?" "Do you wish your house were as good as your neighbor's?" For adolescent boys, "Do you ever have 'wet dreams'?" For girls, "Were you dancing with the young men at the town fair?" For those who were married, "Have you had sexual relations with your spouse for any purpose other than having children?" Or, "Did you use any but the standard position?" Or, "The last time you and your husband (or wife) had sexual intercourse, did you enjoy it or experience any feelings of pleasure?" The theologians debated whether sexual relations within marriage were serious sins, but all agreed that they were sins, at least in principle. Therefore even this most ordinary human activity had to be confessed before the throne of a righteous and angry God.

The church also made it clear that people had to be purged of all the sins they had failed to confess and work off in the here and now. If they did not do so, they would surely pay the price in purgatory, where they would sweat out every unremitted sin before they could see the gates of heaven. Given this situation, there can be little wonder that one of the first things Gutenberg issued from his newly developed movable-type printing press was what the church at the time called an *indulgence*. This was granted in exchange for a "gift" to the church and released the donor from the fires of purgatory for a specified time. Gutenberg's form was much like a modern legal document. It came complete with a blank space for the purchaser's name and another space for how much time in purgatory they had escaped. Indulgences were very popular.

The Danger of Despair

As it did for everyone else, the cycle of sin, confession, and penance played a prominent role in Luther's spiritual life. Confession was required at least annually for all who wished to attend the Mass, but the thought of dying suddenly with several individual sins unconfessed amounted to an unbearable risk for pious people. Sensitive religious leaders did concern themselves with the possibility that such rigorous confessional practices might lead truly pious people to despair. *Despair*—the horrifying thought that God's mercy is not for me or that I have fallen too far for it to help me—was the one unforgivable sin. It was the sin against the Holy Spirit, and no one who died with it in their heart could escape the fires of hell. Moreover, it was feared that, when faced with death, some might indeed despair at the last moment and be lost. This fear was so great that nearly everyone was familiar with artistic depictions of angels and devils wrestling for the soul of someone who was dying.

So the theologians composed more manuals. These instructed priests on how to hear final confessions and how, as they did so, to fend off despair while ushering the dying into the next life. However, in spite of all their worries and second thoughts, the theologians still concluded that the dangers of an incomplete confession far outweighed the chance that a penitent would fall into despair. After all, people actually enjoyed sinning. If one's conscience were troubled, surely it would be relieved by some act of penance, whether several "Our Fathers," an "Ave Maria," or, in the case of those who really wanted to be sure, a pilgrimage to a shrine or the purchase of an indulgence.

The religion that Martin Luther learned was very much like the world in which he lived. Much as the world sometimes added good fortune to a person's labors, in this realm the church added grace to one's good works so they would be complete and acceptable to God. But in each realm, hard work was still essential.

Problems in the Catholic Church Prior to the Reformation

Lewis W. Spitz

Several serious problems in the Catholic church contributed to the success of the Reformation in the early sixteenth century. According to well-known Reformation
scholar Lewis W. Spitz, the popes at this time acted too
often from political and economic motives, behaving
much like typical Renaissance princes. Clergy too often
lacked enough education to perform their jobs, and many
kept common-law wives and had illegitimate children. But
the worst abuses, according to Spitz, concerned the collection of church monies, especially indulgences, which
excused the purchaser from acts of penance or even from
time in purgatory. Though in some respects the church
was as healthy as it had ever been, abuses like these contributed to the acceptance of Reformation ideas. Spitz,
professor emeritus of history at Stanford University, is the
author of *The Protestant Reformation: 1517–1559*, from
which this excerpt is taken.

On the eve of the Reformation the Roman Catholic Church
was the most universal institution and the Christian religion
the most pervasive spiritual and intellectual force in Europe.
It shared its dominance only with the Orthodox Church and
Islam in eastern Europe, and was soon to have missionaries
at work in the New World as well as in Asia and Africa. As

Excerpted from *The Protestant Reformation*, by Lewis W. Spitz. Copyright ©1985
by Lewis W. Spitz. Reprinted by permission of HarperCollins Publishers, Inc.

an institution the church had a hierarchical organization that reached into every parish, and a bureaucracy that rivaled that of kings and emperors. Church law affected public affairs and touched the private life of every individual. The church had great wealth acquired through the centuries by legacies, gifts, bequests, investments, and ecclesiastical dues and taxes. Possibly a third of the real estate in the Holy Roman Empire was held or controlled by the church and in many larger cities a fourth or more of the property in the business section was similarly held. But one must not exaggerate the unity or uniformity of Christendom, for great differences in structure and cultural niveau [sophistication] existed in various parts of Europe, as say between the church in Italy and England. In view of the multitudinous heresies and extremes in the perception of the faith, from the scholastic doctor down to the most superstitious peasant, it is a mistake to conceive of an all-encompassing cultural monism.

The Popes as Politicians

The Renaissance popes asserted the universal claims of the monarchical Roman episcopate, but in reality they increasingly took on the character of Italian Renaissance princes. They were concerned with their political and military control over the Papal States and with the enrichment of their families. The wickedness of popes such as Sixtus IV, Alexander VI, Innocent VIII, has often been exaggerated. There is no real proof, for example, of fornication by one of these popes after his elevation to the papal chair. They did, however, scandalize the faithful and failed to provide spiritual leadership, for their interests ran more to politics and war, art and literature, hunting and luxurious living than to their apostolic duties.

All too many bishops emulated the example of the pontiffs, for they were regularly chosen for political reasons, came from the upper nobility, and were in some cases as much feudal overlords as ecclesiastical leaders. In Germany especially the higher ecclesiastical positions were of great political importance. The archbishops of Mainz, Trier, and Cologne were three of the seven electors of the Holy Roman

Empire. Cathedral chapters in cities such as Augsburg were the special preserve of the local aristocracy. At one time a Bavarian prince became Archbishop of Cologne and held four other sees without even being in priestly orders. . . .

Abuses Among the Clergy

Problems of ignorance, immorality, and irregularities reached down through the lower levels of the secular and regular clergy whose hostility and rivalry were a disturbing element in many dioceses. There is some confusion as to who should be counted as clergy, since the word "cleric" was used to identify a great many men who were not fully ordained priests, such as students, canons, ancillary clergy, and teachers. The clergy constituted a significant part of the population, in many cities, such as Worms, comprising at least 10 percent of the population. Cologne with a population of 40,000 had more than 6,000 clerics, Hamburg with a population of 12,000 had 450 parish priests, and Breslau had more than 400 chantry priests. If the higher members of the hierarchy were drawn from the upper classes, the lesser clergy usually came from families of the lower classes who did not have a tradition of study and learning. Many clerics studied at some prominent church or cathedral or were apprenticed to some literate priest. In England 10 to 20 percent of the clergy with benefices had some university education. In South Germany some 30 to 50 percent had seen the towers of university towns. The Latin of many was poor, hardly adequate for liturgical purposes, but the laity in general did nor seem to demand a high level of reading proficiency in Latin. Despite the jibes of the humanists, who mocked the ignorance of the clergy, there is evidence to indicate that, due in part to the advent of printing, the level of clerical learning was improving. There were some great preachers prior to the Reformation: John of Capistrano, Bernardino of Siena, Girolamo Savonarola, Geiler von Kaisersberg; and towns now began to endow preacherships, not unlike the Puritan lectureships in England at a later day. . . . Since preaching requires higher intellectual gifts than rote performance of ritual, this development suggests an improvement in clerical education. Many of these preachers, the most alert and serious members of the clergy, were to join the Reformation movement.

The most obvious and to some laymen the most egregious abuse was that of clerical concubinage [cohabitation]. In some parts of Europe as many as one-third of the clergy who had taken the vow of celibacy kept concubines. In Italy common-law wives for the clergy were widely accepted. Prominent churchmen even before the Reformation, including Pope Pius II, came out in favor of the marriage of the clergy in order to relieve the situation, but the church was not ready to move in that direction. All too many bishops pre-

The Crisis in Late Medieval Piety

Scholar Steven Ozment argues that medieval Christians aspiring to a purer spiritual life were usually given the clergy or the monastery as a model. Ozment suggests that these models of piety failed to satisfy many on the eve of the Reformation, and that this dissatisfaction spawned a host of late medieval reform experiments prior to what we call the Protestant Reformation.

Whereas in earlier times the monastic life had inspired the laity, by the eve of the Reformation it had become an object of criticism, even ridicule, by reformers and humanists. This was probably owing as much to changing religious needs as to actual abuses within religious houses and clerical ranks, which critics usually exaggerated. A monastically derived lay piety with prominent clerical ideals of obedience and sexual purity seemed incongruous to an increasingly literate, socially mobile urban laity, who prized simplicity, directness, and respectful treatment in all spheres of their lives.

The perceived inadequacy of traditional religion is manifest in the many reforms and experiments that extended from the Waldensians and Franciscans in the thirteenth century to the Hussites and Modern Devotionalists in the fifteenth. Before the Reformation and Counter Reformation redefined Christendom, a multitude of intellectual and devotional options, heterodox and orthodox, were embraced by venturesome laity and

ferred to collect the fines exacted of the clergy for wives and illegitimate children. The monks were derided as a special threat to the wives and daughters of burghers. A common witticism ran, "She entered a convent because she wanted a lover." A particularly sensational incident occurred in the Tyrol, where the daughters of the upper nobility turned their convent into a brothel and had to be evicted by force.

Monetary Abuses

Many abuses related to ecclesiastical fiscalism or cupidity had reached down to the parish level, where they became

clergy. Although the forms of piety were apparently never before so numerous or varied than at the end of the Middle Ages, almost all were restorational in nature, that is, basically attempts to return to the example of the Apostles and revive the moral and ascetic ideals that had transformed the church in earlier times. The reform movements that broke with official church piety and on many points anticipated later Protestant reform continued to conceive lay religious life in terms of traditional, ascetic ideals, as if a purer asceticism could resolve the crisis in late medieval piety. The Reformation while coming in their wake, was not necessarily in their spirit. The Protestant reformers both built on and transcended the religious reforms and experiments of the previous centuries. . . .

What the Reformation did have in common with late medieval reform movements was the conviction that traditional church authority and piety no longer served the religious needs of large numbers of people and had become psychologically and financially oppressive. Luther's inability to satisfy his own religious anguish by becoming a self-described "monk's monk" was an experience many laity also knew in their own way, for they too had sought in vain consolation from a piety based on the penitential practices of monks.

Steven Ozment, *The Age of Reform: 1250–1550*. New Haven: Yale UP, 1980, pp. 220–222.

obvious to all. The catalog of wrongdoing is familiar to any student of the period: simony, nepotism, pluralism, absenteeism. The payment of annates meant that the first year's income of a papal appointment went to the pope. If an appointment to a vacancy in a bishopric or abbacy could be deferred, the income would be appropriated during the interim through reservation by the papal fiscal officer. The sums involved were not insignificant: for Cologne, Mainz, Salzburg, and Trier the amount was 1,000 gulden; for Liège, 7,200 gulden; for Freising, 4,000 gulden; for Minden, 500; for Halberstadt, 100. For the archbishoprics the additional charge for the pallium was 10,000 gulden. These sums could not be paid from the regular income of the see, and so the burden was laid on the people. The parish priests in turn increased exactions on the laity, often charging for services which were part of their sacerdotal duties. Payments were required for dispensations from or the changing of vows for marriages, for annulments of marriages, for the administration of baptism, confession, extreme unction, or burial. Unfortunates caught up in legal processes in the ecclesiastical courts could be bankrupted paying fees and bribes in processes which could be carried by appeals all the way to Rome. Excommunication of an individual or the ban laid on an entire community could be ruinous. Special payments on feast days, charges to see relics, pilgrimages to shrines were frequently required of the faithful as spiritual obligations. In 1492 the Abbot of Deutz commanded Duke Wilhelm of Jülich to force the villagers to go on a pilgrimage and give the customary offerings, because they had refused to do so voluntarily. He threatened to apply "spiritual sanctions" if the duke did not cooperate.

The worst abuse, however, came to be the sale of indulgences, writs given on the payment of money excusing the recipient from deeds of satisfaction or suffering in purgatory upon repentance and confession of sins. While some indulgence preachers emphasized repentance and stirred the consciences of sinners, all too many gave the impression that they were selling the forgiveness of sins for a price. Chantry priests were an especially grievous problem, for they drew their salaries for celebrating the mass for the living or for the souls of the dead, but they usually had no other duties than to say the endowed masses and the office of the dead, so that the devil found work for their idle hands to do. There was little counseling or genuine cure of souls. A further source of hostility between the clergy and the laity was in the economic competition on the part of monasteries and religious brotherhoods. The peasants and the workers and merchants in the cities, who were in an economically difficult situation, were angered at monastic enterprises such as breweries, wineries, mills, tanneries, bakeries, printeries, taverns (often open on Sundays), for the monks could produce and market their wares more cheaply and generally enjoyed tax-free status. A German witticism which went back as far as the year 1200 told of the avaricious priest who read the lesson for the day in this way: "Here beginneth the holy gospel according to the Mark.". . .

Advances in Education

Lay literacy was on the rise and a flood of new municipal schools were being founded, city councils struggling to keep them free of episcopal authority. In a city such as London basic literacy was necessary to participation in commerce and business. The spread of printed books was certainly a major factor in the rise of literacy. At least a thousand printers were at work before 1500 and they produced 30,000 titles for a total output of between nine and twelve million volumes. Nearly half of the books printed before 1500 were religious in nature, including many devotional and sermon books. Three-fourths of them were in Latin, the number of books in the vernacular increasing gradually until the great explosion of vernacular books and treatises in the Reformation period. Moreover, the Bible appeared in the language of the people, at least twenty-nine vernacular Bibles having been printed before 1500, including those in German and even low German. The Archbishop Berthold of Mainz said of printing: "The clergy . . . hailed it as a divine art."

Advances in education are further evident in the founding of new universities. By 1500 there were some seventy-nine

universities in Europe. In England new colleges were added
to Oxford and Cambridge. Popes, prelates, princes, and
cities established new universities. In some cases endowments originally intended for some strictly religious purpose
such as the saying of masses were diverted to support new
colleges and university foundations. Ironically this very rise
in the literacy and learning of the laity became a source of
the criticism directed against the deficiencies of the clergy.
Moreover, just as the church had been the mother of the medieval universities, the university now became the mother of
the Reformation.

Overall Condition of the Church

The upsurge of frenetic religious activity does not prove the
case for a renaissance of the pure Christian faith as such.
There was, to be sure, a new mystical faith reflected in such
movements as the Brethren of the Common Life, in individual mystics such as Catherine of Siena, the English-
woman Margery Kempe, Brigitta of Sweden, Jean Gerson,
or even Lefèvre d'Étaples, and in the work of artists such as
Matthias Grünewald, whose portrayal of the crucifixion for
the Isenheim altar was starkly realistic. The *Pietà*, Christ
taken from the cross and held in the arms of his mother, as
a new German art form reflected a genuine Christocentric
piety. But there is also evidence in many parts of Europe and
on all levels of society of a persistence of paganism, the sur-
vival of Germanic folklore, an inclination toward superstition, the practice of witchcraft, a substratum of materialism,
and a failure to understand or appreciate the transcendent
and otherworldly dimensions of the faith. The extent of
popular theological understanding was not impressive, and
the sense of sin was often fear of damnation rather than deprivation of God. The perception of grace was often distorted into a magical interpretation of the *ex opere operato* or
mechanical and external operation of the sacraments. There
was often more preoccupation with the devil than affection
for God. One student of popular religion in Flanders has
ventured the rather extreme judgment that 40 percent of the
people were Christians of good character and 10 percent

were fervent practitioners, while the rest were indifferent or negligent formal adherents. Catechisms were 80 percent morality, 15 percent dogma, and only 5 percent concerned with the sacraments. The Christian facade concealed an anemic concern with the supernatural. Historical judgments in this area are difficult, dependent as they are upon subjective views of what constitutes pure Christianity. One might argue, for example, that the resurgence of Lollardy, the continuance of Waldensianism, the persistence of Hussitism, the vitality of the Beghards and Beguines, the appearance of flagellants, and other heresies revealed the strength of religious impulses. Certainly the credibility gap between the religious expectations of the people and the ability of the official church to meet those expectations promised little good for the future. But there was still a great deal of health and strength in the old church, and thousands of faithful priests and millions of devout believers sought a more intense religious experience and a pure form of Christianity. The church was perhaps in at least as sound a condition on the eve of the Reformation as it was when it entered the crises of the fourteenth century. But this time the forces against it proved to be even more powerful.

Martin Luther and the Appeal of Protestantism

E. Harris Harbison

In the following account, Reformation historian E. Harris Harbison examines the fundamental role played by Martin Luther in formulating basic Protestant beliefs and in promoting the spread of those ideas throughout Europe in the 1520s. Luther's insight, that sinners are justified only by faith in God, and not by acts such as fasting, penance, or pilgrimages, struck a responsive chord among many European Christians. Luther insisted that the Bible and the individual conscience, rather than the Pope and church councils, are the ultimate authorities in spiritual matters. He also argued that priests are no closer to heaven than ordinary folks, and that the church is a community of believers, not a hierarchical organization centered in Rome. Harbison, a long-time professor at Princeton University, contends here that a central factor in the widespread acceptance of these Protestant ideas was national sentiment, rejecting the power of Rome in favor of local and national power.

The immediate origins of the Protestant Reformation lay in the religious experience of Martin Luther (1483–1546). We will never know precisely what happened to Luther in the years between his becoming a monk in 1505 and his dramatic attack on indulgences in 1517. But we know from his contemporary lecture notes and from his later writings and

Excerpted from *The Age of Reformation*, by E. Harris Harbison. Copyright ©1955 by Cornell University. Used by permission of Cornell University Press.

conversations with friends that he underwent years of harrowing emotional and intellectual tension which finally resulted in a "conversion" experience sometime during these years. The nature of this experience was to determine the main features of Protestant belief and the direction which the Protestant movement took. It is important, therefore—difficult as it is—to sketch briefly the inner struggles of this obscure Augustinian friar and their outcome.

Salvation by Faith

Outwardly, young Martin Luther was one of the most pious and diligent monks in the friary at Erfurt. "If ever a monk got to heaven by his monkery," he wrote twenty years later, "I should certainly have got there." But he was haunted from the beginning by doubts about whether he, a mere man and a sinner, could ever satisfy a righteous God. In spite of fastings, scourgings, and prayer beyond the rule, he could gain no sense of being forgiven. Doubt aroused fear, and fear led to moments of panic and despair. Staupitz, the kindly vicar of the order, could not understand this sensitive and intelligent younger brother who was constantly confessing his minor sins and yet could never quite rid himself of the sense of guilt.

Scholars differ in explaining Luther's predicament. Perhaps his conception of God as a stern and righteous Judge owed something to the character of his father, a hardworking peasant and miner, devoted to his son's welfare but strict and demanding. Perhaps it owed something to stern representations of God in either sculpture or story impressed upon him at an early age. He had taken the vow to become a monk in a moment of panic during a thunderstorm, and the fact that he immediately regretted it but went through with it may have contributed to his later tension. Luther was a high-strung person with keen sensibilities and a sensitive conscience, not the kind to persuade himself easily that he was doing the best he could and that the rest might be left to God (as his spiritual advisers urged). The theological school which dominated the teaching at the University of Erfurt where he had studied put strong emphasis on what were called "good works," a term which included sacramental and ceremonial acts (such as doing penance, fasting, going on a pilgrimage, entering a monastery) as well as acts of charity. The kernel of this teaching was that man through his own effort and will has a large share in determining his ultimate salvation or damnation. In effect, Luther was acting on this teaching, but failing miserably to gain any inner assurance of forgiveness and so of the promise of salvation.

Luther's Insight About Faith

Then something happened. In 1511 Staupitz had seen that Luther was appointed Professor of Bible at the new University of Wittenberg, and for a year or more the thirty-year-old professor had been soaking himself in Scripture. The influence of his friends and his reading began to suggest a solution to his soul's plight. As he remembered it later, it all happened suddenly (some scholars think in the winter of 1512–1513) in the tower room of the Augustinian friary at Wittenberg where he lived, perhaps while he was writing notes for his lectures on the Psalms (which scholars rediscovered only a half-century ago). Here is his own account, written in 1545, of his attempt to probe St. Paul's meaning in Romans 1:17:

> After I had pondered the problem for days and nights, God took pity on me and I saw the inner connection between the two phrases, "The justice of God is revealed in the Gospel" and "The just shall live by faith." I began to understand that this "justice of God" is the righteousness by which the just man lives through the free gift of God, that is to say "by faith.". . . Thereupon I felt as if I had been born again and had entered Paradise through wide-open gates. Immediately the whole of Scripture took on a new meaning for me. I raced through the Scriptures, so far as my memory went, and found analogies in other expressions.

Luther felt he had rediscovered the meaning of St. Paul's conviction that a Christian is saved not by moral or ceremonial "works," but by his faith in the loving and merciful Father who incarnated Himself in Jesus Christ in order to save men. This faith is a "free gift of God." Salvation cannot be deserved or merited, then; it cannot be bought or bargained for by the doing of good works—by fastings and prayer, penances and pilgrimages, or even by becoming a monk. No man can fulfill God's requirements and thus become righteous because all men are sinners, but God counts man's faith (which is His own free gift to man) as the equivalent of righteousness. Luther had tried and failed to merit forgiveness and salvation. At the moment of blackest despair he realized that in the saving of souls literally everything is God's work and nothing is man's. Salvation is the free gift of a loving God to undeserving man.

Scripture and Conscience

Luther was not a systematic or logical thinker. Rather, his thinking was existential, that is, it developed out of his own personal experience and the decisions he had to make in living out his own life. If he had been more logically inclined, he might have concluded immediately that if a Christian is saved by his faith alone, then the whole mediaeval church, with its sacraments and ceremonies, its papacy and its priesthood, was really unnecessary. A man alone in his room with God and God's Word, the Bible, like Luther in his tower room—this would be the true picture of a Christian—not that of a man confessing his sins to a priest, traveling on a pilgrimage, or buying an indulgence to get his dead parents out of Purgatory. This was to be the heart of Protestant belief as it developed later: the Bible and a man's conscience are the channels through which God speaks to human beings, not the Roman Church and its sacraments. But it took personal contact with the practice of indulgences, and later the attacks of enemies, to make Luther realize the full implications of his own religious experience. And even to the end, he never broke with what he thought was the *true* Church of Christ and its sacraments.

The Mainz Indulgence of 1515 was a peculiarly lurid example of the connection between spiritual and financial abuses in the church. The pope proclaimed an indulgence ostensibly to raise money for the building of St. Peter's in

Rome. Actually all but a very small percentage of the money raised found its way into the pockets of the Dominican monks who sold the coveted certificates to the people, of bankers who handled the receipts, and of a great ecclesiastical prince, Albert of Hohenzollern, who owed the pope a large bribe for the privilege of holding three bishoprics when the canon law said that no one might hold more than one. Luther, like the ordinary person, knew nothing of Albert's deal with the pope. He knew only that his students at the University of Wittenberg were flocking across the border of Saxony to buy indulgences in Magdeburg and returning to him convinced that their sins were forgiven. John Tetzel, a particularly unscrupulous Dominican, was preaching to the crowds that "so soon as coin in coffer rings, the soul from Purgatory springs." In indignation born of his own religious experience, Luther drafted 95 Theses attacking the current doctrine of indulgences. The most radical proposition was that "Any Christian whatever, who is truly repentant, enjoys full remission from penalty and guilt, and this is given him without letters of indulgence."

Luther probably had no intention of doing more than start an academic debate on his theses at the University of Wittenberg. But it became evident almost overnight that he had touched on the most sensitive nerve of the whole ecclesiastical organization of his day. The theses were published and devoured by Germans everywhere. The pent-up resentment against papal exactions and ecclesiastical abuses became polarized by his attack. The sale of indulgences fell off sharply, and the Dominicans demanded that Luther be curbed. Step by step, opponents who saw the doctrinal and financial dangers in Luther's criticisms forced him to work out the implications of his position. First he appealed to the pope, but the Medici Leo X was inclined to treat the whole matter as an unimportant quarrel between monks. When Leo's attitude became harder, he appealed from the pope to a general council. Finally a particularly skillful debater, Dr. John Eck, manoeuvred him into declaring that even a general council was fallible—which left him with Scripture and conscience as his only ultimate authorities. This became perfectly clear when he faced the emperor Charles V and the assembled Diet of the empire at Worms in 1521 and replied to the demand that he recant his views with words which were to become famous throughout Europe:

> Unless I am convinced by the evidence of Scripture or by plain reason—for I do not accept the authority of the Pope or the councils alone, since it is established that they have often erred and contradicted themselves—I am bound by the Scriptures I have cited and my conscience is captive to the Word of God. I cannot and will not recant anything, for it is neither safe nor right to go against conscience. God help me. Amen.

Protestant Beliefs

Between 1520, when Luther wrote the tracts and pamphlets which are still the best expression of his religious ideas, and 1530, when the beliefs of the church he founded were summarized in the Augsburg Confession, the main lines of Protestant belief and practice were worked out by Luther himself and his lieutenants in Wittenberg, with some contributions from independent leaders of revolt against Rome such as Ulrich Zwingli in Zurich and Martin Bucer in Strasbourg.

The best general description of Protestantism is still probably that of Ernst Troeltsch: "A modification of Catholicism, in which the Catholic formulation of problems was retained, while a different answer was given to them." In particular, Luther offered relatively new answers to four questions which go far back in Christian history. To the question how is a man to be saved, Luther answered: not by works but by faith. To the question where does religious authority lie, he answered: not in the visible institution known as the Roman Church, but in the "Word of God" contained in the Bible. To the question what is the church, he answered: the whole community of Christian believers, since all are really priests and since every man must be "a Christ to his neighbor." To the question what is the essence of Christian living, he replied: serving God in one's calling, whether secular or ecclesiastical, since all useful callings are equally sacred in the eyes of God. These were the four cen-

tral Protestant beliefs, each closely related to the others: salvation by faith rather than by works, the authority of the
Bible interpreted by the consecrated conscience, the priesthood of all believers, and the service of God in secular as
well as clerical callings. All could be taken to follow from
Luther's original experience of God's saving grace in the gift
of faith.

Recapturing Christian Truth

To sixteenth-century followers of Luther, Protestantism was
essentially a *restoration*. During the Middle Ages—so the
theory ran—Christianity had become encrusted and over-
loaded with doctrines and practices which had nothing to do
with its essence and which came close to obliterating the
Gospel revealed to the early church. It was imperative to go
back to Paul and the Gospels, back to the practices and insights of the Apostolic Age, in order to recapture Christian
truth. The canon law and scholastic theology of recent centuries were satanic corruptions of the primitive Gospel. The
bishop of Rome, far from representing Christ on earth, was
the Anti-Christ prophesied in the Book of Revelation.

To sixteenth-century Catholics, Protestantism was essentially a *revolution*. To deny that Christ had founded his
church on Peter and that the popes were Peter's successors,
to question the divine institution of the seven sacraments, to
say that all believers are equally priests, that all men are
saved or damned by the arbitrary will of God with no respect
to good works or merit—all this was either heresy or blasphemy to loyal sons of the mediaeval church. Luther, not
Leo, was the Anti-Christ—the "wild boar" which was rav-
aging God's vineyards, in the words of the papal bull which
excommunicated the heretic friar in 1520.

Today most historians refer to Protestantism as a *reformation*. In the ordinary sense of moral reform, Protestantism
probably accomplished little. Nor did Luther think of his
movement as aimed primarily at the improvement of clerical
and lay morality. Protestantism is properly described, however, as a reforming or reformulating of the Christian tradition. In attempting to restore first-century Christianity, the

early Protestants were inevitably revolutionists. In going back, they moved forward. And the result was that they gave a new shape to the Christian tradition in almost half of Europe.

The Appeal of Protestantism

One of the most difficult tasks of the historian is to discover how and why a complex set of ideas like those of Luther captures men's minds and so becomes a historical "movement." The simplest explanation is to say that Luther was a "typical" German of his day, with an uncanny feeling for the religious problems of ordinary people, and that his teachings went straight to the hearts of those who were tired as he was of trying to win salvation by good works. There is truth in this, but as an explanation it obviously applies only to a tiny minority of persons who had a religious sensibility and sophistication comparable to Luther's. What of the many others all over Europe—peasants, artisans, merchants, lawyers, priests, monks, and princes—who we know became "Lutherans"?

Among the lowest classes there were many who misinterpreted Luther to mean that God meant men to be free of *all* bonds, social and economic as well as ecclesiastical. They were soon disillusioned when Luther made it clear that what he meant by "the liberty of a Christian" was freedom from the galling restrictions of the Roman Church, not freedom from serfdom or from obedience to secular rulers. But they were awakened and thrilled, nevertheless, by Luther's heroic defiance of authority.

Much has been written about the appeal of Protestantism to the middle classes. The tendency of recent scholarship is to be cautious about generalization on the subject. But Lutheran and particularly Calvinist teachings certainly had special appeal to the merchants and professional people of Europe, particularly in the North. These were the classes which had obvious reasons to dislike papal taxation, to envy the church's wealth, and to despise the luxury and corruption of the nonproductive bishops and monks. Salvation by faith alone, the priesthood of all believers, and serving God in one's calling were attractive slogans to such people—sometimes, but not always, for the purely religious reasons Luther himself would have wished. Not that the ordinary bourgeois was irreligious. More often he was a person deeply immersed in secular pursuits—building up a business, amassing wealth, carrying on a law practice, or serving a monarch—troubled in conscience by the gulf between his worldly interests and the other-worldly ideal imbued in him by the Roman Church. For this reason he might be much attracted by the idea that a man is saved by faith, not by sacramental magic and the buying of indulgences, and that one can serve God just as well as a merchant or magistrate as one can by being ordained priest or monk. Who can estimate the subtle balance of religious and secular motives in the souls of such persons, to whom Lutheranism meant an answer to the question how they might gain salvation and still remain fully in the active world of business competition and human pleasure?

To the German governing classes, the prospects of curbing the independent power of the supranational church in

---

Christians, Not Lutherans

No one was more surprised than Luther himself by the fervor with which his ideas were embraced, both in Germany and in other parts of Europe. In this excerpt from a tract condemning political rebellion, Luther laments the growing tendency for Christians who accepted his basic principles to identify themselves as "Lutherans."

I ask that men make no reference to my name; let them call themselves Christians, not Lutherans. What is Luther? After all the teaching is not mine [John 7:16]. Neither was I crucified for anyone [1 Corinthians 1:13]. St Paul, in 1 Corinthians 3, would not allow the Christians to call themselves Pauline or Petrine, but Christian. How then should I—poor stinking maggot-fodder that I am—come to have men call the children of Christ by my wretched name? Not so, my dear friends; let us abolish all party names and call ourselves Christians, after him whose teaching we hold.

Martin Luther, *A Sincere Admonition by Martin Luther to All Christians to Guard against Insurrection and Rebellion*, 1521. (In Carter Lindberg, *The European Reformations*, pp. 109–110).

their particular dominions, of establishing control over the local clerical hierarchy, of possibly confiscating the lands of monasteries and even bishoprics, had particular appeal. In 1520 Luther appealed to "the ruling class of the German people" to reform the church, since the church would not reform itself. Such an appeal to the secular rulers was nothing new, as we have seen, but it had decisive results for the Lutheran movement. Luther was a peasant and a monk, naturally inclined to think in terms of authority and obedience to lawfully constituted powers. He turned to the princes and magistrates for support, and he was not disappointed. Before his death in 1546 he saw duchy after duchy and city after city in north and central Germany break with Rome, subordinate the local church to the state, dissolve the monasteries, and simplify the church services, all under the leadership and usually at the instigation of the ruling prince or the town council. Luther himself had no intention to preach the "divine right of kings," but the circumstances in which he found himself, together with his own instincts, led him to rely on the powers that be to defend the Gospel. Most of the German rulers who took up his challenge to reform the church profited considerably in terms of political power and wealth.

German National Sentiment

One element in the appeal of Protestantism to all classes of European society, particularly in Germany, was national sentiment. The drain of ecclesiastical taxation was particularly severe in Germany because there was no strong national ruler to stand up against it and the unimpeded abuse was correspondingly resented. This resentment played no part in Luther's own early development, but soon after his attack on indulgences he sensed the support he was receiving from German national sentiment and learned to play upon it. The papacy was wealthy, corrupt—and Italian. It was intolerable, he wrote in 1520, that the pope and cardinals should mulct his countrymen and then refer contemptuously to them as "silly drunken Germans." "If the kingdom of France has resisted it, why do we Germans let the Romanists make fools and monkeys of us in this way?" The appeal of Protestantism to national patriotism was perhaps strongest in Germany, but national sentiment was also a major factor in the appeal of Protestantism to Scandinavians, Englishmen, Netherlanders, and some Frenchmen.

National sentiment is intimately related to language. Within twenty years of the publication of Erasmus' Greek New Testament in 1516 with its preface urging the translation of Scripture into the common tongues of Europe, there were new versions of the Bible in German, French, and English which were to play an important part in the growth of both national sentiment and of Protestant conviction. In 1526 Tyndale began, and in 1535 Coverdale completed a new English version of the Bible which was a steppingstone to the King James Version of 1611, the most influential of all books in the forming of the English mind in the next century. By 1535 there were two new French versions, one in the Catholic spirit by Lefèvre d'Etaples, one in the Protestant by Olivètan. Luther's matchless German Bible, begun in 1522 and completed in 1532, was the greatest of them all if measured by the vigor and vitality of its style and by its influence on a people. Everywhere Protestants became "People of the Book," in an English historian's phrase. The effect of translating the Scriptures into the vulgar tongues was enormous. In an age which knew no television, radio, or even newspapers, the impact of the imagery and wisdom of the Bible upon those able to read their own language was almost revolutionary. In addition to the Bible, theological controversy was carried to the reading public in thousands of printed tracts (Luther's great appeals of 1520, Calvin's own French translation of his *Institutes* in 1541, for example). Cartoons concentrated and focused the gist of the printed word. Services in Protestant churches were conducted in the common tongue. Prayer itself, as a French historian puts it, was "nationalized."

Such were some of the elements, religious and secular, relevant and irrelevant, in the appeal of Protestantism to ordinary people in Germany and elsewhere in Europe. We shall consider the mentality of those to whom Protestantism did not appeal in treating the Catholic Reformation.

The Spread of Lutheranism to 1546

It was partly converted persons, partly printed books and pamphlets, that spread Luther's ideas. Naturally Luther's students and fellow professors at Wittenberg were his first converts, and to the end of his life the university was the nerve center of what came to be called "Lutheranism." The faculty of the university was solidly behind him when he posted his 95 Theses, and his colleagues were his staunchest early supporters, even if some like Melancthon became more conservative, some like Carlstadt more radical, than their leader. After a sharp drop in the 1520's following Luther's excommunication, student enrollment rose steadily at the university, reaching a peak in the 1540's and 1550's. Between 1520 and 1560 some sixteen thousand students went to Wittenberg from all over Germany, returning home as often as not to spread Luther's ideas. Priests and monks were particularly likely to be among the early converts, in addition to students and their families.

Luther's writings in both German and Latin, spread by the printing press, reached others not reached by converted Lutherans. The primary appeal of his thought was limited to Germans and Scandinavians, but his Latin writings were circulated and read in the Netherlands, England, France, Poland, Switzerland, and even in Spain and Italy in the 1520's and 1530's.

The History and Premises of Protestantism

Hans J. Hillerbrand

In this overview of the main figures and events of the Protestant Reformation, scholar Hans J. Hillerbrand identifies the variations in doctrine and approach among different Protestant groups, and he explains the basic Protestant beliefs of *sola fide*, by faith alone, and *sola scriptura*, by Scripture alone. He argues that the Reformation was primarily a religious phenomenon, though one in which political considerations were never entirely absent. According to Hillerbrand, as the Reformation matured, it became gradually more systematic and regimented, as with John Calvin's experiment in Geneva, Switzerland. The emphasis on individual responsibility and personal involvement in religion promoted a sense of freedom and creativity among those who accepted Protestant premises. Hillerbrand is professor of history and religion at Duke University and editor-in-chief of *The Oxford Encyclopedia of the Reformation*.

In order to understand the Protestant Reformation it is necessary to recall that in the time before the storm people were intensely religious. The intensity of religious commitment cannot easily be demonstrated, but all the evidence—the number of religious books, the gifts to religious causes, the frequency of pilgrimages, the membership of voluntary religious societies—suggests that people were as religious as they had always been, and that they took their religion seriously.

There was some deviation from the ideal, and we can easily cite criticisms of the church in which two themes in particular constantly recur: the financial burden imposed by the church and the unspiritual demeanor of the clergy. One must be careful, however, not to generalize too freely. The picture of a church in a state of complete perversion on the eve of the Reformation has little historical basis. Nor is it correct to say that in the early sixteenth century every sensible person yearned for ecclesiastical reform. Abuses were in fact few and far between. More to the point is that this was a generally restless society in which dramatic changes were everywhere taking place. No doubt there was uneasiness about the church, a latent dissatisfaction and disquiet. None of these, however, were pronounced or intense enough to make a religious upheaval inescapable. The generation might well have passed from the scene without having witnessed any kind of ecclesiastical change. A proper admixture of factors was necessary to bring the latent dissatisfaction into the open. When this happened, probably no one was more astounded than the man who had precipitated it: Martin Luther, a youthful and unknown professor of theology of Wittenberg.

Luther's Attack on Abuses

Martin Luther and the publication of his Ninety-five Theses mark the beginning of the Reformation. The theme of these Theses was the doctrine of indulgences, acknowledgedly a minor point of Catholic theology, which Luther meant to expound in a routine academic disputation. The immediate cause of Luther's step had been his disgust with the indulgence proclamation of John Tetzel. This proclamation was part and parcel of a grandiose political, financial and ecclesiastical scheme, and Luther had reached into a hornet's nest. Public excitement was engendered and knowledge of Luther's somewhat esoteric Theses was not restricted to a few theological experts. Since his pronouncement was taken to be directed against the hierarchy and the papacy (which it was not), he increasingly received support from those who were dissatisfied with the general state of ecclesiastical affairs. A controversy evolved which slowly but surely moved to more central issues. By the summer of 1519 the issue was that of religious authority; Luther repudiated the infallibility of both general councils and the pope, and replaced them with *sola scriptura*, Scripture alone.

Luther's proclamation was widely echoed and he became the hero of Germany. A host of disciples joined his cause, some because they had been genuinely touched by his religious message, others because they confused their own religious or even political aspirations with his. While some may have been strange bedfellows—mistaking Luther for a German nationalist or an Erasmian Humanist—their support was real and vastly consequential. By 1521 Luther's "reformation" had become a popular movement.

It also had become heretical. Since the early months of 1518 the wheels of the curial machinery had turned, now slowly, now rapidly, to assess the orthodoxy of the Wittenberg professor. By the summer of 1520 the verdict was reached: the bull *Exsurge Domine* condemned some forty of Luther's teachings as heretical. This should have been the end of the matter. For many reasons, it was not. Thus Luther outlived his excommunication and died peacefully in bed. More than that, he witnessed the establishment of Protestant churches. Once the impossibility of achieving a conciliation with the Catholic church had become obvious, Luther and the other reformers decided to go their own way and their theological pronouncements were translated into ecclesiastical practice. Numerous different questions begged to be answered about such problems as the place of the church in society, the form of worship, or ministerial training.

A House Divided

By that time a host of reformers had appeared on the scene, all in their own way echoing Luther's repudiation of the Catholic church. Multiplicity meant strength, but it also meant diversity, for these reformers did not fully agree with one another's theological positions. Some of the disagreements were innocuous, as, for example, those between Luther and Melanchthon, while others were more consequential, particularly since they soon issued into open controversy and revealed that Protestantism was a house divided against itself.

The most spectacular example was Huldrych Zwingli, the reformer of Zürich. Akin to Luther in a variety of ways, including his basic understanding of the New Testament, he sought to transform the faith and life of the church in Zürich according to his particular understanding of the gospel. He clashed with Luther over the correct interpretation of the Lord's Supper, a controversy that was to dominate the history of Protestantism for many years.

Of equal importance was the emergence of a radical form of Protestantism. Its spokesmen were erstwhile disciples of Luther and Zwingli, men who had become impatient with what seemed to them a slow and haphazard program of reform. They advocated nothing less than a "reform" of the Reformation. In terms of their own positive principles, they were a motley crew, holding to almost as many opinions as there were men. Most numerous among them were the Anabaptists, who advocated the *imitatio Christi*, to be evidenced by believer's baptism, pacifism, and a church composed only of those who had freely and determinedly elected to be Christ's disciples. The story of Anabaptism in the sixteenth century was one of bloody and ruthless persecution, practiced by Catholics and Protestants alike with a grim determination worthy of a better cause. It was a story of martyrdom and of suffering. Since rebaptism was a crime, the legal situation was hopeless for the Anabaptists. It was made worse by the disruption of the unity of society through the Anabaptist postulate of a voluntary church. . . .

Calvin's New Kind of Protestantism

John Calvin, the frail, modest, scholarly reformer of Geneva, was of the second generation of reformers who succeeded in synthesizing a new kind of Protestantism; systematic and persuasive, it proved to be vastly influential in the Anglo-Saxon world. Calvin was one of the outstanding theologians of the century—since there was no dearth of theologians this statement must not be taken lightly—and the systematic exposition of his theological thought, the *Institutes of the Chris-*

tian Religion, is one of the major documents of the Christian tradition. A Frenchman by birth, a lawyer-Humanist by training, a practical reformer in Geneva almost by accident, Calvin conceived of his reformatory work in a broad political setting. Like Zwingli in this respect, he saw direct implications of the gospel for the public and social realm; he set out not only to reform the faith of the Genevan citizens but also to transform the city itself. Some contemporaries thought him eminently successful. In John Knox's well known encomium, Geneva was the "most perfect school of Jesus Christ since the days of the apostles."

Calvin is sometimes described as an ecclesiastical tyrant and Geneva during his time as an ecclesiastical police state. There is some truth to this observation; like all half-truths, however, it is dangerously one-sided. Life was strict and regimented in Geneva; the consistory kept a careful eye on the demeanor of the citizens. But sixteenth-century society in general was circumscribed by numerous rules; in Geneva there was only slightly more regimentation and supervision than elsewhere. Far more important was the different ethos of the Genevan citizens who gladly shared, or at least tolerated, Calvin's vision of the Christian commonwealth. Calvin can hardly have been a tyrant; he faced staunch opposition during his first decade in Geneva and he always depended upon the good will of the Genevan authorities to carry out his program.

The Advances of Protestantism

These various streams of the Protestant Reformation arose from specific theological affirmations, which were expressed in differing ecclesiastical organizations—churches with pastors, people, and a definite polity and way of life. All the Protestant reformers were determined to translate their theological theories into ecclesiastical practice, and all were concerned that theirs should be the legally established religion of their respective commonwealths. Some were more successful than others. In England, . . . the settlement decreed by Queen Elizabeth gave lasting success to Protestantism, and in similar fashion other countries such as Scotland, Scandinavia, and Holland saw the permanent establishment of the Protestant faith. In Germany, the Peace of Augsburg in 1555 brought legal recognition of Lutheranism for those territories whose ruler decided to accept it. The radical expressions of Protestantism never secured such legal recognition, except in isolated instances and on a modest scale. And at some places, such as France or Poland, the struggle for the recognition of the Protestant faith occupied the larger part of the century. Thus, success was varied. At the end of the century, however, the map of Europe was predominantly Protestant; Catholicism seemed to be at its nadir.

A European Religious Phenomenon

Several features characterized the Protestant Reformation of the sixteenth century. First and perhaps foremost is the fact that it was a phenomenon of European dimensions. While the intensity of Protestant belief and the measure of eventual success differed from country to country, virtually all Europe was affected—Italy no less than Sweden, England no less than Poland. In this sense, this was an era with a common temper, affecting all of Europe simultaneously, in contrast to the Renaissance, for example, which never exerted such impact. Reformation scholarship is divided as to whether or not this European movement is to be traced to Martin Luther alone. Students of the Swiss or English Reformation have insisted on the autonomous character of the ecclesiastical transformation in their lands, suggesting that Luther only added further strength and impetus to basically indigenous developments. However, Luther's proclamation undoubtedly had an effect, even if only as a catalyst. It may be that his stand merely encouraged others to speak up boldly, but it was because of his encouragement that the Reformation spread beyond Germany.

A second feature of the Reformation (and it is not unnecessary to mention this) is that it was a religious phenomenon. The slogans of the reformers were religious slogans and their writings theological writings. This is external evidence, it is true, and does not refute the possible objection that religion provided a convenient rationalization for the pursuit of more tangible political or economic goals. But this admittedly attractive argument neglects several persuasive facts; in particular it overlooks the martyrs of the time. These men and women from all religious factions, Catholics, Lutherans, Calvinists, Anglicans, and Anabaptists, reveal intense religious commitment. Many went to the stake for their convictions, and many others who were not put to death suffered physical pain and economic hardship.

Moreover, the acceptance of the Protestant faith was in some instances the least prudent political policy to pursue. This was certainly true in Germany between 1521 and 1525, when it was virtually political suicide to accept the new faith. The peasants' uprising of 1524–1525, with the support it seemed to draw from the Lutheran proclamation, dismayed those charged with the maintenance of law and order. No one knew how the matter would end. In the 1520's the Catholics in Germany possessed a formidable hold on political power that should have given second thoughts to anyone who sought to break with the Catholic church for other than religious reasons. Most rulers possessed as much authority in ecclesiastical affairs as they desired.

Still, it would be naive to suggest that political considerations were completely absent. Indeed, the great theme of the age was, as Ranke observed, the interaction of religion and politics. Religion alone does not suffice as a full explanation for events, for in many ways political considerations intruded upon the ecclesiastical course of events. Zwingli's quest for a Protestant alliance, the formation of the League of Schmalkald, and the ecclesiastical transformation in Poland or France, show that Protestantism was politically involved.

By the same token, however, politics alone is an insufficient guide to understanding these dramatic events: Zwingli's unwillingness to compromise his theological position at the Marburg colloquy on communion even though this meant the abject failure of his political plans, and Luther's unwillingness to become the spokesman for the German people in 1521, are evidence of this.

Religion and politics interacted in countless ways, determining the temper of the age. In their light some men appeared nobler than we are wont to acknowledge, while some lofty ecclesiastical ideals were exposed as being much shabbier than was claimed.

The Central Beliefs of Protestantism

Theologically, the Protestant reformers thought themselves in the authentic Catholic tradition from which, they argued, the papal church had departed. And they were in a sense good Catholics. They accepted the three ancient creeds, so common ground existed between the old and the new church. The trinitarian affirmation or the christological definitions of the early church were never questioned by the reformers. But the Protestant Reformation was not a "reform" movement in the sense of seeking only to clip off certain "abuses" in the church and otherwise accept the status quo. To be sure, Luther and his fellow-reformers now and then talked about the correction of ecclesiastical abuses and initially their efforts may have been so understood by the people. But the real thrust of the reformers was in a different direction—a reinterpretation of the gospel. The reformers propounded a different understanding of the New Testament, and while this understanding had connections with the theological tradition of the Fathers, especially St. Augustine, it can justly be called new. When the Protestants talked about "reform," therefore, they thought not so much about the practical life of the church as about a new theological understanding.

One slogan seemed to express this new understanding most profoundly: the righteousness of faith, or of justification *sola fide*, by faith alone. The reformers attributed man's reconciliation with God solely to the divine offer of forgiveness which was to be appropriated by man through faith: no merits here, no harmonious cooperation between divine grace and human effort. Man, the sinner, is freely accepted by God. This assertion had many ramifications. The notion of the priesthood of all believers stated that all believers have full access to God and do not require the aid of the intermediary priest. In principle this did away with the distinction between clergy and laity and emphasized the fellowship of the Christian congregation.

Equally important was the stress upon *sola scriptura*, Scripture alone, for it propounded a new norm of religious authority. Only the Bible was acknowledged as a true source of Christian truth. This meant the repudiation of the authority of the church—the decisions of church councils, the papal pronouncements, indeed all that the reformers called "human traditions." Only if these ecclesiastical statements agreed with Scripture were they to be accepted as authentic.

There were additional aspects of the Protestant evangel, such as the repudiation of the primacy of the papal office or the acknowledgment of only two sacraments, namely, communion and baptism. The latter affirmation resulted from the reinterpretation of the nature of the sacrament which related the spiritual benefits of the sacrament more intimately to the faith of the individual. The cultural consequences of the Reformation must also be noted. The stress on the Bible as source of Christian truth and the corollary that each man must read it for himself meant that the religious responsibilities of the individual were vastly increased. A more sophisticated theological literacy was mandatory and this led to a determined pedagogical effort; schools were established, and language training was stressed. Behind it lay the Protestant notion of "vocation" which affirmed that all human endeavors, not only the clerical ones, are the fulfillment of a divine call. The swineherd was therefore as much called by God to his work as was the monk. The most menial work, performed in response to God's call, was endowed with religious significance; it was both important in its own right, and related to the divine purpose.

The Protestant Spirit

A further word must be said about what might be called the "Protestant spirit" for it was this "spirit" that caught the imagination of the people perhaps more than the theological doctrines expounded by the Protestant divines. The point of the Protestant proclamation was that religion was to be personal and creative. It called for personal involvement, not merely the affirmation of the dogma of the church or the external participation in its rites. It also called for the bold scrutiny of theological tradition and the willingness to reject it where it did not seem to be in harmony with the biblical message. At this point, one might well add, Catholics are most pronounced in their repudiation of the Reformation. The eminent Catholic historian Joseph Lortz chided Luther for not being "a full listener," that is, for making absolute his own understanding of the faith. Indeed, the reformers appear as the great destroyers—as tearing down the walls of the Romanists, as Luther put it in his tract on *The Babylonian Captivity of the Church:* tearing down the wall of five sacraments, the wall of transubstantiation, of the ecclesiastical superiority over the temporal power, of a celibate clergy. All ecclesiastical affirmations were to be examined creatively in the light of Scripture. Accordingly, an air of freedom surrounded the Protestant proclamation, for such a personal and creative religion left little room for regulations and regimentation. The Christian was a free lord over all things, Luther said, and a dutiful servant of all things.

Two generations ago the German sociologist Max Weber sought to relate the Protestant ethic, especially that of Calvinism, to the rise of capitalism. Subsequent research has tended to be skeptical of his thesis, but about the general cultural significance of the Reformation there should be little doubt. The Reformation was hardly the cradle of the modern world—in a variety of ways its questions were medieval questions—Luther's plea at Worms was hardly a plea for religious tolerance of the autonomy of conscience, and Calvin's economic thought was hardly the paradigm for Adam Smith. This must not obscure the fact, however, that these and many other "modern" notions made their first appearance during the sixteenth century, and the Reformation did its share in stimulating them: Protestantism stressed the centrality of the individual; sought to reduce the intervention of political power in ecclesiastical affairs; cast the glow of "vocation" over formerly menial undertakings; and raised the spirit of free, personal, and creative inquiry. All this could not help but change the face of society.

Chapter 2

The Spread of Protestantism

Turning | Points
IN WORLD HISTORY

Reasons for the Spread of Protestantism

J. Russell Major

While earlier would-be church reformers such as John Wycliffe and Jan Hus failed, Luther succeeded in seeing many of his ideas came to fruition. In the following essay, J. Russell Major, former professor at Emory University, identifies the main reasons for the successful spread of Protestantism. Luther's skill and industry as a writer, the role of the printing press in spreading ideas, and the protection given Luther by political authorities—all these factors provided both the time and means for widespread consideration and acceptance of Protestant views. Luther was also able to tap into nationalist sentiment and resentment against Rome, which led some territorial princes and magistrates to break away from the Roman church. Poverty and the discontent among the peasant class also fueled interest in Luther's stand against church authority.

The rapid spread of Lutheranism and other Protestant denominations was in marked contrast with the limited successes achieved by previous religious leaders like Wyclif and Hus who had also broken with Rome. Many reasons have been given to explain Luther's success.

Luther had nearly every quality essential to a revolutionary leader. His courage and intense conviction enabled him to take his stand against pope and emperor, and his intellectual and argumentative powers often convinced the skeptical. Although many of his sermons and pamphlets now seem unnecessarily violent and vindictive, they made as many friends as enemies. His literary style was superior, and he had genuine gifts as a writer of hymns. Indeed, he was the first person to make congregational singing an important part of the church service. However, it would be hasty to assume that he was a better leader than Wyclif or Hus, whose theological positions were often similar to his own.

Technological and Political Advantages

Luther did have one great advantage that had been denied to his predecessors—the printing press. Their ability to influence people had been limited by the relatively few who could hear their sermons or read the handful of manuscripts that they and their supporters could copy, but the printing press enabled Luther to make the entire Empire his audience. He made special use of small pamphlets from six to eight pages in length that could be sold for very little; some 350,000 copies of these were printed between 1517 and 1520. Woodcuts on the title pages suggested the contents to the illiterate and attracted the attention of those who could read. Quickly they enabled Luther to gain so wide a following that he could have been halted only by the use of a large army.

Another advantage possessed by Luther was that the unusual political situation in Germany gave him time to consolidate his position. The semi-independent status of the Elector Frederick of Saxony enabled him to protect Luther from the wrath of the Church and the secular authorities. Frederick's position was especially strong at the time because Emperor Maximilian was dying when the indulgence question arose; in the interregnum that followed, the pope was more anxious to persuade Frederick to help block the election of Charles V to the imperial throne than he was to get him to punish a rebellious monk. More than three years elapsed after Luther had posted the ninety-five theses before he was excommunicated or placed under the ban of the Empire.

By that time, the Lutheran movement had become so strong that only a large military force could have stamped it out. Charles was in no position to act because war broke out with France that same year and lasted almost continuously until 1544. The Turks besieged Vienna in 1529, and that war continued to sap the imperial strength until 1545. It was not until the following year that Charles was able to take military action against the Protestants. Although he won some initial successes, neither the pope nor the Catholic German princes would give him their wholehearted support for fear that while he was defeating the Protestants he would also make himself political master of the Empire. Finally, renewed French intervention brought an end to Charles's hopes, and he abdicated, leaving to his brother Ferdinand the task of making a religious settlement. By the terms of the Peace of Augsburg, 1555, the individual princes and imperial cities were given the right to decide whether their subjects would be Lutheran or Catholic and those who objected were to be permitted to emigrate. Church lands seized by the Lutherans prior to 1552 were to be retained, but in the future, bishops who became Protestants were to forfeit their lands rather than turn them into secular principalities as they had done before. Protestant sects other than the Lutherans were not recognized, but the existence of a Lutheran church in the Empire was not seriously threatened again until the Thirty Years War (1618–1648).

The Issue of Abuses

The printing press and the advantageous political situation in the Empire gave Luther the time and the means to gather converts, but less obvious factors may also have contributed to his extraordinary success. Most of those who objected only to the abuses in the Catholic church stayed in its fold to work for reform, but the existence of abuses lowered the respect in which the ecclesiastical hierarchy was held and thereby lessened its capacity to combat Protestantism. In addition, the abuses provided Luther and his supporters with propaganda that they never tired of using. Still, bad as they were, the abuses were not so important a factor in the Protestant revolt as might be imagined.

In some respects, the issue of abuses became entangled with the nascent nationalism of the age. At this time, nationalism was a negative force opposing outside interference, more than a positive force drawing different provinces together. The pope, as the head of the one remaining international institution, was constantly under attack. His right to fill many clerical vacancies and to grant indulgences, his claim to receive annates and various other revenues, and his ecclesiastical courts, which served as final courts of appeal in ecclesiastical cases, including divorces, were everywhere unpopular. It was well known that papal favors could usually be purchased, and it was widely believed that the constant flow of money to Rome was hurting local economies. Strong monarchies like those of France, England, and the Spanish kingdoms had been able to reduce papal influence, especially during the conciliar movement, but the emperor had lacked the power to do so effectively. Nowhere was the influence of Rome greater than in the Empire.

This situation provoked the ire of Ulrich von Hutten (1488–1523), an imperial knight whose humanistic studies had led him to Tacitus' (55–118?) description of the early Germans as brave, loyal, and liberty-loving. History, as Hutten saw it, had witnessed a constant struggle between the Latins, represented by the Roman Empire in ancient times and the popes of his day, and the Germans. The Lutheran movement was for him an effort to throw off foreign domination. He enlisted the help of some other imperial knights, including Franz von Sickingen, a mercenary soldier who possessed an army. In 1522, they attempted to secularize the lands of the Archbishop of Trier but were defeated the following year. Their failure, taken with Charles V's decision at the meeting of the *Reichstag* at Worms to remain loyal to Rome, removed the possibility of the Lutheran movement's merging fully with nationalistic forces to create an independent German church.

Economic and Social Factors

It has often been suggested that economic and social factors helped the Protestant cause. Although the peasants in southern and central Germany were, as a whole, becoming more prosperous, higher taxes and increased exactions by the nobility were taking a large part of their gains. They looked to the emperor for support against the great nobles and boldly coupled their economic demands with requests for such Lutheran reforms as the election of ministers by their congregations. Although Luther recognized some justice in their position, he was furious at their efforts to use religion to justify their worldly aspirations and argued that the Bible defended serfdom. By 1524, the peasant movement had become a revolt. In some towns, the lower classes supported the peasants, as did a few of the more radical Protestant ministers, but Luther was violently opposed. Although he was himself of peasant descent, he wrote the virulent pamphlet, *Against the Murdering Hordes of Peasants*, in which he urged the princes to "knock down, strangle, and stab. . . . Such wonderful times are these that a prince can merit heaven better with bloodshed than another with prayer." His advice was hardly necessary. The poorly led peasants were easily defeated, and an estimated 100,000 were slaughtered in the blood bath that followed. Belatedly, Luther called for mercy, but most of the German masses had been permanently alienated.

Many, especially the Marxists, have sought to associate Protestantism with the rise of the middle class. Catholicism, they argued, was an ascetic religion ideally suited for a medieval, feudal, agrarian society, but the growth of a bourgeois capitalistic economy created a need for a new religion that would justify worldly pursuits and business practices such as the charging of interest. Unhappily for the advocates of this point of view, Luther was more conservative in his social and economic outlook than most Catholics and bitterly attacked the pope for permitting usury. No Protestant leader was willing to make more concessions to the capitalists than they already enjoyed in Italy; and Italy, where the middle class was more highly developed than anywhere else in Europe, remained overwhelmingly Catholic.

The Role of Nobles and Princes

Indeed, a higher percentage of the nobility joined the Protestant churches than of any other social class. Some nobles may have hoped to get the lands of the Catholic church or to persuade the Protestants to support their political ambitions, but the risk in abandoning Catholicism was so great during the early stages that it is doubtful whether many, other than the religiously committed, were initially willing to brave the dangers. Only after the territorial prince adopted the new religion or a Protestant military leader had achieved considerable strength would many have been tempted to change their faith for economic or political reasons alone.

The territorial prince and the magistrates of imperial cities undoubtedly played major roles in the spread of Protestantism. The desire to be rid of papal influence and to increase their authority over the local clergy, as well as the desire for the wealth of the Church, commonly prompted rulers to abandon Catholicism. It was a dangerous step to take, however, and most of the German princes and magistrates who turned to Protestantism appear to have done so primarily for religious reasons. In England, where Henry VIII was obviously motivated almost entirely by secular considerations, religious doctrine was not initially changed to a significant degree. Once a ruler decided to become a Protestant, many of his subjects followed his example. Only the most devout put their religious faith ahead of their desire for law and order, which they thought necessitated unquestioned obedience.

Contrasts to Renaissance Humanism

The humanists may have paved the way for Protestantism by their study of philology, by their criticism of scholastic thought, and by their de-emphasis of Catholic dogma and ritual, but here the parallel ceases. The humanists taught a moral code that they found common to Christianity and the writers of classical antiquity. The Protestants taught a religious faith that was exemplified by the incarnation, the crucifixion, and the resurrection. The humanists emphasized that the dignity of man lay in his free will. The Protestants emphasized the depravity of man and insisted that he could do nothing of himself to merit salvation. When Luther began his attack on Rome, many humanists watched hopefully, but as soon as they recognized the character of the new movement, nearly all of the best known of their number decided to remain within the

Catholic Church although some young humanistically trained scholars joined the Protestants. When, in 1524, Erasmus finally entered the fray, it was to decry Luther's denial of free will, but he could have added the Protestant overemphasis on theology and the Protestant willingness to destroy the unity of the Church to his list of grievances.

The aesthetic aspects of the Renaissance were rejected by the Protestants. They regarded most church art as a form of idolatry and secular art as a vain conceit. Only hymn singing received their blessing. Thus, the Renaissance and Protestantism were contrary movements in many respects. They were alike only in that they had several common enemies and each in its own way fostered the development of individualism, the Renaissance by its emphasis on the dignity of man and Protestantism by its emphasis on the direct relationship between man and God.

Therefore, Protestantism was obviously a religious movement. Most of Luther's early support came from those like himself who had been taught by sermons and pictures to fear the flames of hell and who felt unable to merit salvation through their own efforts. To such people, the Protestant doctrine of salvation by faith alone brought a measure of hope. They were most numerous in the north; in Italy, where the religious intensity was less, Luther met with little response.

The Role of the Printing Press in the Reformation

Elizabeth L. Eisenstein

Elizabeth L. Eisenstein, professor of history at the University of Michigan, contends that Protestantism was the first religious movement to fully exploit the potential of the printing press to further its cause. The number of Protestant pamphlets increased exponentially after 1517, and Luther's writings in particular were disseminated throughout Europe in this decade. A phenomenal three hundred thousand copies of Luther's 95 Theses and other writings were printed and sold between 1517 and 1520. According to Eisenstein, Luther and other Protestants saw the printing press as a gift of God provided in order to further the cause of the Reformation. The excerpt that follows originally appeared in Eisenstein's groundbreaking study *The Printing Press as an Agent of Change*.

Between 1517 and 1520, Luther's thirty publications probably sold well over 300,000 copies. . . . Altogether in relation to the spread of religious ideas it seems difficult to exaggerate the significance of the Press, without which a revolution of this magnitude could scarcely have been consummated. Unlike the Wycliffite and Waldensian heresies, Lutheranism was from the first the child of the printed book, and through this vehicle Luther was able to make exact, standardized and ineradicable impressions on the mind of Europe, For the first time in human history a great reading public judged the

Excerpted from *The Printing Revolution in Early Modern Europe*, by Elizabeth Eisenstein. Copyright ©1983 by Cambridge University Press. Reprinted by permission of Cambridge University Press.

> validity of revolutionary ideas through a mass-medium
> which used the vernacular language together with the arts of
> the journalist and the cartoonist.

As this citation from A.G. Dickens suggests, the impact of print, which is often overlooked in discussions of the Renaissance, is less likely to go unnoted in Reformation studies. In this latter field, historians confront a movement that was shaped at the very outset (and in large part ushered in) by the new powers of the press. "The Reformation was the first religious movement," it has been said, "which had the aid of the printing press." Even before Luther, however, Western Christendom had already called on printers to help with the crusade against the Turks. Church officials had already hailed the new technology as a gift from God—as a providential invention which proved Western superiority over ignorant infidel forces.

Although the anti-Turkish crusade was thus the "first religious movement" to make use of print, Protestantism surely was the first fully to exploit its potential as a mass medium. It was also the first movement of any kind, religious or secular, to use the new presses for overt propaganda and agitation against an established institution. By pamphleteering directed at arousing popular support and aimed at readers who were unversed in Latin, the reformers unwittingly pioneered as revolutionaries and rabble rousers. They also left "ineradicable impressions" in the form of broadsides and caricatures. Designed to catch the attention and arouse the passions of sixteenth-century readers, their antipapist cartoons still have a strong impact when encountered in history books today. By its very nature, then, the exploitation of the new medium by Protestants is highly visible to modern scholars.

Moreover, the reformers were aware that the printing press was useful to their cause and they acknowledged its importance in their writings. The theme of printing as proof of spiritual and cultural superiority, first sounded by Rome in its crusade against "illiterate" Turks, was taken over by German humanists trying to counter Italian claims. Gutenberg had already joined Arminius as a native culture hero before he gained added stature for providing Lutheran preachers and princes and knights with their most effective weapon in their gallant struggle against popes. Luther himself described printing as "God's highest and extremest" act of grace, whereby the business of the Gospel is driven forward." From Luther on, the sense of a special blessing conferred on the German nation was associated with Gutenberg's invention, which emancipated the Germans from bondage to Rome and brought the light of true religion to a God-fearing people. The mid-century German historian, Johann Sleidan, developed this theme in an *Address to the Estates of the Empire* of 1542, a polemic which was republished more than once.

> As if to offer proof that God has chosen us to accomplish a special mission, there was invented in our land a marvelous new and subtle art, the art of printing. This opened German

The German Hercules

The printing press played a pivotal role in the dissemination of Luther's ideas, as this brief excerpt from Roland Bainton's biography of Luther makes clear. But Luther's books would not have sold out so rapidly had there not been widespread interest in the ideas themselves. Within just a few years of his 95 Theses, Luther had become an international figure.

In the early years of the Reform a cartoon appeared portraying Luther as "the German Hercules." The pope is suspended in derision from his nose. Beneath his hand cowers the inquisitor Hochstraten, and about him sprawl the scholastic theologians. The caption reveals that Luther had become a national figure. Such prominence came to him only after the Leipzig debate. Why the debate should of itself have so contributed to his reputation is puzzling. He had said very little at Leipzig which he had not said before, and the partial endorsement of Hus might rather have brought opprobrium than acclaim. Perhaps the very fact that an insurgent heretic had been allowed to debate at all was what attracted public notice.

A more important factor, however, may have been the dis-

eyes even as it is now bringing enlightenment to other countries. Each man became eager for knowledge, not without feeling a sense of amazement at his former blindness.

Variations on the German theme were played in Elizabethan England in a manner that has continued to resonate down to the present day. By associating printing with the providential mission of a prospering expansive realm, English Protestants pointed the way to later trends—to revolutionary messianism in the Old World and "manifest destiny" in the New. [As Gabriel Plattes wrote,] "The art of Printing will so spread knowledge, that the common people, knowing their own rights and liberties will not be governed by way of oppression and so, little by little, all kingdoms will be like to Macaria." Protestant divines diverged from Enlightened *philosophes* on many issues. But both viewed printing as a

semination of Luther's writings. John Froben, that hardy printer of Basel, had collected and brought out in a single edition the *Ninety-Five Theses*, the *Resolutions*, the *Answer to Prierias*, the sermon *On Penitence*, and the sermon *On the Eucharist*. In February, 1519, he was able to report to Luther that only ten copies were left, and that no issue from his press had ever been so quickly exhausted. The copies had gone not only to Germany but also to other lands, making of Luther not only a national but also an international figure. Six hundred had been sent to France and to Spain, others to Brabant and England. Zwingli, the reformer of Switzerland, ordered several hundred in order that a colporteur on horseback might circulate them among the people. Even from Rome came a letter to Luther written by a former fellow student, informing him that disciples at the peril of their lives were spreading his tracts under the shadow of the Vatican. He deserved a statue as the father of his country.

Such acclaim speedily made Luther the head of a movement which has come to be known as the Reformation.

Roland Bainton, *Here I Stand: A Life of Martin Luther*, p. 93.

providential device which ended forever a priestly monopoly of learning, overcame ignorance and superstition, pushed back the evil forces commanded by Italian popes, and, in general, brought Western Europe out of the Dark Ages. "The Lord began to work for His Church not with sword and target to subdue His exalted adversary, but with printing, writing and reading," wrote John Foxe in his best-selling Book of Martyrs. "How many presses there be in the world, so many blockhouses there be against the high castle of St. Angelo, so that either the pope must abolish knowledge and printing or printing must at length root him out."

Printing and Protestantism seem to go together naturally, as printing and the Renaissance do not, partly because vestiges of early historical schemes are carried over into present accounts. The new presses were not developed until after Petrarch's death and had no bearing on early concepts of a "rinascita"; they were in full operation before Luther was born and did enter into his views of a religious reformation. In the latter case, moreover, they affected events as well as ideas and actually presided over the initial act of revolt.

When Luther proposed debate over his Ninety-five Theses his action was not in and of itself revolutionary. It was entirely conventional for professors of theology to hold disputations over an issue such as indulgences and "church doors were the customary place for medieval publicity." But these particular theses did not stay tacked to the church door (if indeed they were ever really placed there). To a sixteenth-century Lutheran chronicler, "it almost appeared as if the angels themselves had been their messengers and brought them before the eyes of all the people." Luther himself expressed puzzlement, when addressing Pope Leo X six months after the initial event:

> It is a mystery to me how my theses, more so than my other writings, indeed, those of other professors were spread to so many places. They were meant exclusively for our academic circle here. . . . They were written in such a language that the common people could hardly understand them. They . . . use academic categories.

According to [Reformation scholar Hans Hillerbrand], it is still "one of the mysteries of Reformation history how this proposal for academic disputation, written in Latin, could have kindled such enthusiastic support and thereby have such far-reaching impact.". . .

Use of Marketing Strategies

[Luther's] surprise at the interest he aroused may have entailed self-deception. One of his letters, written in March 1518, reveals his anxious ambivalence over the question of publicity. Although he "had no wish nor plan to publicize these Theses," he wrote, he was willing to have his friends do the job for him and left it to them to decide whether the theses were to be "suppressed or spread outside." Given this choice, did he doubt how his friends would choose? "It is out of the question," writes Heinrich Grimm, "for Luther not to have known of the publication of his theses or for them to have been published against his will." Although Wittenberg was not yet a major printing center, Brother Martin was well acquainted with the new powers of the press. He had already acquired experience editing texts in Latin and German for printers. He had already demonstrated sensitivity to diverse German book markets and discovered that vernacular works appealed to a diversified clientele.

A letter from Beatus Rhenanus to Zwingli in 1519 suggests how the tactics employed by the small Latin-reading audience, whom Luther addressed, might produce distant repercussions in a short time. "He will sell more of Luther's tracts if he has no other to offer," Zwingli was told by Beatus in a letter recommending a book peddler. The peddler should go from town to town, village to village, house to house, offering nothing but Luther's writings for sale. "This will virtually force the people to buy them, which would not be the case if there were a wide selection." The linking of concern about salvation with shrewd business tactics and a so-called hard sell seems to have been no less pronounced in the early sixteenth century than among Bible salesmen today. Deliberate exploitation of the new medium helps to explain the paradox, which is noted in many Reformation studies, that a return to early Christian church traditions somehow served to usher in modern times.

"Rarely has one invention had more decisive influence than that of printing on the Reformation." Luther "had invited a public disputation and nobody had come to dispute." Then "by a stroke of magic he found himself addressing the whole world." [E.G. Rupp] Here is an example of revolutionary causation where normally useful distinctions between precondition and precipitant are difficult to maintain. For there seems to be general agreement that Luther's act in 1517 *did* precipitate the Protestant Revolt. October 31 "continues to be celebrated in Lutheran countries as the anniversary of the Reformation and justly so. The controversy over indulgences brought together the man and the occasion: it signalled the end of the medieval Church." [E.R. Elton] To understand how Luther's theses served as such a signal, we cannot afford to stand at the door of the Castle Church in Wittenberg looking for something tacked there. If we stay at the Wittenberg church with Luther, we will miss seeing the historical significance of the event. As Maurice Gravier pointed out, it was largely because traditional forms of theological disputation had been transformed by entirely new publicity techniques that the act of the German monk had such a far-reaching effect.

> The theses . . . were said to be known throughout Germany in a fortnight and throughout Europe in a month. . . . Printing was recognized as a new power and publicity came into its own. In doing for Luther what the copyists had done for Wycliffe, the printing presses transformed the field of communications and fathered an international revolt. It was a revolution.

The advent of printing was an important precondition for the Protestant Reformation taken as a whole; for without it one could not implement a "priesthood of all believers." At the same time, however, the new medium also acted as a precipitant. It provided "the stroke of magic" by which an obscure theologian in Wittenberg managed to shake Saint Peter's throne.

Zwingli, Calvin, and the Rise of Calvinism

Clyde L. Manschreck

The revolution that ignited with Luther's protest in 1517 expanded quickly to all quarters of Europe. Scholar Clyde L. Manschreck, professor of religious studies at Rice University, examines in this essay the most notable leaders and movements that inspired Luther, each of which deviated in some ways from Luther's agenda. The Anabaptists, Ulrich Zwingli, John Calvin, and John Knox all exerted their own spheres of influence outside of Luther's strongholds of Germany and Scandinavia. Calvin in particular, by the power of his many writings and the audacity of his experiment with Christian government in Geneva, became the most influential Protestant leader in the second half of the sixteenth century.

The explosive reform detonated by Luther reverberated throughout Europe, causing a rift in Christendom greater than that between Roman Catholicism and Greek Orthodoxy. Switzerland especially felt the reverberations. Ulrich Zwingli (1484–1531), about the same time as Luther, began agitations that resulted in widespread evangelical reform in the Swiss cantons. Dissatisfaction with Zwingli's policies prompted the main beginning of the Anabaptists, a group of New Testament Christians who rejected the established church and its ties with sovereignty of state in favor of voluntaryism and individual autonomy in religion. After the death of Zwingli on the battlefield at Kappel, evangelical

Excerpted from *A History of Christianity in the World*, by Clyde L. Manschreck. Copyright ©1985 by Prentice-Hall, Inc. Adapted by permission of Prentice-Hall, Inc., Upper Saddle River, NJ.

leadership in Switzerland shifted to John Calvin (1509–64) whose *Institutes of the Christian Religion* in 1536 and subsequent work in Geneva made him the acknowledged leader of Protestantism. Calvin's impact was primary, Luther's secondary, in the expansion of Protestantism in France, along the Rhine River into Holland, in England, Scotland, and the United States. Calvin's stamp is clearly noticeable in the Reformed Church of the Rhine Valley, Puritanism in England, and Presbyterianism in Scotland. Martin Bucer (1491–1551) and John Knox (1505–72) played important roles in these developments. Long before the end of the sixteenth century, diversity clearly marked Protestantism. The inherent subjectivity in the Protestants' twin authorities of Scripture and conscience led quickly to fragmentation.

Ulrich Zwingli, a native of Wildhaus, came under the influence of religion and humanism early in his life. Being gifted in music, at the age of twelve he almost became a monk in order to train other monks in music. However, he finally chose an alternative route to the priesthood—a humanist education at Vienna and Basel, where he came under the influence of Thomas Wyttenbach and Erasmus—and secured an appointment in 1506 as parish priest at Glarus, a large, wealthy church. In 1510 he published a fable in which he pictured a shepherd (the Pope) protecting his sheep against a marauding leopard (the French) and a stealthy fox (the Venetians). He became a reformer only gradually. His experience as a field chaplain led him to protest Swiss mercenary service for any except the Pope, which endeared him to the papacy, but Zwingli's study of the Bible and the Church Fathers led him also to question some of the church's practices. He wholeheartedly received Erasmus' Greek New Testament in 1516, and his study of it and reading of the sources inclined him toward an Erasmian philosophy of Christ. He grew increasingly critical, so that his departure from Glarus was not entirely voluntary. As the pastor at Einsiedeln for two years, 1516–18, Zwingli concentrated on the Bible and found more fault with Roman Catholicism. He openly attacked pilgrimages and Bernard Samson's selling of indulgences. Current papal authority and practices, he said could not be justified in Scripture.

Nevertheless, in 1518 Zwingli received appointment as Acolyte Chaplain to the Pope which led subsequently to his new pastorate in Zurich, finally enabling him to realize his political and ecclesiastical ambitions. . . . Outward reform in Zurich began in 1522 with Zwingli's vigorous preaching against Lenten fasts and rules. When the Bishop of Constance objected, Zwingli cited scholars and the New Testament, and pressed his point with the city council, which eventually agreed that the New Testament did not impose Lenten fasts but that they should be observed for the sake of good order. That did not satisfy Zwingli and his followers, who in August received a ruling from the council that henceforth all religious customs should be based on the pure Word of God. This undercut the authority of the Bishop of Constance and established civil rule in accordance with the Word as the reform principle of Zurich.

Zwingli's Beliefs

This set the stage for the crucial debates in 1523 for which Zwingli prepared his *Sixty-seven Articles.* He ably argued the authority of the Bible over the church, salvation by faith, the mass as a remembrance not a sacrifice, the right of priests and nuns to marry. He denied that good works merit salvation, that saints should be invoked, that priests mediate between God and man, that monastic vows are binding, that there is a purgatory, that anything is required of a Christian except what the Bible commands. The council implemented these new ideas with new regulations and the turn away from Catholicism was virtually complete. Before the year ended the council forbade images and performance of the mass. In place of the latter, Zwingli instituted the love feast, a memorial in remembrance of Christ. Instead of the golden chalice that he used as a Catholic priest at Glarus, he now celebrated the supper using a simple wooden bowl. Instead of transubstantiation, he held that the elements were purely symbolic and commemorative. He wished to eliminate anything, any creature, that might detract from the worship of the Creator. Consequently he removed from the churches all kinds of or-

naments—clerical robes, tapestries, frescoes, relics, cruci-
fixes, candles, and images. Bell-ringing, chanting, and
organ-playing ceased. In 1527 Zwingli had the great organ
in Zurich dismantled.

Zwingli's best theological work appeared in 1525, a *Commentary on True and False Religion.* He believed the Bible was
authoritative for faith and practice, that the Bible revealed
God's will for all humanity, that the Christian should reject
everything not expressly enjoined in Scripture. He believed
in an omnipotent God who wills and directs us and has foreordained the elect and that election is made known through
a faith experience. But he did not believe in original sin, regarding it only as a moral disease that did not involve personal guilt, and his humanism compelled him to hold that
the Spirit operates outside the sacraments and has inspired
such men as Socrates, Cato, and Hercules. . . .

The Origin of Anabaptists

Earlier in his career Zwingli clashed with some of his co-
workers and instituted one of the most tragic chapters in
church history. Some question remains about the origins of
Anabaptists (so-called for rebaptizing adults). . . . The main
part of Anabaptism originated in Switzerland in reaction to
Zwingli's stand on infant baptism and failure to promote a
genuinely New Testament church. . . .

Soon convinced that infant baptism was not scripturally
justifiable, that baptism was merely a symbol as Zwingli had
preached, that baptismal regeneration of infants was therefore a contradiction, and that Zwingli was not following his
own biblical dictum, they declared that baptism could be
properly administered only to adults who freely believed the
Gospel. This threatened the delicate union of church and
state that Zwingli had learned to manipulate. He feared tam-
pering with infant baptism would arouse antagonism that
could undo the entire reform. . . .

The Anabaptists plagued the mainline Protestants and the
Catholics for one basic reason: they endangered the union of
church and state. They were subversives. Church and state
were so closely linked that any fundamental criticism, any

forming of a new communion, even pacifism, appeared to be seditious. Anarchy might result. If the country were invaded, a large body of citizens could not be counted on to resist. Anabaptists frequently said the threatening Turks were not as bad as bloodthirsty, graceless Christians. In any event, the Bible enjoined them not to resist evil, but to return good for evil, to pray for their enemies. The established church and state rationalized that for the good of society Anabaptists had to be eradicated. The Anabaptists would not accept the absolute sovereignty of either the church or the state: they sought to establish a counterculture based on the Bible. Using a rationale of law and order, Luther, Melanchthon, Zwingli, Bucer, Calvin, Henry VIII, and Queen Elizabeth I subscribed to, justified, and sanctioned violent treatment of the Anabaptists. . . .

A New Champion of Protestants

During these turmoils the foremost leader of the second generation of Protestants emerged—John Calvin (1509–64). He stands midway between Luther and Zwingli in theology, and produced for Protestantism its most comprehensive theological system and model holy community. He and his followers dominated the second phase of Protestantism and clashed violently with Roman Catholicism for control of Western Europe.

Calvin, the son of a secretary to the Bishop of Noyon, France, prepared for a legal career with studies at Orleans, Bourges, and Paris, only to become interested in humanistic studies and eventually to switch to religion. In Paris he came into contact with Jacques Lefevre d'Etaples (1455–1536), a humanist whose commentary on Paul's letters had already raised doubts about transubstantiation as well as the merit of human works. Like many other humanist scholars, Lefevre believed increased knowledge would bring reform to the church. He was not the innovator of a new institution. Around him gathered other scholars who by 1530 had produced the entire Bible in French. Among his admirers was William Farel (1489–1565), who later persuaded Calvin to help in the reform of Geneva. How interested Calvin was in religion in this early period is not known. His first book, a commentary on Seneca's *Mercy*, in 1532, did not touch on religion. But between 1532 and 1534 Calvin underwent a conversion in which he, like Isaiah, experienced the glory of God and the sinfulness of man. In 1533 when Nicolas Cop assumed the rectorship of the University of Paris, Calvin as-

---

Pride and Immorality in the Priesthood

Though it may never have been as extensive as Protestant writers contended, the idea of corruption and abuses by the clergy continued to fuel Protestant indignation throughout the century. In the following excerpt from his Institutes of the Christian Religion, *John Calvin uses, at times, crude language to attack the pride and immorality of Catholic priests.*

Today there is no order of men more notorious in excess, effeminacy, voluptuousness, in short, in all sorts of lusts; in no order are there masters more adept or skillful in every deceit, fraud, treason, and treachery; nowhere is there as great cunning or boldness to do harm. I say nothing about their arrogance, pride, greed, and cruelty. I say nothing about the dissolute license of their entire life. The world is so wearied with bearing these abuses that there is no danger that I should seem to exaggerate unduly. I say one thing that even they cannot deny. There is scarcely a bishop, and not one in a hundred parish priests, who, if his conduct were to be judged according to the ancient canons, would not be subject either to excommunication or at least to deposition from office. I seem to be saying something unbelievable—so far has that former discipline fallen into disuse which enjoined a more exacting censure of the conduct of clergy; but this is entirely so. Let those who serve under the banners and protection of the Roman see go now and boast among themselves of the priestly order! The order that they have, it is clear, is neither from Christ, nor from his apostles, nor from the fathers, nor from the ancient church.

John Calvin, *Institutes of the Christian Religion*, tr. J.T. McNeill, Philadelphia: Westminster Press, 1960, pp. 1096–97.

sisted in the writing of the inaugural speech, which called for a return to the pure Gospel. Both he and Cop fled Paris. Calvin, disguised as a vinedresser, escaped in a basket. In the following year, 1534–35, the zeal of the Paris reformers brought on a persecution in which two hundred were arrested and twenty martyred. This was the persecution that prompted Calvin to write his *Institutes of the Christian Religion*, a small volume in 1536 when first published, but which Calvin greatly enlarged until the final edition in 1559. Since his basic ideas did not change, the book mirrors a lifetime of theological thought. Calvin prefaced it with a plea to Francis I of France (1515–47) to end the persecution of his loyal subjects.

Almost overnight Calvin was hailed as the new champion of the French Protestants. When Calvin's travels brought him to Geneva in 1536, Farel induced him to stay to help make Geneva, which had recently pulled away from Roman Catholicism, a model Christian community. The next two years were rough. Although Calvin produced the *Genevan Confession of Faith*, 1536 and his first *Catechism*, 1537, Roman Catholics, liberals, and libertines mustered sufficient opposition in 1538 to force him and Farel to leave Geneva precipitously. Calvin worked among the refugees in Strassburg for three years, had contact with other religious leaders, wrote his *Reply to Sadoleto*, who was trying to woo Geneva back to Catholicism, and in 1541 was invited to return to Geneva to restore order and stave off the drift to Rome. From 1541 until his death, Calvin molded Geneva, seeking to make it a model Christian community to the glory of God. For twenty-three years he preached, organized, disciplined, and wrote, more in the spirit of the Old Testament than the New. Geneva was a theocracy, directed in the will of God by Calvin.

Calvin's Basic Principles

Calvin took the absolute sovereignty of God as his basic principle. God is omnipotent, free, holy, glorious, just, and good. Human beings are weak, sinful, depraved, corrupt. They are unable to do any works of merit. All deserve to perish. However, through the Incarnation God reestablished contact with humanity, gratuitously granting justification by faith and belief in Christ as the divine Word, Creator, Redeemer, Prophet, Priest, and King. Not all are justified. Only the elect truly hear and believe the Gospel. Election is the work and will of God, from all eternity, and one's realization of election in justification by faith is an act of God and the Holy Spirit. Election is the reason why people respond differently to the preached Word. All are sinners and justly condemned by God, who in his inscrutable wisdom and mercy nevertheless eternally elected to save some through the merits and grace of his Son—salvation for some, reprobation for all others. Why did God elect as he did? Because it pleased him to do so. Election precedes faith: it does not depend on faith; faith, the disciplined life, and one's calling are but manifestations of it. We are saved by God's gratuitous mercy; we are damned by our own depravity. Yet everything is as God ordains. "He governs heaven and earth by his providence, and regulates all things in such a manner that nothing happens but according to his counsel. . . . Predestination we call the eternal decree of God, by which he has determined in himself, what he would have to become of every individual of mankind. . . . Nevertheless God cannot be called the cause of sin, nor the author of evil, nor subject of any guilt. . . . Man falls as God's providence ordains, but he falls by his own fault."

If this doctrine does not meet rational human standards, Calvin replies that God, not puny human reason, is sovereign. God has revealed his will in his inspired Word, which only a few people, like Calvin, with the aid of the Holy Spirit, truly understand.

Discipline in Geneva

Although God's grace is irresistible and irreversible, it may remain unknown. As those who are elected manifest the presence of the Spirit in disciplined morality and calling, this prompted some Calvinists to do good works to convince themselves of election. Because Calvin wanted to glorify God, he rigorously disciplined Geneva's vocations, manners, and morals. In this he was like the Anabaptists and their separated communities. But he joined with this the medieval notion

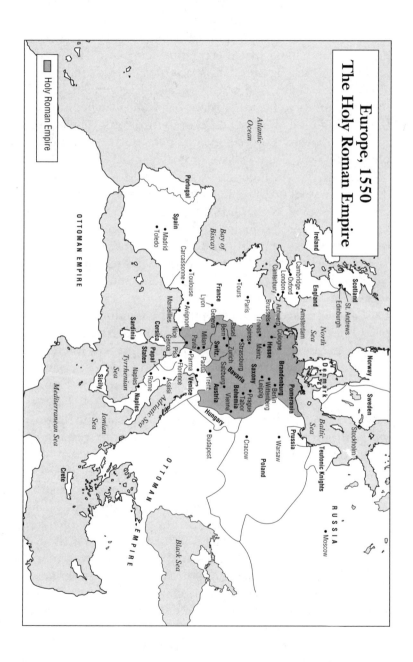

Europe, 1550
The Holy Roman Empire

Holy Roman Empire

that the secular power should cooperate with and protect the church. The result was an extensive and intensive system of social control. He extended his discipline to the entire community, maintaining that there is no adequate means for determining which are true Christians (i.e., elected and grafted into Christ by faith) and which are false. Everyone must have the opportunity to hear the true Word truly preached, and for the glory of God all must conform to his Word. Calvin instituted compulsory enforcement of pure doctrine and discipline; God's sovereign will was not to be mocked.

The instrument of control was a Consistory of twelve elders—laymen of good repute and members of the city council and six ministers that heard reports once a week of moral infractions. Penalties included fines, imprisonment, excommunication, banishment, and death. Between 1542 and 1546, fifty-eight people were executed and seventy-six banished. Adulterers, witches, blasphemers, and traitors were sentenced to death, a child was beheaded for striking his parents, and a critic executed for putting a sign on Calvin's pulpit. Other infractions included profanity, fighting, dancing, playing cards, carousing, laughter or loud noises in church, promiscuous bathing, gambling, theatrical performances, not attending or coming late to services, obstinacy, baptism by midwives, apostasy, and interest in excess of five percent. Pilgrimages, paternosters, idols, papal feasts, and fastings were all forbidden. Saloons were made into restaurants equipped with French Bibles for reading. Houses could be checked without notice at any time. No one, regardless of status, escaped the "fraternal correction" of the Consistory. Even the pastors examined themselves and their fitness for the ministry four times a year. The Consistory operated under the city council, but in 1553 Calvin won the right of the church to excommunicate without any further sanction. Although he had bitter opponents, Calvin dominated Geneva, like a tyrant according to his enemies, like an emissary from God according to his friends and the thousands of refugees who poured into Geneva.

After the massacre of the Waldenses, the burning of twenty-two of their villages in 1545, and the institution of the policy of Henry II of France (1547–59) to exterminate heretics and their books, as many as 5,000 Christians (about thirty percent of the population of Geneva) sought refuge under Calvin. For them Calvin provided jobs, brought in new industries, retrained adults, and established schools so that they might in their vocations properly glorify God and not be a parasitic burden on the community. They formed the bulwark of much of Calvin's power.

Calvin never sought honors for himself. His salary was a mere $600 a year, supplemented with a house, garden, two tubs of wine, twelve bushels of wheat, and enough broadcloth for a new coat each year. He was not ordained. In 1540 he married a widow with two children; his only son died in infancy. Severity marked his domination of Geneva, but in his private life he exhibited love and warmth.

The Death of Servetus

The most noted instance of his control was the execution of Michael Servetus on October 27, 1553. Servetus was a native of Spain, a renowned physician, and a critic of orthodoxy. As early as 1531, while only twenty years of age, Servetus (1511–53) published the results of his early biblical studies in *On Errors of the Trinity*. It was an acrid attack on varying trinitarian theories and contentions prevalent among Catholics and Protestants. He did not find the Trinity in the Bible, did not think three beings in one Godhead could be justified, and felt only disgust for self-serving orthodoxy and ecclesiastical pomposity. If the Christian is to believe only what is in the Bible, then, said Servetus, orthodoxy's "three-headed Cerberus," the Trinity, must go. It has no biblical basis, the Son is not coeternal with the Father, and it is ridiculous to speak of the Trinity as the divine three in one, the same, yet different. The book created a storm of protest, and inasmuch as anti-trinitarianism was, like rebaptism, punishable by death in imperial Roman law, Servetus was compelled to go underground and to live for twenty-two years in France under an assumed name.

In later years Servetus chose Calvin as his special target, corresponding with and writing bitter criticisms of him.

Servetus not only rejected the Trinity, but openly rejected original sin and infant baptism, and lauded the Anabaptist concept of the church as a voluntary community of regenerated believers. When Calvin sent him a copy of the *Institutes* for his instruction, Servetus returned it with copious, contemptuous, marginal notes. Servetus' masterpiece, the *Restitution of Christianity*, appeared anonymously in 1553, but to Calvin he impudently sent a copy under his own name. The *Restitution* was aimed chiefly at Calvin's *Institutes*. It was more than Calvin could stand. Years before he had guessed the identity of his correspondent, but now, through a friend, Calvin exposed Servetus to the Inquisition in France and supplied evidence for his heresy. Servetus was arrested and tried, but escaped from jail just before his sentencing. In effigy he was strangled and burned along with copies of his new book. In his flight toward Naples, he stopped at Geneva, went to church, was recognized, denounced by Calvin, and arrested on charges of heresy. How much Calvin's struggle for political power in 1553 affected his actions is not known, but the outcome is certain. The Genevan Council found Servetus guilty of obstinately spreading heresy and sentenced him to death by burning. Seven years earlier Calvin had vowed that if Servetus ever came to Geneva he would not leave it alive. On the day after sentencing, Servetus was chained to a stake, his book fastened to his arm, sulphur and straw rubbed into his hair. But the straw and fagots were damp and Servetus died only after half an hour of agony and screaming. At the end he cried, "O Jesus, Son of the Eternal God, have pity on me!"

Defending the Persecution of Heretics

Theologians and governments approved, including Melanchthon, Bullinger, Wittenberg, Basel, Berne, and Zurich. Heresy threatened the body politic; it was like a rotten limb that had to be amputated; the heretic could mislead and poison others. Harsh immediate action was necessary.

However, not all approved, and when the clamors reached Calvin, he wrote his *Defense of the Orthodox Trinity Against the Errors of Michael Servetus*, 1554, upholding the necessity of severely dealing with heretics in order to glorify God. The best criticism of Calvin was Sebastian Castellio's anonymous *Concerning Heretics* (1554). In it Castellio pleaded for the right of conscience in religion. The burning of heretics is far removed from Christ's spirit and words, and there are always the dangers that someone will be mistaken for a heretic or that a heretic will be punished more than Christian discipline requires. "To kill a heretic," he said, "is not to defend a doctrine, but to kill a man."

Servetus was not the first nor the last to be put to death in Calvin's Geneva, only the most famous. In 1903 some loyal "sons of Calvin" erected an "expiatory monument" on the site of Servetus' execution.

Despite the obvious criticisms that can be leveled against Calvin's excesses and harsh discipline, his religion of the majestic sovereignty of God attracted thousands of followers. Calvinists increased phenomenally in Holland, France, Scotland, and England, and also in parts of Germany, Poland, Hungary, and America. They suffered martyrdom by the thousands in their push against Roman Catholicism, particularly in Holland and France. Part of the appeal lay in the doctrine of election and God's providence, in the consummate skill with which Calvin expounded it, in the inherent democratic tendencies in the city-state of Geneva and the synod, in the paradoxical dynamic of Calvinism, in its biblically based insights into human nature and destiny. Calvin would have attributed its success to providence, to God's inscrutable will for the world.

The Reformation in England and Scotland

Karl H. Dannenfeldt

The Reformation in England took shape in a curious way. King Henry the VIII, a staunch defender of Catholicism, was unable to convince the Pope to grant him a divorce from his wife. To achieve this divorce, which Henry saw as a practical political move in order to conceive an heir to the throne, Henry broke away from the Church in Rome and declared himself head of a separate church of England. However, the rituals and teachings of the church Henry founded remained very similar to those of Catholicism until twenty years later when Henry's son Edward VI took the throne. England's distinctive brand of Protestantism did not fully take shape until the Elizabethan Settlement of 1559, shortly after the accession of Queen Elizabeth to the throne. The progress of Protestantism in England and Scotland is ably traced here by Karl H. Dannenfeldt, former academic vice-president at Arizona State University and author of several studies of both the Renaissance and the Reformation.

The reformation in England had been long in preparation. In the 14th century, waves of anticlericalism had swept the country, Wycliffe had thundered his warnings against the papacy, and the statutes of Provisors and Praemunire had drastically curtailed papal jurisdiction over England. Papal control over the English church became even weaker when the strong Tudor dynasty came to power in 1485 after the War of the Roses. Nationalism had grown during the Hundred Years' War with France, and such feeling came in conflict with the international sway of the papacy. The people of England readily accepted the English translation of the New Testament by William Tyndale, and Luther's works were widely distributed and debated in England. Yet it is doubtful whether England would have made a complete break with the papacy if Henry VIII had not encountered difficulties in securing an annulment of his marriage to the Spanish royal princess, Catherine of Aragon.

Henry VIII and Reform

Henry, well trained in theology and of unquestioned orthodoxy, was perturbed that his marriage with Catherine had produced no male heirs but only a princess named Mary. Since Catherine had been his brother's widow, their marriage had been possible only by papal dispensation as contrary to canon law and certain portions of Scripture (Lev. 20:21). Henry thought God had evidently not blessed the union. A male heir seemed absolutely necessary to perpetuate the dynasty. In 1527, after 18 years of marriage, Henry requested an annulment from Pope Clement VII. Because the pope feared reprisals from Catherine's powerful Spanish family, he hesitated. Henry decided to take the matter in his own hands. In 1529 he summoned Parliament, and during the ensuing six years this "Reformation Parliament" carried out his plans to sever the English church from Rome. In 1531 the king secured from the clergy recognition as the "Protector and Supreme Head of the English Church and Clergy . . . as far as the law of Christ allows." Parliament next moved against the payment of annates to the pope and by the Act in Restraint of Appeals removed the pope's spiritual jurisdiction over England. In 1533 Henry secured a dissolution of his marriage to Catherine from Thomas Cranmer, archbishop of Canterbury and primate of the English church. The king then married Anne Boleyn, a union that also failed to produce the desired male heir. Their only child was the princess Elizabeth. When the pope excommunicated

Henry and declared the marriage of Henry and Anne invalid, and thus their child illegitimate, papal revenues from England were cut off completely. In the Act of Supremacy (1534), Parliament confirmed the king as "the only supreme head on earth of the Church of England, called *Anglicana Ecclesia*." The act also declared that he should "have and enjoy, annexed and united to the imperial crown of this realm, as well the title and style thereof, as all honours, dignities, preeminences, jurisdictions, privileges, authorities, immunities, profits and commodities to the said dignity of supreme head of the same Church belonging and appertaining." It became treasonable to deny the king this position and title. John Fisher, bishop of Rochester, and Sir Thomas More, the author of the famous *Utopia*, were executed for not accepting the king as head of the church. In general, however, the substitution of the king for the pope created little disturbance.

The Dissolution of the Monasteries

The supremacy of the king was first exercised in the dissolution of the monasteries of England on the pretext of corruption. The dissolution, a real break with the ecclesiastical past, provided the crown with considerable much-needed money and at the same time eliminated possible centers of propapal feelings. The dispossession of all the monks and friars was carried out with efficiency and little suffering. In 1536 those houses having an annual income of less than 200 pounds were declared dissolved by Parliament, which resolved "that it is and shall be much more to the pleasure of Almighty God and for the honour of this his realm that the possessions of such spiritual religious houses, now being spent, spoiled and wasted for increase and maintenance of sin, should be used and converted to better uses, and the unthrifty religious persons so spending the same to be compelled to reform their lives." In the following years the larger monasteries shared the same fate. Many of the monastic properties were given away by the king or sold at bargain prices to the local gentry, who thus became strong supporters of the king's antipapal policies.

In all the actions taken by Henry and Parliament, political, economic, and national motives had been uppermost. The king was not anti-Catholic; he still considered himself a good Christian in the Catholic tradition and had not instituted any changes in doctrine or services. Lutheran influence was spreading in England, however, and the appearance in 1535 of the Bible in the translation of Miles Coverdale led to open discussion of the issues. By the king's order, an English Bible was placed in every parish church, available for reading by laymen. But Henry was not attracted to Luther's views. In order to secure unity in religion, Parliament, under Henry's guidance, enacted the Act of Six Articles (1539). This reaffirmed the traditional tenets of transubstantiation, celibacy, private masses, auricular confession, and Communion under one element. Persecution of those suspected of Protestantism followed.

Edward VI and Cranmer

Henry VIII died early in 1547 and was succeeded by the young Edward VI, his son by Jane Seymour, his third wife. The Council of Regency was predominantly Protestant, and Edward was educated by Protestant tutors. Under the regency of the moderate Protestant Edward Seymour, duke of Somerset, England began to move along the road of doctrinal and liturgical change. The Act of Six Articles and the statutes against heresy were repealed. In 1549 an Act of Uniformity required the use of the First Prayer Book in the churches of England. This book, largely the work of Archbishop Thomas Cranmer, provided new services in place of the customary Latin Mass and the monastic "hours." It was written in beautiful English and drew much on these traditional services as purged by the Lutheran Reformers. However, Cranmer, unlike the Lutheran Reformers, did not merely translate and purge the old Latin texts. He was a creative liturgical writer himself. His phrasing allowed for considerable latitude of interpretation. The services centered on the Psalms, Scripture readings, and appointed collects in an attempt to return to the ancient services of the Christian church in a condensed, simplified, and purified form. In the Lord's Supper, both the bread and the wine were given to the communicants: "Graunt us therefore (gracious lorde) so to eate the flesche of thy dere sonne Jesus Christ, and to drynke his bloud in these holy Misteries, that we may continuallye dwell in hym, and he in us, that our synfull bodyes may bee made cleane by his body, and our soules washed through hys most precious bloud."

The English Reformation was deliberately conservative and conciliating so far, but under the growing influence of Bucer and the Swiss, iconoclasm now began in England. Altars and images were removed from the churches. Marriage of the clergy was legalized. When the duke of Northumberland overthrew Somerset in 1549, Protestantism moved more rapidly towards the Reformed types. This was aided by the arrival in England of a number of religious refugees from the continent. The Second Prayer Book of Edward VI, again produced by Cranmer and made compulsory by the Second Act of Uniformity (1552), was more Zwinglian in tone. Vestments were abolished, and the Lord's Supper was to be received primarily "in remembrance." It was stressed that the Mass was not a sacrifice, since Christ by His death on the cross had "made there (by hys one oblacion of hymselfe once offered) a full, perfecte and sufficiente sacrifice, oblacion, and satisfaccion, for the synnes of the whole worlde. . . ." Congregational participation was limited to the litany; there was no singing of hymns. In the six years of Edward's reign, England moved gently and with no Catholic martyrs from Catholicism to Reformed Protestantism. However, the English Reformation, imposed as it was from above, was suddenly brought to a halt by the death of Edward in July 1553.

Mary Tudor and the Catholic Reaction

By law, Edward's successor was Mary Tudor, the daughter of Henry and Catherine of Aragon. Mary was passionately Roman Catholic, and Parliament acceded to her wishes by repealing almost all of the religious statutes that had been passed since 1529. It would not restore the confiscated church lands, now in the possession of many of its members, or recognize the supremacy of the pope. As her demands increased and when she even married Philip of Spain, the heir to the throne of a country that was fast becoming England's major enemy, Mary's popularity declined rapidly. Persecutions of Protestants began in 1555, after Parliament had revived the heresy laws. The martyrs burned at the stake numbered about 300 and were drawn from all classes of society. The most prominent of the victims were the Protestant bishops Latimer, Ridley, and Hooper and Archbishop Cranmer. Mary's persecutions won her the nickname "Bloody Mary." Many others, the Marian exiles, fled to the continent and settled as colonists in Geneva, Frankfurt am Main, Strasbourg, and elsewhere. On the continent they came more strongly under the growing influence of Calvinism. Mary died in 1558, her plans for a complete restoration of the pre-1529 religious establishment frustrated by the opposition of Parliament and the people of England.

The Elizabethan Settlement

Mary Tudor was followed by her 25-year-old half-sister Elizabeth I, daughter of Henry VIII and Anne Boleyn. Elizabeth's primary concern in her domestic and foreign policies was national unity under a strong monarch. Theological considerations were secondary. Religious differences were for a time tolerated. The Marian exiles returned home. Calvinism came to be a growing influence. The new queen was not identified with any religious group, though she did like the vestments and drama of the Roman Catholic ritual. Yet she was naturally opposed to the papacy that had declared her illegitimate. Unlike her predecessor, Elizabeth moved cautiously, recognizing that the vast majority of the common people were still Roman Catholic but that the middle class and many prominent persons were Protestant in sympathy. She appointed moderate Protestants as officials. In order to secure a Protestant clergy, Parliament passed in 1559 an Act of Supremacy that revived many of the Reformation statutes of Henry VIII and Edward VI. This act, among others, gave the queen the title of the "only supreme governor of this realm . . . as well in all spiritual or ecclesiastical things or causes, as temporal," avoiding the more offensive term "Supreme Head of the Church." All clergy, judges, and high officials had to swear that they accepted the subordinate position of the church to the crown; those who refused to take the oath were deprived of their offices. The somewhat Zwinglian Second Prayer Book (1552) was slightly revised to include more Catholic passages and ambiguous phrases, and this Elizabethan Book of Common Prayer was to be followed by all. Absence from religious service was punishable by fine. Elizabeth insisted on the retention of certain Catholic usages, as the wearing of white surplices by the clergy and their being called "priests." The traditional role of the bishops in confirmation and ordination was carefully preserved.

So conservative and cautious was Elizabeth in her religious policy that the popes hesitated for a long time in denouncing her. In 1570, however, Pius V excommunicated the "Pretended Queen of England and those heretics adhering to her." The bull also declared that Englishmen did not owe obedience to her and the present laws of England because she had "forbidden the prelates, clergy and people to acknowledge the Church of Rome" and "the observance of the true religion."

Central to the Elizabethan Settlement in religion are the moderate Thirty-nine Articles, enacted by Parliament in 1571. Showing less conservatism than Lutheranism and leaving room for individual interpretation, these articles have remained the authoritative statement of Anglican doctrine ever since. They recognize only two sacraments and define the Lord's Supper in a Calvinistic manner as "a parttakyng of the body of Christe, and likewyse the cuppe of blessing, is a parttakyng of the blood of Christe. Transubstantiation is repugnaunt to the playne wordes of scripture. The body of Christe is geuen, taken, and eaten in the Supper *only after an heauenly and spirituall maner*" (italics ours). The articles enjoin infant baptism and adherence to the Apostles', Nicene, and Athanasian creeds. According to the articles, general councils are to be called only by order of the rulers, as in the early Christian centuries. All councils can err. Marriage of the clergy is permitted. . . .

Many Englishmen were dissatisfied with the Elizabethan

Settlement. The conservatives, while often antipapal for nationalist reasons, disapproved of the doctrinal changes. On the other hand, many Protestants thought that the settlement, basically a compromise for unity's sake, was too conservative and too close to Roman Catholicism. The returning Marian exiles, numbering over 500, especially attacked the settlement. These nonconforming Calvinists were called Puritans, for they wanted to "purify" the Anglican Church of the "vestiges of popery" that remained in ritual and in the episcopal church government. As opposition grew and as propapal plots aimed at deposing Elizabeth occurred, the government took stern action with stringent laws against treason, for religious and political convictions were inextricably intertwined. During the last 20 years of Elizabeth's reign, about 250 Roman Catholics were executed, chiefly for treason. As the Puritans grew in strength and as their literature became more abusive, Parliament passed the Act Against Seditious Sectaries (1593) for "the preventing and avoiding of such great inconveniences and perils as might happen and grow by the wicked and dangerous practices of seditious sectaries and disloyal persons." Those over the age of 16 who did not attend services given according to the laws of England were to be imprisoned. Many fled to Holland. However, by the end of Elizabeth's rule in 1603, Roman Catholics and Puritans were still strong enough to cause difficulties for the Anglican government in the 17th century.

Protestantism Comes to Scotland

The Puritans found more sympathy for their views in the land to the north of England, for Calvinism had become firmly established in Scotland, then independent from the English. Here, too, there had been a long preparation for the advent of Protestantism. The moral and spiritual state of the clergy was worse in Scotland than elsewhere. Dissatisfaction with the wealthy hierarchy and dissolute clergy was strong among the independent-minded Scots, and Wycliffe's views had found sympathetic understanding. Despite official prohibition and suppression, Luther's works were widely read and his ideas preached. Protestantism found strong support among the barons, and religious differences became part of the struggle of the nobility against a combination of crown and hierarchy. King James V died in 1542, leaving his week-old daughter Mary Stuart as queen of Scots. There was a brief period during which Protestantism was favored by the regency, but the country soon came under the control of Cardinal David Beaton, who followed a pro-French and anti-English policy. The young Mary was sent to France to be raised by the Guises, a powerful and conservative Catholic family. The cardinal's repression of the growing Protestant and pro-English movement, especially his execution of the courageous preacher George Wishart, led to his own murder at St. Andrews in May 1546.

The little band of armed conspirators, secure in the castle of St. Andrews, received as their chaplain a refugee priest named John Knox. This 32-year-old disciple of Wishart had at times protected his teacher with a two-handed sword, and now he became an implacable fighter for Calvinism. When the arrival of a French fleet forced the group in the castle to surrender, Knox and his companions were made galley slaves. Released early in 1549, Knox went to England and began his real work as a reformer under Edward VI. Again his work was interrupted, this time by the accession of Mary Tudor in 1554. Knox fled to Frankfurt and then went to Geneva, where he spent some time with Calvin; he also stayed with Bullinger at Zurich. After a short visit to England, where he married, and to Scotland, where he preached for nine months, Knox returned to Geneva, the "perfect school of Christ," to minister to other English-speaking refugees. During his absence a few Scottish noblemen, later called the Lords of the Congregation, formed in 1557 the first Scottish Covenant. In this covenant they committed their lives and fortunes "to establish and maintain the Word of God" in Scotland. In 1558 Mary Stuart married Francis, the dauphin who was soon to be king of France; in the same year Mary Tudor died and was succeeded by Elizabeth. The Marian refugees now returned to England, and Knox would have gone there also; but Elizabeth was offended by his violent political tract, *The First Blast of the*

Trumpet against the Monstrous Regiment of Women, which Knox had directed against the governments of Mary Tudor and Mary of Guise, the wife of the former James V and then the regent of Scotland.

Calvinism Triumphs

Knox returned to his homeland, where he led the forces of Calvinism against the regent, who was attempting to repress the Reformation. All Europe awaited the outcome of this contest, for it was not an internal affair alone; it involved not only the future of Scotland but Protestant England and Roman Catholic France as well. European Protestantism hung in the balance, for Mary Stuart was now queen of France and threatened to tie Scotland to Catholic France and thus isolate Protestant England. However, the arrival of an English fleet and army led to the surrender of the French troops in Scotland. The regent, Mary of Guise, had died in June 1560. Emboldened by victory, the Scottish Parliament ratified in the same year the 25 articles of the Calvinist Confession of Faith prepared by Knox and his associates. They also cut Scotland's ties with Rome, annulled previous anti-Protestant acts, and condemned the Mass. A Book of Discipline was also prepared, and although it was not approved by Parliament, its proposals for the government of the Scottish church were accepted by the General Assembly of the church. This work provided a constitution and disciplinary rules for the Reformed Church of Scotland. The government of the church was organized on the principle of democratic assemblies, beginning with the parish church and extending upward through the synods to the General Assembly. Representative leadership in church government was developed through the elected and ordained elders, or presbyters. The endeavor was to follow the New Testament pattern of church government and worship. The Scottish church with its presbyterian system thus differed from the Anglican episcopal church with its bishops and more "Catholic" forms of worship. This difference was to be a source of conflict between the two nations in the 17th century. The principle of popular (representative) leadership in Scotland, however, meant that the church there had a much greater impact on the lives of the people. The English clergy, often drawn from the ranks of the younger sons of the nobility and not too well educated for the ministry, were also less popular and less respected than their Scottish counterparts.

The Reformed Church of Scotland had no sooner been established in 1560 than it was confronted by the return of the Catholic Mary Stuart in August 1561. Her husband, Francis II of France, had died in 1560 at the age of 16. Both Elizabeth of England and the Scots, most of whom were now Calvinists, feared that the French-educated queen would attempt to use force and the support of her Guise relatives in France to bring her land back to Catholicism and place it under the influence of France. In that country the wars between the crown and the Huguenots were beginning. However, the shrewd and self-confident young queen did not follow the advice of her counselors to use French troops to repress Protestantism in her realm. Instead, she tried persuasion and dissimulation and held a series of conferences with Knox and his colleagues. Nothing was accomplished by these means, for the fiery Knox could not be persuaded or intimidated. The General Assembly continued to meet without the permission of Mary. In 1567 Mary's husband, Lord Darnley, was murdered. The Queen then hastily married the unscrupulous Earl of Bothwell, but the Scottish nobles refused to allow him to become king. Instead, Mary was deposed and her infant son was crowned as James VI. Parliament declared that all future kings must swear to maintain Protestantism in Scotland. It also recognized the authority of the General Assembly of the Church of Scotland. Mary fled to England, where she was eventually executed for complicity in plots to overthrow Elizabeth.

The Reformations in England and Scotland Compared

While both England and Scotland rejected Roman Catholicism, the reformations that resulted took different forms. The English Reformation was an act of state in which the monarch and Parliament held final authority in discipline and doctrine. The episcopal form of church government and more traditional forms of worship were retained. The Anglican Church was a compromise between the extremes of continental Protestantism and Roman Catholicism. The definition of the compromise took long to evolve. On the other hand, the Scottish Reformation was a more radical and quicker break with the past. The Scottish nobles, with the support of the people, brought into being a church firmly based on Calvinism, with a representative church government, independent of secular authorities, replacing the episcopal hierarchy. Scottish ministers were mostly sons of God-fearing and Bible-reading commoners and were highly respected for their learning. The Presbyterian church services, based on the Genevan services, became known for their austere simplicity and the singing of psalms and other Scripture in vernacular paraphrase. Both ministers and services were somewhat in contrast to what was the rule in the Church of England.

The Anabaptists and Their Heritage

Roland H. Bainton

One of the most problematic aspects of the Reformation is the Anabaptists, a breakaway segment of Protestants. According to noted scholar Roland H. Bainton, formerly professor of history at Yale University, the Anabaptists separated themselves from society, which they saw as hopelessly corrupted. The Anabaptists believed in an absolute separation of church and state, and tried to have nothing to do with the state. From both Catholic and Lutheran perspectives, this view bordered on anarchy and would lead to the breakdown of organized society. As Bainton observes, the Anabaptists were killed by the thousands throughout Europe for these views, and they were virtually eradicated from Germany.

The Reformed Church was to find its most influential embodiment in French Switzerland under Calvin at Geneva. But his movement can better be understood if first attention be given to the emergence of the third type in the Anabaptists. Their movement arose in Zwingli's own circle as the result of an effort to carry through more consistently the program of the restoration of primitive Christianity. The word Reformation is usually referred to the Lutheran movement, the word Reformed to the Zwinglian and Calvinist. The word "restored" would be the most appropriate to apply to those who by opponents were called Anabaptists. Their great word was "Restitution." Much more drastically than any of their contemporaries they searched the Scriptures in order to recover the pattern of the early church.

Rejection of Society

What struck them was that the primitive church had been composed only of heartfelt believers and so far from being united with the state was rather persecuted, despised and rejected, a church of martyrs. So always, said the Anabaptists, must the true Church be reviled, rejected, and crushed. To this the Catholics and equally the Lutherans and Zwinglians replied that of course the Church was persecuted in an age when the government was hostile, but after the conversion of the emperor why should hostility continue? The state had become Christian and the Church could affiliate with the state and embrace the community. The Anabaptists retorted that the formal conversion of the emperor did not Christianize the state. The world remains the world, and if Christians are well spoken of, the explanation can only be that they have abandoned their witness. In the words of an Anabaptist hymn writer:

> "Yes," says the world, "there is no need
> That I with Christ should languish.
> He died for me and by his deed
> He saved me from this anguish.
> He paid for me, this faith can see.
> Naught else need be.". . .
>
> O brother mine, it is not so fine.
> The devil said this to thee.

The Anabaptist view rested upon pessimism with regard to the world and optimism with regard to the Church. The world—that is, society at large—will always be the partner of the flesh and the devil, but the Church must walk another road and must exemplify within her fellowship the living and the dying of the Lord Jesus. She must be a community of the saints whose members, though not perfect, yet aspire to perfection and strive mightily. The complaint against the Lutherans and the Zwinglians was that they had not produced a sufficient improvement in life. Promptly came the retort that the Anabaptists were reverting to monasticism and seeking again to win heaven by their good deeds, to which the answer was that they were not seeking to fulfill the law in order to be saved but rather to give proof of their faith by exhibiting its fruits. The kernel of Anabaptism was an ethical urge. If the Catholic Church had improved its morals they might not have found it too hard to return to her fold, whereas Luther said that his objection to the Catholic Church centered not on the life but on the teaching.

A Strict Ethics

The Anabaptists called for a strict morality, and there can be no question that they achieved it. The testimony of their opponents is eloquent. Zwingli said of them, "At first contact their conduct appears irreproachable, pious, unassuming, attractive. . . . Even those who are inclined to be critical will say that their lives are excellent." Zwingli's successor, Bullinger, said that they denounced covetousness, pride, profanity, the lewd conversation and immorality of the world, drinking, and gluttony. A Catholic observed in them "no lying, deception, swearing, strife, harsh language, no intemperate eating and drinking, no outward personal display, but rather humility, patience, uprightness, meekness, honesty, temperance, straightforwardness in such measure that one would suppose they had the Holy Spirit of God."

One notes in these testimonies the witness to their sobriety. The movement for total abstinence from alcoholic beverages stems from these groups. Not even Catholic monasticism had called for total abstinence. Luther most assuredly did not, but neither did Calvin or Knox. The Anabaptists moved in this direction.

Upsetting Church Structure

But if they were so exemplary why did the theocracy of Zurich in the year 1525, with the full approval of Ulrich Zwingli, pronounce against them the death penalty by drowning? Why was Felix Manx, one of the first leaders, sunk in the lake? Why was the old law of the Code of Justinian revived, which visited death upon those who repeated baptism and upon those who denied the Trinity? The Anabaptists did insist on adult baptism only, but was that enough to outweigh their Christian living and a warrant for exterminating them like superfluous puppies? . . .

The first Anabaptists, to be sure, were not disturbing the peace but they did upset the whole structure of the Church, state, and society. Their theory of the Church made of it a conventicle [an assembly of like-minded people] and not a church of the community. Christianity, they said, demands a quality of living which can be and will be achieved only by heartfelt Christians who have truly died with Christ to sin and risen with him to newness of life. One cannot expect persons, merely because they have been dipped in infancy, to show forth the excellency that was in Christ Jesus, and baptism ought not to be given to babies because it is not a sign of membership in a Christian society, not a rite of initiation, but a visible token of that inward regeneration which has already taken place. In baptism, declared the Apostle Paul, we die and rise with Christ and this experience cannot come at birth, but only through an adult conversion and commitment. Those alone who have had this experience constitute the Church and all others would still belong in the world even though an ocean of water had been poured over them. Infant baptism consequently is no baptism at all, but only "a dipping in the Romish bath." To call these people Anabaptists, that is re-baptizers, was to malign them, because they denied that baptism was repeated, inasmuch as infant baptism is no baptism at all. They called themselves simply Baptists, not re-Baptists. The offensive name was fastened on them in order to bring them under the penalty of the Justinian Code against the Donatists.

Separation of Church and State

The Church, then, according to these so-called Anabaptists, must be a gathered society, to use the terminology later current among the Congregationalists, and cannot coincide with the community unless of course the community be restricted to adult believers, as was sometimes the case in Anabaptist colonies. An unweeded city like Zurich could never be regarded as the new Israel of God because Zwingli had not instituted a sufficient purge. The Church is to be kept pure by discipline and the expulsion of those who do not exemplify the pattern of Christ's conduct. The religious ban, however, was to be the only penalty. The arm of the state should never be invoked. Religious liberty was thus a tenet of the Anabaptists, and they were the first church to make it a cardinal point in their creed.

Furthermore church and state should be separate, inasmuch as the state is concerned with everyone in the community, whereas the Church consists only of the saints. The state was ordained because of sin, but the Church was created for the saved. These propositions entailed the dissolution of the whole structure of medieval society. Luther and Zwingli had never gone so far and recoiled the more because the Anabaptists went on to say that the true Christians must not only forswear an alliance with the state, but must have nothing whatever to do with it, since the world is the world and remains without hope of ever being Christianized. Luther agreed that society cannot be Christianized, but nevertheless believed that Christians must accept the office of magistrate in order to restrain outrageous villainy. The Anabaptists retorted that the state has indeed been ordained of God on account of sin and to restrain sin, but should be left to be administered by sinners.

Such a position of itself entailed a withdrawal from political life and the separation became all the more marked because the ethic of the Sermon on the Mount was taken literally and made incumbent upon all Christians. The Catholics took it literally but conserved it only through a vocational division whereby its rigoristic precepts applied solely to the monks. Luther rejected this division, insisting that Christian morality is demanded of all, but he regarded the Sermon on the Mount rather as a disposition than a code. The Anabaptists agreed with the Catholics in taking the counsels to the letter and with Luther as to the single standard. Hence all Christians became monks. There was this difference, however, that the Anabaptists did not reject marriage. They repudiated war and capital punishment. Under no circumstances would they wield the sword, nor would they go to law. They would take no oath, for Christ said "Swear not at all," and some held all things in common.

Pacifism and Abstention from Society

Their whole manner of life was summed up by a Swiss chronicler who was himself impressed although not persuaded: "Their walk and manner of life was altogether pious, holy, and irreproachable. They avoided costly clothing, despised costly food and drink, clothed themselves with coarse cloth, covered their heads with broad felt hats; their walk and conduct was altogether humble. . . . They carried no weapon, neither sword nor dagger, nothing more than a pointless bread knife, saying that these were wolf's clothing which should not be found on the sheep. They would never swear an oath, not even upon demand of the government. And if anyone transgressed, he was excluded by them."

Here, then, was a program not only of religious liberty and the separation of church and state, but also of pacifism and complete abstention from public life. The Anabaptists for the most part were not revolutionary—there were indeed a few marauders who because they left their children unbaptized were called Anabaptists, and there were a few among the early Anabaptists who would not go the whole way on the repudiation of the sword. The great majority, however, obeyed the government in matters not directly contrary to their tenets, disobeyed when conscience required, and suffered meekly whatever penalties were imposed.

Persecution and Death

Those who thus held themselves as sheep for the slaughter were dreaded and exterminated as if they had been wolves. They challenged the whole way of life of the community. Had they become too numerous, Protestants would have been unable to take up arms against Catholics and the Germans could not have resisted the Turks. And the Anabaptists did become numerous. They despaired of society at large, but they did not despair of winning converts to their way.

Every member of the group was regarded as a missionary. Men and women left their homes to go on evangelistic tours. The established churches, whether Catholic or Protestant, were aghast at these ministers of both sexes insinuating themselves into town and farm. In some of the communities of Switzerland and the Rhine valley the Anabaptists began to outnumber Catholics and Protestants alike. Would not the growth of people with such views be even more of a menace to public security than the demolition of a city wall? In 1529 the imperial meeting at Speyer declared with the concurrence alike of Catholics and Lutherans that the death penalty should be inflicted upon the Anabaptists.

Menno Simons, one of their later leaders, reported the outcome.

> Some they have executed by hanging, some they have tortured with inhuman tyranny, and afterwards choked with cords at the stake. Some they roasted and burned alive. Some they have killed with the sword and given them to the fowls of the air to devour. Some they have cast to the fishes. . . . Others wander about here and there, in want, homelessness, and affliction, in mountains and deserts, in holes and caves of the earth. They must flee with their wives and little children from one country to another, from one city to another. They are hated, abused, slandered and lied about by all men.

After recording the deaths of 2173 of the brethren, an Anabaptist chronicler proceeds:

> No human being was able to take away out of their hearts what they had experienced. . . . The fire of God burned within them. They would die ten deaths rather than forsake the divine truth.

> They had drunk of the water which is flowing from God's sanctuary, yea of the water of life. Their tent they had pitched not here upon earth, but in eternity. Their faith blossomed like a lily, their loyalty as a rose, their piety and candor as the flower of the garden of God. The angel of the Lord battled for them that they could not be deprived of the helmet of sal-

vation. Therefore they have borne all torture and agony without fear. The things of this world they counted only as shadows. They were thus drawn unto God that they knew nothing, sought nothing, desired nothing, loved nothing but God alone. Therefore they had more patience in their suffering than their enemies in tormenting them.

Their situation is poignantly described in an Anabaptist hymn:

Sheep without shepherd running blind
Are scattered into fight
Our house and home are left behind,
Like birds we fly by night,
And like the birds, naught overhead
Save wind and rain and weather,
In rocks and caves our bed.

We creep for refuge under trees.
They hunt us with the bloodhound.
Like lambs they take us as they please
And hold us roped and strong-bound.
They show us off to everyone
As if the peace we'd broken,
As sheep for slaughter looked upon,
As heretics bespoken. . . .

Few of those who had the temerity to attend an Anabaptist conference could expect to die in bed. Most of the more sober leaders were eliminated in a few years by fire, water, and sword. One has only to examine an Anabaptist hymnbook to see over against the names of the authors the notation: "Drowned 1525, burned 1526, beheaded 1527, hanged 1528," and so on. Sometimes whole congregations were taken; the leaders especially were struck down and the people left without a shepherd.

The Fanatics Take Over

Then the less balanced spirits came to the fore. Those who had lived under the continual shadow of death in caves and desolate places of the earth began like Muentzer to dream

dreams of the birds of the heaven coming to devour the car-
casses of the oppressors, of the return of the Lord to vindi-
cate the saints, of the New Jerusalem from which the
144,000 of the redeemed should go out to slaughter the un-
godly. Whether the Lord would accomplish all this by Himself, or whether men should assist, was not altogether clear.
Dates for the return of Christ were set and places selected as
the New Jerusalem. Melchior Hoffman predicted that in the
year 1533 he would be imprisoned for six months in Strasbourg and then the Lord would come. Only the first half of
the prediction was fulfilled, and Hoffman languished in
prison, speedily forgotten even by his own party. But his
ideas moved down the Rhine and in 1534 the town of Muenster in Westphalia was selected as the New Jerusalem. Here
for the first and only time the Anabaptists succeeded in taking over municipal government, and not without violence.
Under all the strains pacifism succumbed. The Anabaptists
marched into the market place prepared to be as sheep for
the slaughter, but armed with swords just as a reminder of
what they might do if they chose. Whereupon a revelation
from the Holy Ghost instructed them to choose that which
they might. Catholics and Lutherans were expelled; the
saints began their reign.

Leadership fell to those who sought to restore not only
the New Testament but also the Old. They were like
Zwingli in stressing the continuity between the new and the
old Israel of God. But then they began to revive the eccen-
tricities of the prophets and the immoralities of the patri-
archs. Some Anabaptists in Holland ran around naked in imitation of the prophet Isaiah who walked naked as a sign.
Another Anabaptist, also in imitation of Isaiah, went to the
fireplace and lifted a hot coal to his lips. Instead of being able
to say like the prophet, "Woe is me, I am undone, for I am a
man of unclean lips," he was too burned to say anything for
a fortnight. At Münster the aberration took the form of a re-
instatement of polygamy after the example of Abraham,
Isaac, and Jacob. Catholics and Lutherans combined to exterminate the New Jerusalem. The town was taken and all
the new Davids and Enochs and Elijahs were put to the rack

and the sword.

The whole ugly episode discredited Anabaptism. Despite the fact that for the first ten years under frightful provocation they had been without offense, yet when a handful of the fanatics ran amuck the entire party was besmirched with the excesses of the lunatic fringe, and well into the nineteenth century historians of the Reformation did little more than recount the aberrations of the saints rampant.

Survival and Restored Principles

Despite constant vigilance Anabaptism was not extinguished. Nor did the excesses pervert the character of the movement as a whole. Menno Simons, the founder of the Mennonites, and Jacob Hutter, the founder of the Hutterites, repudiated all of the Muenster vagaries: polygamy, revolution, and date-setting for the return of the Lord. Anabaptism revived its original principles of a sect separated from the world, committed to following the pattern of the New Testament in simplicity, sobriety, poverty, meekness and long-suffering. Menno declared that true Christians must "crucify the flesh and its desires and lusts, prune the heart, mouth and the whole body with the knife of the divine word of all unclean thoughts, unbecoming words and actions." There must be no adornment with gold, silver, pearls, silk, velvet and costly finery. Swords must be beaten into plowshares and love extended even to enemies. Charity must be given to all, and though the faithful be despoiled of their goods they must turn not away.

For the most part in Europe these groups could find no abiding place. In Holland and Switzerland a few survived at the price of a measure of conformity. In Germany they were stamped out. This is one of the greatest tragedies of German history. If only Lutheranism could have been subject to the stimulus of the criticism and competition of the sects, it could never have become so complacent and allied to the established order. The Anglican Church owes an incalculable debt to the Nonconformists. So completely were the Anabaptists exterminated that few Lutherans are aware that the principles of British dissent originated on German soil.

The Anabaptist Heritage

The Anabaptists, however, do survive. They maintained themselves by following the frontier and keeping aloof from bourgeois civilization, industrialism, imperialism, and nationalism. They sought the fringes where social totalitarianism had not yet imposed conformity and the community of the saints could live unmolested. Poland and Moravia for a time offered an asylum. Tolerant noblemen were willing to admit tillers of the soil without asking too many questions about their religious convictions. In Moravia religious communist societies with an international complexion were established in small groups of about a hundred. The ideal was not the improvement of the standard of living as in modern communism, but rather to live in accord with Franciscan poverty but on a family basis. The resemblance to monasticism is obvious save for celibacy and later the Shakers were to introduce celibacy in a Protestant community, but the Mennonites and Hutterites have never done so. How close they were, however, to monasticism appears in the case of one group of Anabaptists in Moravia, who in the period of the Counter Reformation were offered the choice of exile or toleration of their entire mode of living on the one condition that they accept the Mass. The Catholic Church regarded them as a quasi-monastic community.

Those who did not conform, and they were the majority, had to suffer repeated exiles. Some went west, some went east. Pennsylvania received a considerable migration. Other bands traversed northern Germany to Poland, Hungary and Transylvania and at length to Russia, until in the late nineteenth century new pressures in the east occasioned fresh movements to the west, to Manitoba, Indiana, Nebraska, and Paraguay. Eternal Abrahams, they have ever loins girt ready to go they know not whither.

On the western frontiers the Anabaptists have preserved their pattern more truly than in the Old World. During the past four centuries they have succeeded amazingly in maintaining a community life of their own, cut off from all the corruptions of the world. The buttonless coats, the broad hats, the flowing beards of the Amish set them apart even on their occasional excursions into society. These peculiarities serve like a uniform to distinguish the wearer and guard him against seduction. All the encroachments of modern society have been stoutly resisted—the railroad, the telephone, the automobile, the movie, the newspaper, especially the comic strips, and even the tractor. Naturally, too, the state school has been regarded as a peril to the community pattern. The old ways have been best preserved where the isolation is greatest and where the opposition is most acute. A segregated community thrives on persecution. It needs something like the ghetto for the preservation of its own morale. Contact with the outside and fraternization insidiously induce conformity. Then the children begin to dress and think like others and to go over to the world. The sect thus becomes the church and the old witness survives only in a warm piety and a nostalgic singing of martyr hymns.

Chapter 3

The Cultural and Social Context of the Reformation

Turning | Points

IN WORLD HISTORY

Humanism and the Reformation

Alister E. McGrath

According to scholar Alister E. McGrath, professor of history at Oxford University, Renaissance humanism exerted a profound formative influence on the Reformation. One fundamental premise of the humanists was *ad fontes*, the return to the fountains or original sources of the great writers and thinkers of the classical past. When translated into the religious sphere, this concept meant a return to the original texts of the oldest Christian writers, such as the church fathers, and above all, to the Bible itself. The leading Northern European humanist Erasmus influenced all the early reformers in one way or another, and his publication of the first printed Greek New Testament was a crucial stepping-stone for Protestants in their common goal of providing reliable translations of the Bible into each of the languages of Europe.

Of the many tributaries which contributed to the flux of the Reformation, by far the most important was Renaissance humanism. Although the Reformation may have begun in the cities of Germany and Switzerland, there are excellent reasons for suggesting that it may well have been the inevitable outcome of developments in fourteenth-century Italy as the movement we now know as the 'Italian Renaissance' gained momentum. . . .

When the word 'humanism' is used by a twentieth-century writer, we are usually meant to understand an anti-religious philosophy which affirms the dignity of humanity without any reference to God. 'Humanism' has acquired very strongly secularist, perhaps even atheist, overtones. It is perhaps inevitable that many students approach the theme 'Humanism and the Reformation' on the basis of this twentieth-century understanding of the word 'humanist'. The scene seems set for the confrontation of religion and atheism. Yet that confrontation never materializes. As we shall see, however, remarkably few—if any—humanists of the fourteenth, fifteenth or sixteenth centuries correspond to our modern understanding of 'humanism'. Indeed, they were remarkably religious, if anything concerned with the *renewal* rather than the *abolition* of the Christian church. The word 'humanist' had a meaning in the sixteenth century which is quite different from the twentieth-century meaning of the word, as we shall see shortly. To anticipate a little, it is now clear that humanism was generally theologically neutral in the Renaissance. The reader is asked to set aside the modern sense of the word 'humanism', as we prepare to meet this phenomenon in its late Renaissance setting. . . .

Back to the Sources

The literary and cultural programme of humanism can be summarized in the slogan *ad fontes*—back to the original sources. The squalor of the medieval period is bypassed, in order to recover the intellectual and artistic glories of the classical period. The 'filter' of medieval commentaries—whether on legal texts or on the Bible—is abandoned, in order to engage directly with the original texts. Applied to the Christian church, the slogan *ad fontes* meant a direct return to the title-deeds of Christianity—to the patristic writers, and supremely to the Bible.

The slogan, however, does more than specify the sources to be used in the rebirth of civilization. It also specifies the attitude to be adopted towards these sources. It is necessary to remember that the Renaissance was an era of discovery, both geographical and scientific. The discovery of the Americas fired the imagination of the late Renaissance, as did new insights into the functioning of the human body and the natural world. And so classical sources were read with a view to rediscovering the experiences they reflected. In his *Aeneid*, Virgil described the discovery of new and strange lands—and so late Renaissance readers approached Virgil with a sense of expectation, for they too were in the process of discovering *terrae incognitae*. Galen was read in a new light: he described the gaining of physiological insights to a generation who were repeating that experience in their own day and age. And so it was also with scripture. The New Testament described the encounter of believers with the risen Christ—and late Renaissance readers approached the text of scripture with the expectation that they too could meet the risen Christ, a meeting which seemed to be denied to them by the church of their day.

This point is often overlooked, but holds the key to the humanist reverence for ancient texts. For the humanists, classical texts mediated an experience to posterity—an experience which could be regained by handling the text in the right way. The new philological and literary methods developed by the thinkers of the Renaissance were thus seen as a way of recapturing the vitality of the classical period. For the Christian church, this opened up a new, exciting and challenging possibility—that the experience of the first Christians, described in the New Testament, could be regained, and transferred to a much later point in history. It is this factor, perhaps more than any other, which helps explain the remarkably high regard in which humanists were held in reforming circles throughout Europe. It seemed to many that the sterile form of Christianity associated with the Middle Ages could be replaced with a new vital and dynamic form, through the study of scripture. *Ad fontes* was more than a slogan—it was a lifeline to those who despaired of the state of the late medieval church. The Apostolic Age, the Golden Age of the church, could once more become a present reality.

It is perhaps difficult for some modern readers to empathize with this sense of excitement and anticipation. Yet to enter into the thought-world of Europe on the eve of the Reformation, we must try to recapture this sense of expectation. To many individuals and groups throughout Europe, it seemed that a new day in the history of the church was about to dawn, in which the risen Christ would be restored to the church. It seemed to many, such as Luther, that God in his providence had given the church the key (in the new humanist textual and philological tools) by which the New Testament experience of Christ could be unlocked and made available.

The Ideals of Northern European Humanism

At this point, we must pause to clarify one important point. The 'humanism' which affected the Reformation is primarily *northern European humanism*, rather than *Italian* humanism. We must therefore consider what form this northern European movement took. . . .

Three main themes dominate northern European humanism. First, we find the same concern for *bonae litterae*—written and spoken eloquence, after the fashion of the classical period—as in the Italian Reformation. Second, we find a religious programme directed towards the corporate revival of the Christian church. The Latin slogan *Christianismus renascens*, 'Christianity being born again', summarizes the aims of this programme, and indicates its relation with the 'rebirth' of letters associated with the Renaissance. Although [Swiss historian Jacob] Burckhardt is unquestionably right to state that the Renaissance led to a new emphasis upon the subjective consciousness of the individual, northern European humanists supplemented this new emphasis upon the individual with a recognition of the need to reform the communities (both church and state) to which the individual belonged. It is worth noting at this point that the Renaissance emphasis upon the subjective consciousness of the individual is particularly linked with the doctrine of justification by faith. . . . Third, northern European humanism was strongly pacifist during the early sixteenth century, largely in reaction to the tragedy of the Franco-Italian war. The quest for international peace and mutual understanding was espoused by most humanists at the time, particularly in Switzerland, which was caught up in the disastrous Franco-Italian war. Distaste for papal political manoeuvring was an important element in the background to the Swiss Reformation.

Erasmus of Rotterdam

One figure stands head and shoulders above other northern European humanists, not least in terms of his influence upon both the German and Swiss reformations—Erasmus of Rotterdam. Although the direct influence of Erasmus upon Luther and Calvin is less than might be expected, many other Reformers (such as Zwingli and Bucer) were heavily influenced by him. It is therefore essential that his considerable contribution to the thought of the Reformation be considered in some detail. . . .

The most influential humanist writing to circulate in Europe during the first decades of the sixteenth century was Erasmus' *Enchiridion Militis Christiani*, 'Handbook of the Christian Soldier'. Although the work was first published in 1503, and then reprinted in 1509, the real impact of the work dates from its third printing in 1515. From that moment onwards, it became a cult work, apparently going through twenty-three editions in the next six years. Its appeal was to educated lay men and women, whom Erasmus regarded as the true treasure of the church. Its amazing popularity in the years after 1515 may allow us to suggest that a radical alteration in lay self-perception took place as a result—and it can hardly be overlooked that the reforming rumbles at Zurich and Wittenberg date from so soon after the *Enchiridion* became a bestseller. Erasmus' success also highlighted the importance of printing as a means of disseminating radical new ideas—a point which neither Zwingli nor Luther overlooked, when their turns came to propagate such ideas.

The *Enchiridion* developed the attractive thesis that the church of the day could be reformed by a collective return to the writings of the fathers and scripture. The reading of scripture on a regular basis is put forward as the key to a new lay piety, on the basis of which the church may be renewed and reformed. Erasmus conceived his work as a lay person's guide to scripture, providing a simple yet learned exposition of the 'philosophy of Christ'. This 'philosophy' is really a form of morality: the New Testament concerns the knowledge of good and evil, in order that its readers may eschew the latter and love the former. The New Testament is the *lex Christi*, 'the law of Christ', which Christians are called to obey. Christ is the example whom Christians are called to imitate. Yet Erasmus does not understand Christian faith to be a mere external observance of some kind of morality. His characteristically humanist emphasis upon inner religion leads him to suggest that reading of scripture *transforms* its reader, giving him a new motivation to love God and his neighbour.

Laity, Not Clergy

A number of points are of particular importance. First, Erasmus understands the future vitality of Christianity to lie with the laity, not the clergy. The clergy are seen as educators, whose function is to allow the laity to achieve the same level of understanding as themselves. There is no room for any superstitions which give the clergy a permanent status superior to their lay charges. Second, Erasmus' strong emphasis upon the 'inner religion' results in an understanding of Christianity which makes no reference to the church—its rites, priests or institutions. Why bother confessing sin to another human, asks Erasmus, just because he's a priest, when you can confess them directly to God himself? Religion is a matter of the individual's heart and mind: it is an inward state. Erasmus pointedly avoids any reference to the sacraments, for example. Similarly, he discounts the view that the 'religious life' (in other words, being a monk or a nun) is the highest form of the Christian life: the lay person who reads scripture is just as faithful to his calling as the pious monk.

The revolutionary character of Erasmus' *Enchiridion* lies in its daring new suggestion that the recognition of the Christian vocation of the lay person holds the key to the revival of the church. Clerical and ecclesiastical authority is discounted. Scripture should and must be made available to all, in order that all may return *ad fontes*, to drink of the fresh and living waters of the Christian faith, rather than the murky and stagnant ponds of late medieval religion.

Erasmus, however, came to recognize that there were serious obstacles in the path of the course he proposed, and was responsible for a number of major developments to relieve them. First, there was a need to be able to study the New Testament in its original language, rather than in the inaccurate Vulgate translation. This necessitated two tools, neither of which was then available: access to the Greek text, and the necessary philological competence to handle the text.

A New Translation of the New Testament

The second difficulty began to be relieved through Erasmus' discovery of Lorenzo Valla's fifteenth-century notes on the Greek text of the New Testament, which Erasmus published in 1505. The first was resolved through the publication by Erasmus of the first printed Greek New Testament, the *Novum Instrumentum omne*, which rolled off Froben's presses at Basle in 1516. . . .

The Christian church has always attached particular importance to certain rites or forms of worship, which are referred to as *sacraments*. Two such sacraments were recognized by the early church as 'dominical' (in other words, as going back to Jesus Christ himself). These were baptism, and the sacrament now known by a variety of names, such as 'the Mass', 'the Lord's supper', the 'breaking of the bread', or 'the eucharist'. By the end of the twelfth century, however, this number had increased to seven. The additions to the list now included matrimony and penance. The development and consolidation of the sacramental system of the church is one of the most important aspects of medieval theology.

Erasmus' new translation of the New Testament seemed to many to call this entire system into question. For example, the inclusion of matrimony in the list of sacraments was justified on the basis of a New Testament text—as translated by the Vulgate—which spoke of marriage being a *sacramentum* (Ephesians 5:31-2). Erasmus followed Valla in pointing out that the Greek simply meant 'mystery'. There was no reference whatsoever to marriage being a 'sacrament'. One of the classic proof texts used by medieval theologians to justify the inclusion of matrimony in the list of sacraments was thus rendered virtually useless.

Similarly, the Vulgate translated the opening words of

Jesus' ministry (Matthew 4:17) as *'do penance,* for the Kingdom of heaven is at hand', with a clear reference to the
sacrament of penance. Erasmus, again following Valla,
pointed out that the Greek should be translated as *'repent,*
for the Kingdom of heaven is at hand'. In other words,
where the Vulgate seemed to refer to the sacrament of
penance, Erasmus insisted that the reference was to a psychological attitude—that of 'being repentant'. Once more,
an important justification of the sacramental system of the
church was challenged. . . .

For the Reformers, however, these developments were
nothing less than providential. As we have seen, the Reformers wanted to return to the beliefs and practices of the early
church—and if Erasmus' new translation of the New Testament helped demolish medieval additions to those beliefs and
practices, then so much the better. Humanist biblical scholarship was therefore regarded as an ally in the struggle for the
return to the apostolic simplicity of the early church. . . .

Tensions Between Reformation and Humanism

It will be obvious that humanism had a decisive contribution
to make to the Reformation. Humanist and Reformer alike
rejected scholastic theology, in favour of a more simple theology based upon scripture and the fathers. We have already
seen how humanism made decisive contributions to the development of the Reformation, through making available reliable editions of the New Testament and the fathers. Yet
tensions remained between humanism and both wings of the
Reformation. Five areas may be singled out for comment.

1 *Their attitude to scholastic theology.* The humanists, the
Swiss Reformers and the Wittenberg Reformers had no hesitation in rejecting scholasticism. In this respect, there is a
strong degree of affinity between the three movements. The
humanists, however, rejected scholasticism because of its un-
intelligibility and inelegance of expression: a simpler and
more eloquent theology was required. Similar attitudes are
evident within the Swiss Reformation, indicating strong
affinity with humanism at this point. The Wittenberg Reformers however (especially Luther and Karlstadt), had no

difficulty in understanding scholastic theology: their rejection of scholasticism was based on their conviction that its theology was fundamentally wrong. Where the humanists and Zwingli dismissed scholasticism as an irrelevance, the Wittenberg Reformers regarded it as the most important obstacle in the path of a reforming theology.

2 *Their attitude to scripture.* All three groups held that scripture held the key to reform of the church, in that it bore witness to Christian belief and practice in its original form. For the humanists, the authority of scripture rested in its eloquence, simplicity and antiquity. The Swiss and Wittenberg Reformers, however, grounded the authority of scripture in the concept of the 'word of God'. Scripture was seen as embodying the commands and promises of God, thus giving it a status over and above any purely human document. The phrase *sofa scriptura,* 'by scripture alone', expresses the basic Reformation belief that no source other than scripture need be consulted in matters of Christian faith and practice. A further tension exists between the Swiss and Wittenberg Reformers: the former regarded scripture primarily as a source of moral guidance, whereas the latter regarded it primarily as a record of God's gracious promises of salvation to those who believed.

3 *Their attitudes to the fathers.* For the humanists the writers of the patristic period represented a simple and comprehensible form of Christianity, lent authority by their antiquity and eloquence. In general, humanists appear to have regarded the fathers as being of more or less equal value, in that all dated from roughly the same period of antiquity. . . .

The Wittenberg Reformers Luther and Karlstadt, however, regarded Augustine as pre-eminent among the fathers. The humanists employed two criteria in evaluating the fathers: antiquity and eloquence. Thus Erasmus' preference for both Origen and Jerome is justified by the elegance of their writings, in addition to their antiquity, in common with the other patristic writings. The Wittenberg Reformers, however, used an explicitly *theological* criterion in evaluating the fathers: how reliable were they as interpreters of the New Testament? On the basis of this criterion, Augustine was to be preferred, and Origen to be treated with some suspicion. The humanists were not prepared to use such an explicitly theological criterion in evaluating the relative merits of the fathers, thus heightening the tension between these two movements.

4 *Their attitudes to education.* In that the Reformation witnessed the birth of a series of new religious ideas (or, at least, ideas which were new to most people in the sixteenth century), it was essential to both the Wittenberg and Swiss reformations that a major programme of religious education be undertaken. Humanism was essentially an educational and cultural movement based upon reform of the liberal arts, with the result that most early sixteenth-century humanists were professional educators. It is therefore interesting to note that most northern European humanists joined the cause of the Reformation, not necessarily because they approved of its *religious* ideas, but because they were attracted strongly by its *educational* ideals. The tension is obvious: the Reformers were concerned with the religious ideas being taught, viewing the educational methods as the means to that end—whereas the professional humanist educators were primarily concerned with the development of educational techniques, rather than the ideas being taught.

5 *Their attitude to rhetoric.* As we have seen, humanism was concerned with eloquence, both written and spoken. Rhetoric was thus studied as a means to this end. The Reformers, in both Germany and Switzerland, were concerned with the promotion of their religious ideas through the written word (e.g., as in Calvin's famous *Institutes of the Christian Religion*) and the spoken word in sermons (Luther and Calvin both being, by all accounts, superb preachers). Rhetoric was therefore the means to the end of the propagation of the ideas of the Reformation. Recent studies, for example, have emphasized how Calvin's style is heavily influenced by rhetoric. Both humanist and Reformer, therefore, regarded rhetoric highly—but for different reasons. For the humanists, rhetoric promoted eloquence; for the Reformers, it promoted the Reformation. Once more, we encounter superficial similarities between the two groups, which mask profound differences.

Distinctions Made Clear

On the basis of our discussion so far, it will be clear that the Swiss wing of the Reformation was influenced to a far greater extent by humanism than its counterpart at Wittenberg. Even at Wittenberg, however, the new programme of study of the Bible and Augustine appeared to many to be thoroughly humanist in inspiration. With the benefit of hindsight, it is very easy for us to distinguish Luther and Karlstadt from the humanists—yet *at the time*, this distinction was virtually impossible to make. To most observers, Luther and Erasmus were engaged in precisely the same struggle. We have one very famous illustration of this misunderstanding of Luther by humanists. In 1518 Luther delivered the famous Heidelberg Disputation, in which he developed a radically antihumanist and antischolastic theology. One of his audience was the young humanist Martin Bucer, later to become a leading Reformer in the city of Strasbourg. Bucer wrote with enthusiasm to his humanist correspondent Beatus Rhenanus, declaring that Luther merely stated Erasmus' views, but did so more forcefully. As a close examination of that letter indicates, Bucer seems to have misunderstood Luther on virtually every point!

The full extent of the tension between humanism and the Reformation only became fully apparent in 1525. In this year, both Zwingli and Luther composed attacks on Erasmus, both concentrating their attention on the concept of the 'freedom of the will'. For both Reformers, Erasmus' teaching of the total freedom of the human will led to a grossly overoptimistic conception of human nature. With the publication of Zwingli's *Commentary on True and False Religion* and Luther's *On the Bondage of the Will*, the tensions that had always been in existence between humanism and the Reformation were made obvious to all.

The Reformation and the Rise of National States

Owen Chadwick

It remains an open question whether the Reformation would have survived had it not gained the support and protection of various European princes and monarchs. Owen Chadwick, former professor of history at Cambridge University, contends in this essay that the embrace of Protestantism and the growing power of princes were complementary developments. Princes and monarchs enhanced their own prestige and power by rejecting the control of the Catholic Church at Rome. They also gained control over the vast wealth and landholdings of the church in their own countries. As the unity of Christendom in Europe collapsed, the system of national independent states arose to take its place.

But what was it that made the call to reformation more potent and more revolutionary in the early sixteenth century than a hundred years before? Was it simply that the abuses were worse ? That corruption so rotted the carcass that the hollow body collapsed in the moment when it was pushed ?

The evidence upon this point, though hard to judge, suggests not. The Reformation came not so much because Europe was irreligious as because it was religious. The medieval Church begat repeated waves of fervent idealism, and was doing so again. The abuses now condemned were always abuses and always condemned at the bar of public opinion. A lot of parish priests were ignorant in 1500, a lot of parish

priests were ignorant in every age. The reformers were
under an illusion in looking back towards a golden age. The
Church came to dominate western Europe in rough times,
and the scars of that roughness could still be seen upon it.
Most of the abuses were not so much worse. What was new
was the extent of men's awareness of the defects in Church
order and the possibility of remedy.

In certain areas, and in certain practices, there had been
decline during the fifteenth century. The new world of
credit afforded opportunities to the self-seeker beyond the
wilder dreams of his predecessors. There was a new blatancy
in non-residence, in piling up ecclesiastical offices, in keeping concubines, in drawing the pay of a priest without being
ordained as a priest. 'We Italians,' wrote Machiavelli, 'are
more irreligious and corrupt than others . . . because the
Church and its representatives set us the worst example,' and
there may be a truth somewhere in the complacent self-
accusation. But there was plenty of reforming idealism even
in the Italy of the later Renaissance.

Continuing Religious Devotion

What is undoubted is the extent of religious practice. Henry
VIII was said to hear three masses on days when he was
hunting and sometimes five on other days; and the devout
Margaret Beaufort heard six masses every day. . . .

The strong and popular devotion to the Virgin was accompanied by a marked growth in the cult of the saints and
their relics, and of pilgrimage to their shrines. Ill-regulated
fervour could be superstitious or even demonic. In 1500
more witches were being tortured and burnt, more Jews
were being persecuted. But superstition was no innovation.
Since the darkest ages peasants had consumed the dust from
saints' tombs or used the Host as an amulet or collected pretended relics or believed incredible and unedifying miracles
or substituted the Virgin or a patron saint for the Saviour. In
1500 they were ardently doing these things. What was new
was not so much the practice as the way in which the leaders
of opinion were beginning to regard it.

In short, the perpetual gap between the religions of the

literate and the illiterate was widening till it could hardly be bridged. While popular devotions, mingled with popular superstition, seemed to be almost uncontrollable by bishops or by theologians, while the ardour of the people was seeking the emotional cult, the printing press was at work publishing more than 100 editions of the Bible between 1457 and 1500.

We must therefore seek other explanations than the simple theory that the Church was too bad to continue, and consider two special circumstances: the increasing control of kings over their kingdoms, and the improved education of the intelligent minds of the western world.

The Power of Government

Kings Henry VII and Henry VIII were more powerful in England than any of their predecessors. King Ferdinand and Queen Isabella in Spain likewise; the kings of Portugal and Denmark, certain German princes, and even the German Emperor, were less weak than their recent predecessors. Government, though not modern, was becoming a little more modern. The pace varied from land to land. In England the private armies of the barons had been exhausted in the Wars of the Roses and the lords thereafter weakened by the Tudors; in France the feudal nobility remained great enough to divide the realm; in Poland the nobility was gaining control over the king. But the foundations of a civil service, of an improved machinery for administration and justice at the centre, the use of trained lawyers—these ingredients of a modern state marked the constitutional development of several realms during that age. And around these more effective governments was gathering the idea of the nation, the half-conscious and yet patriotic loyalty of their peoples.

The relation between this and the success of a Protestant revolt is undoubted but not easy to define. It might be said broadly that in England, and in Denmark, the Reformation came because limitation of the power of the Church was necessary to the further development of efficient government. Efficient government demanded restraint upon papal intervention, upon ecclesiastical privilege and exemptions, upon the legal right of an authority outside the country to levy taxes. In all the states of western Europe, and not only in the states which would later become Protestant, this began to happen before 1500.

The Control of the Church

But this connexion between constitutional development and the Protestant revolt, which looms so large in English history that it dwarfs every other consideration, was not a general rule throughout Europe. Before the Reformation began, the kings of Spain and France partially satisfied their need to control the Church. In 1478 the Pope granted to the Spanish sovereigns the right to set up and direct the Inquisition: a system of courts which effectively controlled the churchmen of the land and was under the immediate authority, not of the Pope or the bishops, but of the king. The inquisitors had power over all religious orders and (after 1531) over bishops, and there was no appeal to Rome from their verdicts. The kings of France, like the kings of England, but with more success, limited the interference of the Pope during the fifteenth century. In 1516, after long interviews between the Pope and King Francis I, was signed the Concordat of Bologna, which determined the legal relation of Pope and Crown until the French Revolution of 1789. The king secured the right of appointment to all the higher posts in the Church of France, and placed within narrow limits the right of appeal by the clergy to the see of Rome. He could now nominate to 10 archbishoprics, 82 bishoprics, 527 abbeys, and numerous priories and canonries, and as dispenser of these favours and their endowments he was indirectly in control of the property of the Church. When he wanted ecclesiastical money, his methods need not even be devious.

In the fifteenth century the kings of England were already controlling the appointments to bishoprics. Even the weak emperor Frederick III in Germany, even the weaker kings of Scotland, obtained this right of nomination to many sees. The Republic of Venice fought several battles with Rome to the same end. The Popes were slowly losing actual (not theoretical) authority over the churches in the different states,

the appointments to higher posts, the right to levy contributions and to maintain the immunity of ecclesiastical estates
from taxation, and the right to hear appeals without interference. But it is certain that the Popes had never before
given away so much authority as by allowing the Spanish Inquisition and by granting the Concordat of Bologna to the
French king. The Pope was becoming weaker because the
governments were becoming stronger. And the stronger the
government, the more helpless lay the vast wealth and possessions of the Church and the more dangerous to vested interests and to corruption was the cry for reform.

The Reformation was not always a means by which legit-
imate sovereigns strengthened their hold upon their states.
The contrary is sometimes true. In many lands the Protestant revolt was associated with a political revolt against an
external or foreign sovereign—as in Scotland, the Netherlands, Sweden, some of the Swiss cities, some of the German
princedoms seeking freedom from imperial supervision.
Even the English political revolution against the Pope was a
faint reflection of the discarding of a foreign master.

The Increasing Power of Princes

As the power of the prince was increasing and the power of
the Pope decreasing, Church reformers looked to the government for effective power to reform. Reform needed a
knife to cut through the legal knots which protected established abuse. In the tangle of rights and prescriptions, the
conflict of legal systems secular and ecclesiastical, the rival
jurisdiction of courts, the constant opportunity for delaying
tactics, the powerlessness of the diocesan system, and the anarchy in some parts of the ecclesiastical administration, the
idle and the vicious flourished comfortably. You wished to
reform a monastery? If you went to the provincial of the
order, or the bishop, or the Pope, you would probably end
in years of frustrating litigation, at the end of which little
good had been done; but if you went to the king, he might
break rudely through the tangle and order the monks to be-
have or begone. The best of reformers, at least in Spain, England, France, Germany, wanted the sovereign to act. He

alone possessed the power to act effectively.

The Cardinal d'Amboise, empowered by the king to conduct a reformation in France, needed fortifying for reform with a Bull (from Pope Alexander VI) giving him full authority as papal legate. Thus armed with weapons from the heads of Church and State, he conducted an admirable reformation of several monastic houses and congregations. In 1501 he determined to reform the Cordeliers at Paris, and commissioned two bishops to visit and reform the house. When the commission arrived, the friars hurried away to the chapel, exposed the blessed sacrament, and began singing psalms. The two bishops waited for four hours and then, frustrated, went away. Next day they came back with the Provost of Paris, a hundred archers, and a band of constables. Again the friars fell to their psalms. They were stopped, and the papal bulls and royal decrees were read to them. They replied by quoting extracts in a contrary sense from their charters and the canon law. After a prolonged deadlock, and a different commission composed of Cordeliers, the Cardinal at last secured a measure of reform in the house.

The State as Ally of Reform

In the tangle of law, the reformer, though he needed papal power, needed royal powers also. He carried with him the decrees of the king as well as the bulls of the Pope, and he might need the king's guards. In modern language, though the State had always been necessary to the reform of the Church, it was becoming ever more necessary as its own power grew more effective, more sovereign.

The old ideal of a unity in Christendom was collapsing before the rise of the national states. The Vatican still trumpeted forth the claims of an Innocent III or Boniface VIII to world dominion. In 1493 Pope Alexander VI, as lord of the continents, divided the newly discovered world of America and the Indies between Spain and Portugal. In a European conflict Popes might still talk of deposing enemy kings from their kingdoms. Before a solemn audience of Alexander VI in St Peter's, Chieregato repeated the age-long interpretation of the two swords of power, the spiritual sword wielded by the Church and the temporal sword wielded by the State at the behest of the Pope. These vast pretensions corresponded to little enough in the cold reality of European politics. The Pope could sometimes secure what he wanted, but by diplomacy, no longer by decree. Bulls might thunder forth, and were still potent when they thundered, but behind the scenes there had been bargaining. To achieve anything important in France, Spain, Portugal, England, parts of Italy, parts of Germany, the Pope must secure the cooperation or the complaisance of the effective ruler. This was the age when the See of Rome first found it desirable to retain ambassadors (nuncios) in the European capitals. The first permanent nunciatures were set up at Venice in 1500 and at Paris in 1513. Men no longer bowed before the dread rebukes of the Church. They arranged them, compromised with them, argued about them, even bought them against their enemy—for in 1500 they were decidedly worth buying.

As the system of European states grew into manhood, the Italian needs and responsibility of the Papacy loomed larger relatively to the international responsibility. Like the other rulers of Europe, the ruler of the Papal States had to establish efficient control over his territories. The officials of the see needed to be Italian; popes were made to sign promises before election that all the Roman offices should go to Romans; the number of Italian cardinals steadily increased. To retain a majority of Italian cardinals was also to keep at a distance the pressure which kings might seek to exercise through their national cardinals. During the fifteenth century there were only two non-Italian popes, and one of them was Alexander VI Borgia. There was one more non-Italian pope, Adrian VI, who reigned briefly in 1522–3. There was not another till 1978. It was hardly conceivable that a non-Italian could effectively perform the Italian duties of the Pope.

Economic Conditions and the Reformation

Bard Thompson

While they cannot fully explain the Reformation, economic considerations clearly played an important role in creating the fertile soil in which the Reformation took root. Bard Thompson, former professor emeritus of church history at Drew University in Madison, New Jersey, focuses on the economic and social conditions in Germany on the eve of the Reformation. Because the feudal system was falling apart, both peasants and the knightly class were disaffected and resentful and more open to the changes the Reformation promised.

The Protestant Reformation began in 1517 in the university town of Wittenberg, in the German principality of Saxony. Already by 1521 it had spread to Zurich, in German-speaking Switzerland. From the French-speaking section of Switzerland, and specifically through the city of Geneva, it entered France. It traveled northward along the Rhine, into the Low Countries, into Scandinavia, and into Poland. Even in the 1520s, it crossed the Channel into England and entered Scotland. Only the staunchly Catholic nations of Spain and Italy were impervious to Protestantism, and only the Lutherans' own awkward treatment of the German peasants prevented the Reformation from attaining strength in the southern and southeastern sections of Germany.

Europe began the sixteenth century Catholic; it left the sixteenth century part Catholic, part Protestant, with a variety of evangelical parties competing with the old church and with each other, often vociferously, for a corner on religious truth. Europe began the sixteenth century still under the overarching umbrella of Christendom, with a more or less common set of religious and political assumptions; it left the sixteenth century a mass of new national states and territorial principalities, many with only tenuous connections to the papacy, if any at all. Europe began the sixteenth century with a capitalist economy based on the commerce and industry of the towns and the raw materials furnished by farms; it left the sixteenth century with a capitalist economy vastly changed and enlarged by colonial expansion into virtually every corner of the world. Europe began the sixteenth century already aware of the challenge that the Renaissance had posed to medieval culture; it left the sixteenth century with the prospects of a modern secular culture, which Protestantism unwittingly made possible, and with the prospects of an age of science, for which the Renaissance was a major preparation.

A Popular Movement

Unlike the Renaissance, which appealed principally to the elite, the Reformation was a vast popular movement that touched every segment of society. It was the first such movement of the post-Gutenberg era, that is, the first in which the printing press could be used as an instrument of persuasion. From 1500 until the beginning of the Reformation, German printers issued an average of forty books a year; once the Reformation began, however, that number increased to five hundred books a year. Luther's writings were literally snatched from the hands of booksellers. The combination of the Reformation and the printing press produced a great diffusion of knowledge and inaugurated what Oswald Spengler called the modern "book and reading culture." Printing in the service of religion reinforced some radical new ideas such as "the priesthood of all believers"—in other words, the idea that every believer is a priest—suggesting that the combination of personal faith and access to religious knowledge through the invention of printing empowered everyone to be a priest. Printing and the idea of the priesthood of all believers also encouraged literacy and education, including systems of public education, apart from which no one could even begin to acquire religious wisdom, much less become sophisticated in it. . . .

The Erosion of Feudalism

The Europe of the Reformation consisted of 65–80 million inhabitants. The prevailing economic system was capitalism. The bourgeois classes, normally associated with capitalist economies, flourished in the towns and cities, which continued to grow in the sixteenth century. New technologies in mining, shipping, and printing invigorated the economy. This setting, however, included two sorts of displaced and disaffected people. The lesser nobility had no place left to them in the exorable erosion of feudalism and were literally a superfluous people. The peasants, especially those of Germany, were an exploited people who sought some better stake in the money economy. Both parties were susceptible to revolutionary tendencies, and both contributed to the course of the Lutheran Reformation and to the emergence of the Anabaptist tradition. . . .

The Reformation began in Germany and throughout its first generation was a peculiarly German institution. It will be useful, therefore, to consider briefly the pre-Reformation history of Germany.

In the years after 1300, while France and England were developing into strong, centralized states under royal governments, Italy and Germany were both giving way to political particularism—Italy to the particularism of northern Italian city-states, Germany to the particularism of territorial princes. It is simply inappropriate to speak of a German "nation" before the time of the emperor Maximilian (1493–1519), and not until 1870 was there a national state called Germany.

In other words, as feudal structures were eroded by a money economy and by the vigorous economic life of the towns, there appeared in Germany, not a strong national government, but a system of princely states, or territories, and a gaggle of free cities, loosely federated under a parliament (the Diet) and the sovereignty of an emperor. The

German territorial states, being virtually independent, greatly diminished the power of the central government and bred a form of cultural provincialism of which many Germans, including Luther, were ashamed. . . .

A Chaotic Political System

If the territorial states seemed to add up to a system of political and social security, they did not. Pre-Reformation Germany suffered untold turbulence and lawlessness for the lack of a national government. The princes contended against each other in endless feuds and aggrandizements. Leagues of cities arose to defend the autonomy of the towns against overbearing princes. The knightly class, which had been rendered obsolete by the introduction of mercenary

The Favor of Princes

In this brief excerpt, noted British scholar G.R. Elton suggests that the Reformation was less than modern in the way it looked to the past for inspiration and its ideals. The success of the Reformation is primarily explained by the protection it received from various European princes.

In some ways the Reformation is more remote from the present day than the century or so that had preceded it. The fundamental intellectual attitude of the Reformation involved the doctrine of a decline from an ideal in the past and a devoted attachment to theology and ecclesiology at the expense of other studies; neither of these is a characteristic element in western thought after 1700. Admittedly it will be well to remember that besides the stream directly issuing from the Reformation there flowed a sizeable river of writings concerned with secular things and increasingly 'scientific' in its methods of analysis and interpretation. As one might expect, there are both traces of established modes of thinking and faint hints of great changes to come. Substantially, however, the Reformation was conservative—even backward-looking—in thought: since it was avowedly intent on restoring a lost condition, it could hardly be anything else.

armies paid for out of public taxes, manifested great restless-
ness and resentment and attempted to assert independent
power in fiefs still controlled by the knights. Throughout
the fifteenth century there were revolutionary expressions
among the German peasants, which will be described below.
In the absence of a strong, national government, prosecution
of crimes and the maintenance of public order was often left
to vigilantes; peace making was assigned to the fragile efforts
of the so-called *Landfrieden*, local agreements resembling the
medieval Peace of God.

Of all of the disaffected classes in Germany, the peasants
were the most restless. They arose from the agrarian and
feudal organization of the Middle Ages. In the money economy in which they increasingly found themselves, the peas-

---

The desire for spiritual nourishment was great in many parts
of Europe, and movements of thought which gave intellectual
content to what in so many ways was an inchoate search for
God have their own dignity. Neither of these, however, comes
first in explaining why the Reformation took root here and vanished there—why, in fact, this complex of anti-papal 'heresies'
led to a permanent division within the Church that had looked
to Rome. This particular place is occupied by politics and the
play of secular ambitions. In short, the Reformation maintained itself wherever the lay power (prince or magistrates)
favoured it; it could not survive where the authorities decided
to suppress it. . . .

The Reformation was successful beyond the dreams of earlier, potentially similar, movements not so much because (as the
phrase goes) the time was ripe for it, but rather because it found
favour with the secular arm. Desire for Church lands, resistance to imperial and papal claims, the ambition to create self-
contained and independent states, all played their part in this,
but so quite often did a genuine attachment to the teachings of
the reformers.

G.R. Elton, *The New Cambridge Modern History: Vol. II*, 1962.

ants discovered that most of the time-honored duties expected of them had been converted into money equivalents. Whatever gains the peasants made, whether in prosperity or in personal freedom, were immediately offset by a clamor for more prosperity and more civil rights. In the Rhineland, where the peasants were comparatively better off, the revolutionary sentiment was therefore the most intense. There the *Bundshuh*, the dreaded secret society of peasant revolutionaries, operated with especially awesome effect.

Widespread Dissatisfaction

The German world into which Luther was born was a world on the verge of upheaval. It is no wonder that, at first glance, most Germans, even the German peasants, mistook Luther to be a national hero, "the nightingale of Wittenberg," as Hans Sachs said, sent to lead Germans into a new era of hope and national purpose. Much of the resentment expressed by many classes of German society was focused against the Roman Catholic Church. Princes sought to exploit church lands and wealth; cities resented the princes of the church who, in some instances, governed them; town councils disliked the courts of law run by the church and bridled at episcopal control over the religious, moral, and social manners of the burghers; knights blamed the church for draining off the wealth of the empire by taxes, enriching Rome and Italy at the expense of Germans; peasants were convinced that bishops and abbots were among their principal oppressors; and virtually everyone denounced the taxation imposed by the church as a denigration of national dignity and an exploitation of German resources.

Yet, at the same time, largely through the rediscovery of Roman law by Renaissance scholars, the princes of the territories of Germany, by appealing to the absolute power of the *princeps* in Roman law, began to assert their own authority over religious affairs in their realms, the authority of the Catholic bishops notwithstanding. Thus, by the time of Luther, the crucial axiom *cuius regio, eius religio* (who rules the realm, his shall be the religion) could be used to admit the Reformation, or not to admit the Reformation, into the various territorial states of Germany. Meanwhile a quite similar development had taken place in the cities, as town councils began to insist on being able to control religious affairs within their corporate limits.

Aided and abetted by ardent nationalists among the German humanists—Ulrich von Hutten, for example—the chorus of hatred against the Church of Rome grew louder and louder as the fifteenth century yielded to the sixteenth. Almost every imperial diet that met during the century before Luther received a *gravamen*, or formal slate of grievances, compiled by the various classes of German society against the Church of Rome.

Luther's Influence on Attitudes Toward Sex and Marriage

Steven Ozment

Some of the most important changes resulting from the Reformation concerned sex, marriage, and family life. Protestants rejected clerical celibacy, nunneries, and monasteries. They believed that ministers and all Christians should be allowed to marry. This position raised the status of marriage as an institution, and elevated the dignity of women generally, according to the Harvard historian Steven Ozment. Ozment contends that the endorsement of marriage, with the mutuality and companionship involved, constituted a revolution in sexual attitudes. He claims that the Catholic glorification of the monastic life as the highest calling of Christians became a glorification of marriage and family in Protestant hands. Though this attitude did not constitute an endorsement of equal rights for women, it set the stage for more egalitarian treatment for women, as well as more liberal innovations such as free choice of a marriage partner and divorce.

Unlike the old clergy, the new clergy married, virtually en masse. From the outset they demanded the right to marry; for both Saxon and Swiss reformers, clerical marriage was as prominent a tenet as justification by faith. In making it so, the reformers attempted to set an example of Christian life for the laity in domestic as well as in spiritual matters. Nothing caught the new clergy up more personally in the Reformation's transition from theory to real life than the institution of marriage. In the new families they created these clergy found an emotional warmth and intimacy that had escaped them in the cloisters and parishes of the old church. Possessed of wives and soon with children, Protestant clerics became self-styled marriage counselors and child psychologists, as freespoken and dogmatic in domestic matters as in divine. But marriage also put their religious thinking to a test celibate clergy had been able to avoid. Even a man as self-assured as Martin Luther discovered that life within a family had a way of rewriting theology.

When we think of Martin Luther, we understandably think first of the monk and theologian who wanted to reform the church, a great man of God seemingly obsessed with sin and the devil and lost in otherworldly pursuits. But the monk and the theologian who wrote the Ninety-five Theses and threw an inkwell at the devil was also a husband and the father of six children. Problems of marriage and family life preoccupied Luther even before he married in 1525. While still a celibate priest, he wrote extensively on the subject. He portrayed marriage as an institution as much in crisis as the church and no less in need of reform. He describes marriage as "universally in awful disrepute," with peddlers everywhere selling "pagan books that treat of nothing but the depravity of womankind and the unhappiness of the estate of marriage"—a reference to misogynist and anti-marriage sentiments popular among his contemporaries. Women and marriage were widely ridiculed in proverbs and jokes; the biblical stories of the downfall of Adam, Samson, and David at the hands of women had gained popularity; and the advocates of virginity and celibacy never missed an opportunity to remind the lovestricken of the sacrifices and suffering that marriage and parenthood entailed.

It may seem surprising to learn that Martin Luther was a leading defender of the dignity of women and the goodness of marriage. He is perhaps too well known for his famous jesting comments on the meaning of woman's anatomy. "Women have narrow shoulders and wide hips," he quipped one evening at the table; "therefore they ought to be domestic; their very physique is a sign from their Creator that he intended them to limit their activity to the home." Luther, however, also deserves to be known as the century's leading critic of Aristotle's depiction of women as botched males (Aristotle's theory assumed that a perfect generative act would always result in a male offspring). Luther also criticized the church fathers (Jerome, Cyprian, Augustine, and Gregory) for "never having written anything good about marriage."

Sexual Chastity in Marriage

Like the church fathers, the clergy of the Middle Ages were obsessed with chastity and sexual purity. Saint Augustine portrayed sexual intercourse in Paradise as occurring without lust and emotion, Adam and Eve calmly reflecting on God as their sexual organs chastely fulfilled the marital duty. Approximation of such self-control, to the point of suppressing human sexual desire in imitation of Christ, had inspired the monastic life. The clergy not only attempted to live up to such ascetic ideals in their own lives, they also wanted to model the private sexual lives of the laity on them.

Consider, for example, a vernacular catechism from 1494, which elaborates the third deadly sin (impurity) under the title: "How the Laity Sin in the Marital Duty." According to the catechism, the laity sin sexually in marriage by (1) unnatural acts and positions, contraception, and masturbation; (2) desiring sex with another while performing it with one's spouse; (3) desiring sex with another while not performing it with one's spouse; (4) refusing the marital duty without an honest reason, thereby forcing a spouse to enter an illicit relationship to satisfy unfulfilled sexual need; (5) having sex in forbidden seasons (periods of penance, particularly Lent, during menstruation and the final weeks of pregnancy, and when a mother is lactating); (6) continuing to have sex with a known adulterous spouse; and (7) having sex for the sheer joy of it rather than for the reasons God has commanded, namely, to escape the sin of concupiscence and to populate the earth.

Luther and the first generation of Protestant clerics rejected the patristic tradition of ascetic sexuality in both their theology and their personal lives. This rejection was as great

Luther's View of Parenthood

Luther commented throughout his career on the virtues of family life over the sterility of the monastic life. Some social historians find Luther's most enduring legacy in his radical, positive view of marriage and the family.

Along comes the clever harlot, namely natural reason, looks at married life, turns up her nose, and says: Why, must I rock the baby, wash its diapers, change its bed, smell its odour, heal its rash, take care of this and take care of that, do this and do that? It is better to remain single and live a quiet and carefree life. I will become a priest or a nun and tell my children to do the same.

But what does the Christian faith say? The father opens his eyes, looks at these lowly, distasteful and despised things and knows that they are adorned with divine approval as with the most precious gold and silver. God, with his angels and creatures, will smile—not because diapers are washed, but because it is done in faith.

Martin Luther, *Concerning Married Life*, 1522. (Cited in Hans J. Hillerbrand, *The Reformation: A Narrative History*, p. 5)

a revolution in traditional church teaching and practice as their challenge of the church's dogmas on faith, works, and the sacraments. They literally transferred the accolades Christian tradition had since antiquity heaped on the religious in monasteries and nunneries to marriage and the home. When Saint Jerome, writing in the fourth century, compared virginity, widowhood, and marriage, he gave virginity a numerical value of one hundred, widowhood, sixty, and marriage, thirty. "Faith, not virginity, fills paradise," the Wittenberg pastor Johannes Bugenhagen retorted in the 1520s. "Saint Jerome's unfortunate comment, 'Virginity fills heaven, marriage the earth,' must be corrected," agreed the Lutheran poet Erasmus Alberus; "let us rather say, '*Connubium replet coelum*, Marriage fills heaven.'"

The first generation of Protestant clerics did not advocate equal rights for women in all walks of life, and none passes the stern tests posed today by modern feminist scholars, who depict the Reformation as having done women more harm than good, despite, or perhaps because of, the reformers' very positive evaluation of marriage. Idealizing women as wives and mothers, Protestants are accused of closing down wherever they could the contemporary institutions that allowed early modern women to have "an existence of their own in a more or less satisfying way"—namely, the cloister and the bordello. The claimed result [Dagmar Lorenz argues]: "an enormous impoverishment of previously provisioned women and the creation of a vast army of female beggars."

This harsh judgment is made from the perspective of the most egalitarian segment of twentieth-century society. When the domestic policies of Protestants are viewed less anachronistically against the religious culture and domestic practice of the Middle Ages, they are seen to address issues of great relevance to the well-being of sixteenth-century women and to have assisted the efforts then under way to reform the institution of marriage.

Celibacy and Marriage

Luther and his followers regarded the cloister, with its glorification of virginity and celibacy, as the chief expression of the age's antifeminism and hostility to marriage. When Protestant towns and territories dissolved cloisters and nunneries, they did so in the sincere belief that they were freeing the women there from sexual repression, cultural deprivation, and domination by inferior and abusive male clergy and religious. Among the leaders of the Reformation, it was widely believed that in most cases women had been placed in cloisters against their will and without full understanding of the consequences. They also believed that nuns were more easily bullied by their superiors than monks, and had far greater difficulty breaking their vows and returning to the world when they chose to do so. The reformers had no concept whatsoever of the cloister as a special "woman's place," where women might gain a degree of freedom and authority denied them in the secular world, while at the same time escaping the drudgery of marriage, the domination of hus-

bands, and the debilities of serial pregnancies and motherhood. Had such an argument been made to them, the reformers would surely have condemned it as an unnatural and
unchristian attempt on the part of women to escape their
God-given responsibilities in life. . . .

Luther rejected the cloister altogether as a proper solution to the problem of unmarried daughters, especially the
younger daughters of noblemen and wealthy burghers. He
insisted that fathers at every social rank had a responsibility
to make proper marriages for all of their children and to
avoid the mismatch of the cloister. He actively encouraged
fathers to remove their daughters from convents, and he tac-
itly approved the use of force to that end. In 1523, for example, he praised a Torgau burgher, Leonhard Koppe, who
successfully plotted the escape of his daughter and eleven
other nuns, among them Katherine von Bora, Luther's future wife, from the cloister at Nimbschen near Grimma.
Koppe regularly delivered herring to the cloister and apparently smuggled the sisters out in empty herring barrels.
Luther published a pamphlet account of the deed as an example for all parents with children in cloisters, comparing
Koppe's freeing of the sisters with Moses' deliverance of the
children of Israel from Egypt. He admonished parents to
consider the plight of women placed in cloisters while they
were still "young, foolish, and inexperienced." The great
majority, he believed, discovered at puberty that they could
not suppress their sexual desire and need for male companionship. In light of such facts, only "unmerciful" parents and
"blind and mad" clergy could permit girls to suffer and waste
away in cloisters: "a woman is not created to be a virgin, but
to conceive and bear children."

Attacks on Monasticism

To document his charges against the cloister, Luther encouraged the publication of exposés by renegade nuns. One
impressive example is Florentina of Ober Weimar, a noblewoman who had been placed in the cloister at age six. Discovering at fourteen that she lacked the aptitude for celibate
vows, she so informed her superior, only thereafter to find

herself forced to abide by the rules of the cloister and to endure ostracism, ridicule, imprisonment, and even thrashings whenever she again attempted to gain her release.

As far as Luther was concerned, opportunities for marriage abounded; the rapid marriage of numbers of former monks and nuns in the 1520s was proof enough. Where the Reformation succeeded, new laws prohibited boys and girls from entering cloisters, and the majority of monks and nuns already there were either pensioned off or returned to their families, those among them wishing to marry receiving permission immediately to do so.

The Issue of Secret Marriages

It was not the celibate ideal alone that Protestants believed threatening to the stability of contemporary marriage and family life. The marital legislation of the medieval church seemed to them equally menacing. Luther accused church law of encouraging immature and unhappy marriages by its recognition of so-called "secret" marriages. These were private unions entered into by youths of canonical age (at least twelve for girls and fourteen for boys) without the knowledge and consent of their parents and apart from any public witnesses. The medieval church sanctioned such unions grudgingly in an attempt to control premarital sex and to bring marriage, at its inception, under the moral authority of the church. . . .

For Lutherans, the secret marriages of youth indicated a cavalier approach to the most serious of life's decisions and the most important of human institutions. "When the honeymoon is over," warned the Eisenach reformer Jacob Strauss, "and one has to contend with the body of a sick mate, then we discover how lasting is the fidelity of a marriage based on lust." Among both Lutherans and Zwinglians, new marriage laws required both parental consent and a public witnessing of the vows, normally in church, before a marriage could be deemed fully licit. As important as such measures were, they did not put an end to clandestine marriages. Confronted by youth in love who had sexually consummated their relationship and might even be expecting a child, Protestants found themselves recognizing marriages undertaken without parental consent as readily as Catholics had done.

The Right of Choice in Marriage

Although Luther opposed the private marriages of youth, he strongly defended the right of young people to marry whomever they pleased. Learning of parents who forced their children into unwanted marriages with unhappy consequences for all, he devoted a special tract to the subject in 1524. As the title indicates, he believed that marriage should be a family decision respecting the wishes of all family members, but especially of those most directly involved: *Parents Should Neither Compel nor Hinder the Marriage of Their Children and Children Should Not Marry Without the Consent of Their Parents.* He advised youth confronted with the "outrageous injustice" of a planned forced marriage to turn to their local magistrates for help when informal appeals through relatives, friends, or a sympathetic parent failed. Youth who found all such efforts frustrated were advised to flee to another land and there marry their chosen mate at will.

As for parents confronted with a marriage they could neither willingly accept nor easily prevent (or dissolve), Luther advised that they state their objections frankly, but permit the marriage to occur without their approval, thereby letting obstinate children learn by experience the wisdom of their parents. As a husband and a parent, Luther appreciated both the difficulty of separating young lovers and the futility of forcing two people to live together against their will. If, as he believed, men and women were supposed to find in marriage "the things they naturally desire, namely, sex and offspring, a life together, and mutual trust," then to force two people together (or apart) against their will threatened both the purpose of marriage and social order beyond it.

As for the church's many impediments to marriage, Luther condemned them as "only snares for taking money," and he derided those who imposed them as "merchants selling vulvas and genitals." He recognized as valid only those impediments of consanguinity and affinity set forth in Leviticus

18:6–18. This position made it possible for Lutherans to accept such previously forbidden marriages as those between first cousins, step-relations, and the siblings of deceased spouses and fiancees, and to deny altogether impediments based on contrived spiritual and legal grounds such as godparentage and adoption. According to Luther, "one may take as (one's) spouse whomsoever (one) pleases, whether it be godparent, godchild, or the daughter or sister of a sponsor (i.e., a godparent) . . . and disregard those artificial, money-seeking impediments."

The politicians of the age were not as bold in domestic matters as the new theologians, and the laws and institutions of marriage did not in fact change as rapidly or as radically during the sixteenth century as the reformers had decreed they might in the 1520s and 1530s. The biblical impediments for the most part remained, and newly created marriage courts, which became predictably more conservative with age, rigidly supervised domestic morality. Still, it is a gross exaggeration to say that Luther removed the pope from the bedroom only to put the state there. Foundations were laid in Protestant lands for both a more realistic and a more charitable treatment of marriage. On the one hand, new laws made immature marriages more difficult to contract, while, on the other, mature and disciplined marriages became less vulnerable to arbitrary spiritual harassment. The domestic surveillance encouraged by the Reformation had the stability of marriage and family, not impossible religious ideals, at heart.

The Benefits of Marriage

Luther liked to turn traditional criticisms of women and marriage back onto the clerical critics themselves. He once described marriage, for example, as the only institution in which a chaste life *could* be maintained, and he insisted that "one cannot be *un*married without sin," arguments that could only have baffled the defenders of celibacy. Nothing seemed to Luther to be a more natural and necessary part of life than marriage. "Marriage pervades the whole of nature," he disarmingly points out; "for all creatures are divided into male and female; even trees marry; likewise, budding plants; there is also marriage between rocks and stones." Living at a time in which most people married comparatively late (women in their early twenties, men in their mid- to late twenties), he praised the early marriages (at nineteen) and high fertility of the Israelites. He condemned women who shunned motherhood because children might diminish their leisure and pleasure. "Our savior Christ did not despise motherhood," he reminded the advocates of the solitary life, "but took flesh from the womb of a woman."

Luther had a high regard for the ability of women to shape society by molding its youth and civilizing its men through the institution of marriage. He joined the moralists of his age in praising women as mothers, for filling the earth with life, and as wives, for taming the beast within their husbands. "A companionable woman brings joy to life," he told his table companions one evening; "women attend to and rear the young, administer the household, and are inclined to compassion; God has made them compassionate by nature so that by their example men may be moved to compassion also." Even when Luther seemed in jest to denigrate women, he could still bestow on them a high compliment. Once at table he declared, "Eloquence is not to be praised in women; it is more fitting that they stammer and babble." These unkind comments came after he had told a visiting Englishman (possibly the reformer Robert Barnes), who knew no German, that he should learn German from Luther's wife Katie because she was the more fluent, indeed, "the most eloquent speaker (*facundissima*) of the German language." On more than one public occasion, Luther described Katie as his "lord": "I am an inferior lord," he would say, "she the superior; I am Aaron, she is my Moses." He bore her outspoken criticism of his poor business instincts and misplaced charity with respect and good humor. Once he compared "household wrath," by which he meant a fight with his wife, with the wrath of God in politics, where war and death threaten, and in religion, where the soul and heaven are at stake, and drew the following conclusion: "If I can survive the wrath of the devil in my sinful conscience, I can withstand the anger of Katharine von Bora." He also acknowledged his respect for her abilities in his last will and testament. Ignoring the traditional German practice of appointing a male trustee to administer a deceased husband's estate on behalf of his widow and children, he directly designated her "heir to everything."

The Example of Luther's Wife

Katharine von Bora earned such respect from her husband, whom she surpassed in virtually all worldly matters. Modern feminist scholars who today praise the cloister as the ideal place for women in the Middle Ages may do so because the cloistered life seems at a distance to have been so much like the modern academic life of women—that is, a protected and privileged life, free from the cares of the real world, allowing educated women both power and the leisure to pursue their own thoughts. Katharine von Bora fled that life for one she believed held even greater opportunities for the women of her age. She became a model housewife and an accomplished businesswoman. To increase their income, she remodeled the old cloister in which she and Martin lived so that it would accommodate up to thirty students and guests. She also expanded the cloister garden and repaired the cloister brewery. She became locally famous as a herbalist, and her beer was so renowned that Luther once took samples to the electoral court. He dubbed her "the morning star of Wittenberg," as her day began at 4:00 A.M., much like that of the wife of a butcher or a merchant. As the Luthers' example indicates, Protestant women could work outside the home as readily as women in previous centuries, despite increasing restrictions in the sixteenth century on women's vocational opportunities as a result of growing inflation and new state bureaucracy.

Luther obviously meant it when he said, "there is no bond on earth so sweet nor any separation so bitter as that which occurs in a good marriage." His comments on marriage leave the impression of an experienced husband who had given the matter considerable thought. Take, for example, the following analysis: "In the beginning of a relationship love is glowing hot; it intoxicates and blinds us, and we rush forth and embrace one another." But once married, we tend to grow tired of one another, confirming the saying of Ovid: "We hate the things that are near us and we love those that are far away."

> A wife is easily taken, but to have abiding love, that is the challenge. One who finds it in his marriage should thank the Lord God for it. Therefore, approach marriage earnestly and ask God to give you a good, pious girl, with whom you can spend your life in mutual love. For sex [alone] establishes nothing in this regard; there must also be agreement in values and character.

An Emphasis on Companionship

Luther here expresses a point of view broadly shared by the moral authorities of his day, both Protestant and Catholic. Physical attraction may well play a role in the creation of a marriage, but it is no foundation for a lasting relationship. A mutual willingness to make sacrifices is what holds a marriage together over time. So when seeking a spouse, the most important question was always whether the object of one's desire was also a person worthy of respect and trust, that is, a person with companionable qualities and the ability to keep his or her word. According to Luther, both he and his wife to be had "begged God earnestly for grace and guidance" before they married. They had in fact long been associated in Wittenberg between 1523 and 1525. Their relationship had engendered much gossip, as Luther was a constant visitor at the home of Lucas Cranach, where Katharine, a renegade nun under Luther's supervision, lodged. Luther twice attempted unsuccessfully to arrange other marriages for her. According to Catholic pamphleteers, they "lived together" in Wittenberg before they married. Whatever the truth of this particular gossip, such practices were not uncommon among clergy at the time. Zwingli made public his secret marriage to a widow only a short time before the arrival of their child.

Because of the importance attached to companionship in

marriage, the reformers tolerated bigamous attachments as a solution to loveless marriages, particularly among powerful rulers, whose protection they needed and whose reckless behavior they could not curb anyway. They also endorsed for the first time in Western Christiandom genuine divorce and remarriage. Although the reformers viewed marriage as a spiritual bond transcending all other human relationships, it did not in their opinion create a permanent state. A marriage could definitively end this side of eternity and a new one begin for separated spouses. In his earliest writings on such matters, Luther expressed "great wonder" that the church forbade people to remarry who were irreconcilably separated and living apart because of one partner's adultery. "Christ," he pointed out, "permits divorce for adultery and compels none to remain unmarried [thereafter]; and Saint Paul would rather have us [re]marry than burn [now with lust and later in hell]."

The Issue of Divorce

In the medieval church, divorce had meant only the separation of a couple from a common bed and table, not the dissolution of the marriage bond and the right to marry again. As long as both lived and the marriage was not annuled, a "divorced" couple remained man and wife in the eyes of the church and were so treated by law where the church prevailed. In practice, this situation meant that the turmoil of a failed marriage might never end for a couple.

Protestants, by contrast, generally permitted divorce and remarriage on five grounds: adultery, willful abandonment, chronic impotence, life-threatening hostility, and willful deceit (such as when a presumed virgin is discovered after marriage to have given birth previously to an illegitimate child or to be pregnant by another man). Most Protestant writers sympathized with the position of the Strasbourg reformer Martin Bucer, who declared no proper marriage to exist where affection was not regularly shared and all conversation had ceased. . . .

Protestant marriage courts did not permit divorce and remarriage to occur without first making every effort to reunite an estranged couple and revive the dead marriage. All concerned deemed reconciliation preferable to divorce in every case. Despite lip service to harsh biblical punishments, pastors actually discouraged extreme penalties for adultery, lest an estranged couple be driven even farther apart, as might happen when an adulterer was punished by exile or by fines that impoverished him. When a table companion once expressed to Luther the belief that adulterers should be summarily executed, Luther rebuked him with a local example of how harsh punishment had done more harm than good to a couple. A pious wife, who had borne her husband four children and had never been unfaithful, one day committed adultery. For the transgression, the enraged husband had her publicly flogged. Afterward, Luther, Pastor Bugenhagen, and Philipp Melanchthon tried to persuade the couple to reconcile. The husband was willing to take her back and let bygones be bygones, but the wife had been so humiliated by the flogging and the resulting scandal that she abandoned her husband and children and wandered away, never to be seen again. "Here," Luther comments, "one should have pursued reconciliation before punishment." Chronic and willful public adultery, however, was treated harshly and without regret.

Both spiritually and socially, Lutheran theology held the community formed by a husband and a wife to be society's most fundamental. The marriage bond was too important to be allowed to stand when all conversation, affection, and respect between a husband and a wife had irretrievably broken down. And the same bond was also too important to allow a marriage to dissolve without a fight to save it. Protestants gained the right to divorce and remarry in the sixteenth century, but it remained a difficult one to exercise.

Protestant Attitudes About Women

Merry E. Wiesner-Hanks

According to Merry E. Wiesner-Hanks, professor of history at the University of Wisconsin at Milwaukee, Protestant contributions to the liberation and well-being of women can be easily overstated. While some nuns, for example, eagerly embraced the closing of their nunneries, many others resisted it strenuously. Though attitudes to marriage may have improved in some quarters, Wiesner-Hanks points to the legacy of chauvinistic and patriarchal attitudes that remained unchanged, especially belief in the inferiority and subjection of women to men. While some opportunities and roles—such as pastor's wife, domestic missionary, etc.—were expanded by the Reformation, other opportunities for religious expression and fulfillment were curtailed. The author concludes that, while women's activities expanded in the early years of the Reformation, they became more restricted as the Reformation became more institutionalized.

Since the late 1960s, women's history has developed as a new field of historical inquiry as scholars have begun systematically to examine the experiences of the half of the human population that had been largely left out of traditional historical scholarship. This research has involved both the reinterpretation of well-known texts and images and the discovery of new sources that provide evidence of women's lives.

Excerpted from "Women," by Merry E. Wiesner-Hanks, from *The Oxford Encyclopedia of the Reformation, 4-Volume Set*, edited by Hans J. Hillerbrand. Copyright ©1996 by Oxford University Press, Inc. Used by permission of Oxford University Press, Inc.

Both types of research are ongoing in Reformation scholarship. Theologians and intellectual historians are reexamining the writings of major and minor reformers to discover their ideas about women and other related subjects such as marriage, motherhood, sexuality, and the family. . . .

Historians of women have also begun to explore women's responses to the Reformation, responses of both words and actions. Women were not simply passive recipients of the Reformation message, but left convents, refused to leave convents; preached; prophesied; discussed religion with friends and family; converted their husbands, left their husbands; wrote religious poems, hymns, and polemics; and were martyred on all sides of the religious controversy. . . .

The Reformers' Ideas About Women

Much disagreement has arisen in the late twentieth century among scholars in their assessments of the religious reformers' ideas about women. One of the reasons for this is that many of the most important religious leaders of the period were not consistent, expressing strongly negative opinions of women at some points and very positive ones at others. For example, Martin Luther notes at one point, "There is nothing better on earth than a woman's love," and at another, "Women are created for no other purpose than to serve men and be their helpers. If women grow weary or even die while bearing children, that doesn't harm anything. Let them bear children to death; they are created for that." A second is that other leaders, such as John Calvin, expressed their view of women only obliquely while considering other issues, so that their opinions must be extrapolated and require a high degree of interpretation. A third is that many contemporary scholars have strong personal or religious convictions regarding certain religious leaders or the denominations they founded, so that it is sometimes difficult for them to accept the opinions they find. Despite the contradictions and ambiguities in the writings of religious thinkers, and the differences of opinion among modern scholars, however, one can make some generalizations about the impact of religious change on ideas about women.

Though they broke with the institutional structure and denounced many of the theological ideas of the Catholic church, the Protestant reformers did not break sharply with the medieval scholastic theologians in their ideas about women. For Luther, Zwingli, Calvin, and the leaders of the English Puritans, women were created by God and could be saved through faith; in that respect women and men were spiritually equal. In every other respect, however, women were to be subordinate to men. Women's subjection was inherent in their very being and was present from creation—in this the reformers agreed with Aristotle and the classical tradition, though Luther in particular denounced the ideas of Aristotle on other matters and saw the scholastic attempt to reconcile Aristotle and the Bible as misguided.

Most reformers accepted Eve's principal responsibility for the Fall and thought this had made women's original natural inferiority and subjection to male authority even more pronounced. Protestants generally supported Paul's teaching that women should be silent in church, though Calvin, alone among sixteenth-century leaders, noted that this teaching was determined by tradition and custom rather than divine commandment and so might be open to change; but he did not see this change happening in the near future or make any practical attempts to bring it about. A few small Anabaptist groups that emphasized the importance of divine revelation took the visions of their female members seriously, although not until the seventeenth-century Quakers did any group officially allow women to hold positions of religious authority.

New Views of Celibacy and Marriage

The Protestants did break with official Catholic teachings on the relative merits of celibacy and marriage and wrote large numbers of tracts trying to convince men and women to marry and advising spouses (particularly husbands) how best to run their households and families. It is in this pro-marriage literature that one finds the most positive statements about women, for the writers recognized that many of their readers were former priests and monks who had been trained to regard marriage, sexuality, and women in general as destroyers of their spiritual well-being. The writers used the story of Eve being created out of Adam's rib as proof that God wanted women to stand by the side of men as their assistants and not be trampled on or trod underfoot (for then Eve would have been created out of Adam's foot); these directives always mention as well, however, that women should never claim authority over men, for Eve had not been created out of Adam's head.

Protestant marriage manuals, household guides, and marriage sermons all stress the importance of husbandly authority and wifely obedience. For almost all Protestants, this obedience took precedence over women's spiritual equality; a woman's religious convictions were never grounds for leaving or even openly disagreeing with her husband, though she could pray for his conversion. The only exceptions to this generalization were some radical reformers who did allow women to leave their unbelieving spouses, but the women who did so were expected to remarry quickly and thus come under the authority of a male believer. Women were continually advised to be cheerful rather than grudging in their obedience, for in doing so they demonstrated their willingness to follow God's plan. Men were also given specific advice about how to enforce their authority, which often included physical coercion; in both Continental and English marriage manuals, the authors use the metaphor of breaking a horse for teaching a wife obedience. Though the opinions of women who read such works were not often recorded, one gets the impression from private letters that women knew they were expected to be obedient and silent, for they often excused their actions when they did not conform to the ideal. Such letters also indicate, however, that women's view of the ideal wife was one in which competence and companionship were as important as submissiveness.

Marriage and Control

The Protestant exhortation to marry was directed to both sexes, but particularly to women, for whom marriage and motherhood were a vocation as well as a living arrangement. Marriage was also regarded as a way for women to control their sexual urges, which in the sixteenth century were regarded as much stronger than men's. Unmarried women were thus suspect, both because they were fighting their natural sex drives and because they were upsetting the divinely imposed order, which made woman subject to man. It is important to recognize, then, that the Protestant elevation of marriage is not the same as, and may in fact directly contradict, an elevation of women *as women*.

The opinions of Protestant leaders about marriage and women were not contained simply in written works but were communicated to their congregations through marriage sermons and homilies; because people in many parts of Europe were required to attend church, there was no way they could escape hearing them. Their opinions were also reflected in woodcuts and engravings that illustrated religious pamphlets, an important tool in the spread of Protestant ideas. The ideal woman appears frequently in both sermons and illustrations: sitting with her children, listening to a sermon or reading the Bible, dressed soberly and with her hair modestly covered. Negative depictions also appear: the nun who quotes her psalter while her attention is elsewhere; the priest's concubine; prostitutes or women dressed extravagantly buying indulgences or expensive rosaries; disobedient wives being beaten by their husbands.

Catholic Response

Catholic reformers responded to the Protestant elevation of marriage by reaffirming traditional doctrine and emphasizing that the most worthy type of Christian life was one both celibate and chaste. Spouses who took mutual vows of chastity within a marriage or left marriage to enter cloisters were praised. Catholic authors also realized, however, that despite exhortations to celibacy, most women in Europe would marry, and so wrote marriage manuals to counteract those written by Protestants. The ideal wife they described was exactly the same as that proposed by Protestant authors—obedient, silent, pious—and their words give clear indication that they still regarded women as totally inferior. Thus the opinions of learned Catholic authors about

women, as well as about marriage, tended to reaffirm traditional negative ideas, though the harshest criticisms were
generally reserved for specific women who challenged male
authority in some way rather than simply being addressed to
women in general in the style of Tertullian or Jerome.
Catholic leaders from the late sixteenth century on often
recognized that women were useful allies in the fight to reconvert or hold areas to the Catholic faith, so they did not
openly express the type of harshly misogynist ideas that were
common in pre-Reformation writers.

Women's Opportunities

Just as scholars disagree about the reformers' ideas, they also
debate the impact of these ideas, for the Protestant and
Catholic Reformations both expanded and diminished
women's opportunities. In terms of the Protestant Reformation, the period in which women were the most active was
the decade or so immediately following an area's decision to
break with the Catholic church or while this decision was
being made. During this period, many groups and individuals tried to shape the new religious institutions. Sometimes
this popular pressure took the form of religious riots, in
which women frequently participated. In 1536 at Exeter in
England, for example, a group of women armed with shov-
els and pikes attacked workers who had been hired by the
government to dismantle a monastery. Sometimes this popular pressure took the form of writing, when women and
men who did not have formal theological training took
Luther's notion of the "priesthood of all believers" literally
and preached or published polemical religious literature explaining their own ideas.

Women's preaching and publishing of religious material
stood in direct opposition to the words ascribed to Paul (*I
Tim*. 2: 11–15) that ordered women not to teach or preach,
so that all women who published felt it necessary to justify
their actions. The boldest, such as Argula von Grumbach, a
German noblewoman who published a defense of a teacher
accused of Lutheran leanings, commented that the situation
was so serious that Paul's words should simply be disre-

garded: "I am not unfamiliar with Paul's words that women should be silent in church, but when I see that no man will or can speak, I am driven by the word of God when he said, 'He who confesses me on earth, him will I confess and he who denies me, him will I deny.'" Ursula Weyda, a middle-class German woman who attacked the abbot of Pegau in a 1524 pamphlet, agreed, as did Marie Dentière, a former abbess who left her convent to help the cause of the Reformation in Geneva and published a letter to Marguerite d'Angoulême in 1539 defending some of the reformers exiled from that city. Katharina Zell, the wife of one of Strasbourg's reformers and a tireless worker for the Reformation, asked that her writings not be judged according to the standards of a woman but simply according to the standards of a divinely inspired Christian.

Zell's wish was never granted, and women's writings were always judged first on the basis of gender. Argula von Grumbach's husband was ordered to force her to stop writing, and Marie Dentière's pamphlets were confiscated by the very religious authorities she was defending. Once Protestant churches were institutionalized, polemical writings by women (and untrained men) largely stopped. Women continued to write hymns and devotional literature, but these were often published posthumously or were designed for private use.

Women's actions as well as their writings in the first years of the Reformation upset political and religious authorities. Many cities prohibited women from even getting together to discuss religious matters, and in 1543 an act of Parliament in England banned all women except those of the gentry and nobility from reading the Bible; upper-class women were also prohibited from reading the Bible aloud to others. Class as well as gender hierarchies were to be maintained at all costs, though women's diaries reveal that this restriction was rarely obeyed and that they frequently read the Bible to themselves and to others.

The Power of Class

The ability of a woman to act out her religious convictions was largely dependent on class in reality as well as in theory.

Though none of the reformers differentiated between noblewomen and commoners in their public advice or writings, in private they recognized that noblewomen had a great deal of power and made special attempts to win them over. Luther corresponded regularly with a number of prominent noblewomen, and Calvin was even more assiduous at trying to win noblewomen to his cause. Their efforts often succeeded, for in a number of cases female rulers converted their territories to Protestantism or influenced their male relatives to do so. In Germany, Elisabeth of Brunswick-Calenburg brought in Protestant preachers and established a new church structure; in France, Marguerite d'Angoulême and her daughter Jeanne of Navarre supported Calvinism through patronage and political influence; in Norway, Inger of Austraat, a powerful and wealthy noblewoman, led the opposition to the Norwegian archbishop, who remained loyal to Catholicism. The most dramatic example of the degree to which a woman's personal religious convictions could influence events occurred in England, when, after Mary Tudor attempted to wrench the country back to Catholicism, Elizabeth created a moderately Protestant church. In all of these cases political and dynastic concerns mixed with religious convictions, in the same way they did for male rulers and nobles.

A Domestic Activity

Once the Reformation was established, most women expressed their religious convictions in a domestic rather than a public setting. They prayed and recited the catechism with children and servants, attended sermons, read the Bible or other devotional literature if they were literate, and served meals that no longer followed Catholic fast prescriptions. Women's domestic religion often took them beyond the household, however, for they gave charitable donations to the needy and often assisted in caring for the ill and indigent. As it had been before the Reformation, most women's charity was on a case-by-case basis, but there are also examples from Protestant areas of women who established and supported almshouses, schools, orphanages, funds for poor widows, and dowry funds for poor girls. The secularization of public welfare that accompanied the Reformation did give some women the opportunity to create permanent institutions to deal with social problems; evidence from wills indicates that women were, perhaps not surprisingly, more likely than men to make bequests that specifically benefited other women.

The women whose domestic religious activities were most closely scrutinized in the first generation of the Protestant Reformation were the wives of the reformers. During the first few years of the Reformation, they were still likened to priests' concubines in the public mind and had to create a respectable role for themselves, a task made even more difficult by the fact that many were, in fact, former nuns. They were often living demonstrations of their husbands' convictions and were expected to be models of wifely obedience and Christian charity. The women whose status was most tenuous were the wives of English bishops. Not only were many forced into exile or, worse yet, repudiated by their husbands during Mary's reign, but their marriages were not formally approved by Elizabeth, so that their children could always be declared bastards. Bishops were expected to live like wealthy noblemen and were accorded high rank at all ceremonial occasions, but their wives had no rank whatsoever. Long after Continental pastors' wives had succeeded in making theirs a respectable position, bishops' wives in England still had not achieved even legal recognition despite all their efforts at maintaining pious households.

Religious Martyrs

No matter how much it was extolled in Protestant sermons and domestic conduct books, the vocation of mother and wife was not enough for some women, whose religious convictions led them to leave their husbands and continue to express their religious convictions publicly, even at the cost of their lives. One of the most famous of these was Ann Askew, an English woman who was tortured and then executed for her religious beliefs in 1546. Askew was one of the few women martyrs to come from a gentry or middleclass background. Of the people executed for religious reasons during the reign of Mary Tudor in England, one-fifth were women, and most of these were quite poor; wealthy people who opposed Mary fled to the Continent.

Most of the women executed for religious reasons in early modern Europe were Anabaptists. The interrogations of Anabaptists are one of the few sources we have for the religious ideas of people who were illiterate. From these records, it is clear that many women could argue complicated theological concepts and had memorized large parts of the Bible. Anabaptist women actively chose the path of martyrdom, often against the pressure of family members, and the records of their trials reveal a strong sense of determination. Their strength of purpose may now appear heroic, but to many of their contemporaries Anabaptist women seemed demonically inspired, and in some ways the interrogations of Anabaptists parallel later witchcraft interrogations. In both cases, young women were stripped naked before they were tortured and were asked not only to confess their beliefs but also to name accomplices; the beliefs they were accused of were viewed as so pernicious that normal rules of legal procedure did not apply; most of those accused were poor.

Restricted Roles and Choices

At the same time that it created new roles for women—religious polemicist, pastor's wife, domestic missionary, philanthropist, martyr—the Protestant Reformation also rejected many of the activities that had previously given women's lives religious meaning. Religious processions that had included both men and women, such as that of Corpus Christi, were prohibited, and laws restricted the celebration of baptisms, weddings, and funerals, all ceremonies in which women had played a major role. Lay female confraternities, which had provided emotional and economic assistance for their members and charity for the needy, were also forbidden, and no all-female groups replaced them. The new charitable funds founded by women for women often had men as their overseers, and in any case did not bring together women of different classes as comembers the way confraternities had, but made sharp distinctions between the bestower and recipient of charity. The reformers attempted to do away with the veneration of Mary and the saints, though women continued to pray to Mary and Saints Anne and Margaret, the patron saints of childbirth, for centuries. The Protestant martyrs replaced the saints to some degree as models worthy of emulation, but one was not to pray to them, and their names were not given to any days of the year, which stripped the calendar of celebrations honoring women.

The Protestant rejection of celibacy had the greatest impact on female religious, both cloistered nuns and women who lived in less formal religious communities. One of the first moves of an area rejecting Catholicism was to close the monasteries and convents, either confiscating the buildings and land immediately or forbidding new novices and allowing the current residents to live out their lives on a portion of the convent's old income. In England and Ireland, where all monasteries and convents were taken over by the Crown, most nuns got very small pensions and were expected to return to their families, though not all did. Many Irish nuns fled to religious communities on the Continent or continued to fulfill their religious vows in hiding while they waited for the chance to emigrate. In many cities of the Netherlands, the convents were closed, their assets liquidated, and the women given their dowries and a pension. . . .

Women in the Netherlands and England, denied the possibility of remaining in their convents, [often] continued to live together, letting their formal religious affiliation remain a matter of speculation, both for contemporaries and for historians. The Protestant championing of marriage and family life, which some nuns accepted with great enthusiasm as a message of liberation from the convent, was viewed by others as a negation of the value of the life they had been living; they thus did all in their power to continue in their chosen path.

Chapter 4

The Catholic Reformation and Counter-Reformation

Turning Points

IN WORLD HISTORY

The Impact of Ignatius of Loyola and the Council of Trent

Bruce L. Shelley

The Catholic response to the Protestant upheaval came in three prominent developments: Pope Paul's reform commission of 1534; the creation of a new militant religious order, the Jesuits, in 1540; and the Council of Trent, which extended off and on from 1545 to 1563. Bruce Shelley, professor of church history at Denver Theological Seminary, provides here a useful overview of these three responses. The most important outcome of the Pope's reform commission was the call for a general church council. The ensuing Council of Trent and the founding of the Jesuits are two of the most significant events in the shaping of modern Catholicism. The Jesuits, under the leadership of Ignatius of Loyola, provided tremendous energy and impetus for missionary and educational activity. The Council of Trent addressed the central tenets of Protestantism, such as the idea of justification by faith alone, and decisively rejected each one, thus codifying the distinctions between Catholic and Protestant that continue to this day.

In 1521, the year that Martin Luther stood before the Emperor Charles V at the Diet of Worms, a young Spanish nobleman was fighting on the emperor's borderlands against the invading French at Pamplona. A cannonball shattered one of his legs. During a long, painful convalescence, he turned out of boredom to two popular inspirational works, one on the lives of the saints and the other a life of Christ. With these his long process of conversion began.

Months later, at the Benedictine abbey of Montserrat, he exchanged his gentleman's clothes for a rough pilgrim's garb and dedicated his sword and dagger to the shrine's Black Virgin. For nearly a year, in a little town called Manresa, thirty miles north of Barcelona, he gave himself to an orgy of austerity: begging door to door, wearing a barbed girdle, fasting for days on end. For months he endured the terrible depressions of the mystic's dark night of the soul, even contemplating suicide at one point. But what followed was the mystic's singular reward, an immense breakthrough to spiritual enlightenment. In a wave of ecstatic illumination one day at the River Cardoner, the wounded nobleman, Ignatius Loyola, became, in his own words, "another man."

Loyola (1491–1556) reduced his rebirth at Manresa to a plan for spiritual discipline, a military manual for stormtroopers at the service of the pope. The result was the Jesuits, the Society of Jesus, the greatest single force in Catholicism's campaign to recapture the spiritual domains seized by Protestantism.

How did the Church of Rome respond to the Protestant challenge? It didn't, not immediately. But when it finally realized the seriousness of the revolt, it called upon its spiritual warriors; it convened a new, militant council; and it reformed the machinery of the papal office. Faced by the rebellion of almost half of Europe, Catholicism rolled back the tide of Protestantism until by the end of the sixteenth century Protestantism was limited roughly to the northern third of Europe, as it is today.

Some historians have interpreted the Catholic Reformation as a counterattack against Protestantism; others have described it as a genuine revival of Catholic piety with few thoughts of Protestantism. The truth is the movement was both a Counter Reformation, as Protestants insist, and a Catholic Reformation, as Catholics argue. Its roots run back to forces before Luther's time, but the form it took was largely determined by the Protestant attack.

Strange as it may seem the mystical experience was a large part of Catholicism's recovery. The sixteenth century produced a remarkable variety of Catholic saints: the English lawyer and statesman, Thomas More; the cheerful and imaginative missionary to the Calvinists, Francis of Sales; the somber reforming archbishop of Milan, Charles Borromeo; the rapturous Spanish mystic, Teresa of Avila, and most influential of all, the Spanish soldier of Christ, Ignatius Loyola.

Even before Luther posted his theses on the church door a distinguished and aristocratic group at Rome had formed a pious brotherhood called the Oratory of Divine Love. Their guiding belief was that the reformation of the church and society begins within the individual soul.

The Oratory was never large in number, perhaps 50, yet it had enormous influence. It stimulated reform in the older monastic orders and contributed leaders to the Church of Rome as it laid plans for a general council to deal with internal reform and the Protestant heresy. Among the members of the Oratory who later emerged as significant figures were Jacopo Sadoleto, who debated with Calvin; Reginald Pole, who tried under Bloody Mary to turn England back to Rome; and Gian Pietro Caraffa, who became Pope Paul IV.

Throughout the 1520s and 1530s, however, the Church of Rome took no significant steps toward reform. The question is why? Why was she so slow to respond to the Protestant challenge?

One simple answer is politics. The Emperor Charles V and the popes fought a running battle over the calling of a general council that stretched over two decades. Luther had called for a council of the church as early as 1518. The idea gained the support of the German princes and the emperor, but the popes had fears of such an assembly. They remembered too well the councils at Constance and Basel. They also knew that many in Germany had in mind a council without the pope.

The Role of Politics

Equally important, the popes in the 1520s and 1530s were preoccupied with secular and political affairs. Clement VII

(1523–1534) is a prominent example. He regarded concern for the Papal States in Italy as a supreme law, and his passion for papal political fortunes drew him into an alliance with France against Charles V, leader of the Hapsburg interests in Italy. The pope's treachery and disloyalty enraged Charles, and he threatened Clement with a trial before a general council unless he broke his alliance with Francis I, King of France.

To show the pope he meant business Charles ordered his troops to march on Rome. As it turned out he got more than he had planned. The commanders of his troops were killed. As a result, the rough and undisciplined Spanish and German mercenaries were leaderless when they stormed Rome on 6 May 1527. Their pillaging, plundering, and murdering in the Eternal City lasted for weeks. The pope took refuge in the Castle of St. Angelo, but finally had to surrender and endure half a year of harsh imprisonment. Many considered this sack of Rome a terrible visitation by God, a clear call to repentance and change in the worldly papacy.

A Reform Commission

No serious reform came until Pope Paul III (1534–1549) ascended to the papal throne. Paul appeared to be a most unlikely candidate for spiritual leadership. He had three illegitimate sons and a daughter, four striking reminders of his pursuit of pleasure. The sack of Rome, however, seems to have sobered him. He realized that the time had come for reform to begin in the House of God. He started where he felt a change of heart was most urgently needed, in the College of Cardinals. He appointed to the college a number of champions of reform. Among them were leaders in the Oratory of Divine Love: Sadoleto, Pole, and Caraffa.

Paul, then, appointed nine of the new cardinals to a reform commission. The head of the commission was another former member of the Oratory, Gasparo Contarini. A peacemaker by temperament, Contarini stood for reconciliation with the Protestants and advocated a return to the faith of the apostles.

After a wide-ranging study of conditions in the Church of Rome, the commission issued in 1537 a formal report, *Ad-*

vice . . . Concerning the Reform of the Church. Disorder in the
Church, the report said, could be traced directly to the need
for reform. The papal office was too secular. Both popes and
cardinals needed to give more attention to spiritual matters
and stop flirting with the world. Bribery in high places,
abuses of indulgences, evasions of church law, prostitution in
Rome, these and other offenses must cease.

Call for a General Council

Pope Paul took action on a few of these items, but his most
significant response was a call for a general council of the
Church. After intense negotiations he agreed with the emperor on a location for the assembly, a town in northern Italy
under imperial control called Trent.

Even then, however, no council assembled for years, because Francis I did everything in his power to prevent such
a gathering. In his passion for leadership of Europe he feared
a council would only strengthen Charles's hand. Francis
even stooped to inciting the Turks against the emperor. Two
wars between Francis and Charles delayed the opening of a
council until 1545, almost three decades after Luther's theses appeared.

By 1545 Rome was under the spell of a new austerity. Reform was on the rise. The immoralities of Paul's younger
days were no longer acceptable behavior. The pope's new
rigor was apparent in the institution of the Roman Inquisition and in the Index of prohibited books—works that any
Catholic risked damnation by reading. All the books of the
Reformers were listed, as well as Protestant Bibles. For a
long time merely to possess one of these banned books in
Spain was punishable by death. The Index was kept up to
date until 1959 and was finally abolished by Pope Paul VI.

Ignatius Loyola

It was this city, a new militant Rome, and this pope, Paul III,
who approved Ignatius Loyola's new Society of Jesus. These
daring soldiers of Christ promised the pope that they would
go wherever he might send them "whether to the Turks or
to the New World or to the Lutherans or to others, be they

infidel or faithful." They said it and they meant it, for the Jesuits were a fitting likeness of their founding general.

As a boy Ignatius had left the gloomy castle of Loyola near the Pyrenees to enter the court of his father's noble friend. He had grown into little more than an engaging "playboy," spending his days in military games or reading popular chivalrous romances, his nights pursuing less noble adventures with local girls.

But all that was before Ignatius met God at Manresa. Martin Luther emerged from his spiritual struggle convinced that the human will is enslaved, that man cannot save himself. God, and God alone, must deliver him. Loyola came out of his struggle believing that both God and Satan are external to man, and man has the power to choose between them. By the disciplined use of his imagination man can strengthen his will so as to choose God and his ways.

One of Loyola's spiritual exercises, for example, aimed to make the horrors of hell real: "Hear in imagination the shrieks and groans and blasphemous shouts against Christ

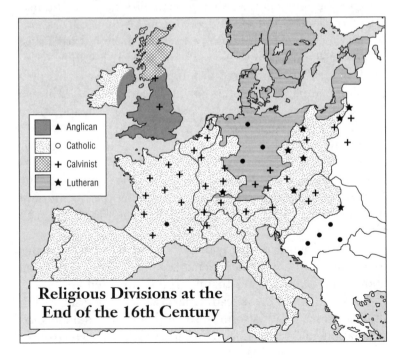

Religious Divisions at the End of the 16th Century

our Lord and all the saints. Smell in imagination the fumes of sulphur and the stench of filth and corruption. Taste in imagination all the bitterness of tears and melancholy and growing conscience. Feel in imagination the heat of the flames that play on and burn the souls." The same technique, of course, could be used to represent the beauties of the Nativity or the glories of heaven. By proper discipline the imagination could strengthen the will and teach it to cooperate with God's grace.

For Ignatius personally, surrender to the will of God meant more education. He entered a school in Barcelona to sit with boys less than half his age to study Latin, then threw himself into a dizzying year of courses at the University of Alcala. Out of it came his conviction that learning must be organized to be useful. The idea eventually grew into the Jesuits' famed plan of studies, which measured out heavy but manageable doses of classics, humanities, and sciences.

A Passion for Sainthood

Ignatius became such a fervent evangelist that the Inquisition imprisoned and examined him more than once about his life, teaching, and theology. Perturbed, he left for Paris, where he spent seven years at the university, became "Master Ignatius," and gathered around him the first of his permanent companions: Peter Faber, Diego Laynez, Alfonso Salmeron, Simon Rodriguez, Nicholas Bobadilla, and above all, the young Spanish nobleman, Francis Xavier.

Ignatius shared with them his remarkable program for sainthood, his *Spiritual Exercises*. A distillation of his own religious experiences during and following his conversion, the *Exercises* prescribe four "weeks" of meditations, beginning with sin, death, judgment, and hell, and then moving on to Christ's life, death, and resurrection.

Ignatius intended a path to spiritual perfection: rigorous examination of conscience, penance, and a resolute amnesia about guilt once the spiritual pilgrim confronted God's forgiveness. The *Exercises* became the basis of every Jesuit's spirituality. Later popes also prescribed them for candidates for ordination, and Catholic retreats applied them to lay groups.

In his *Portrait of the Artist As a Young Man*, James Joyce describes his young hero, Stephen Dedalius, reduced to horror by a sermon on hell. "A wave of fire swept through his body . . . flames burst forth from his skull." After he had gone to confession, however, "the past was past." That is just the way Ignatius planned it. "Send no one away dejected," Loyola wrote. "God asks nothing impossible." Thus, his followers became the great apostles of the possible.

The Society of Jesus

In 1540, Pope Paul III approved the little Society of Jesus as a new religious order. In Ignatius' metaphor, they were to be chivalrous soldiers of Jesus, mobile, versatile, ready to go anywhere and perform any task the pope assigned. As a recognized order, they added to their earlier vows of poverty and chastity the traditional vow of obedience to their superiors and a fourth vow expressing their special loyalty to the pope. They gave command to a Superior General elected for life. Their choice for the first General was Ignatius.

The aim of the order was simple: to restore the Roman Catholic Church to the position of spiritual power and worldly influence it had held three centuries before under Innocent III. Everything was subordinated to the Church of Rome because Ignatius believed firmly that the living Christ resided in the institutional church exclusively.

Perhaps the most fascinating feature of the Jesuits was their perilous attempt to live energetically *in* the world without being *of* it. Loyola wanted them to be all things to all men, and they nearly succeeded.

Their efforts have rallied defenders who assign them the highest posts in heaven and critics who consign them to the lower regions of hell. Writing to Thomas Jefferson in 1816, John Adams said, "If ever any congregation of men could merit eternal perdition on earth and in hell, it is the company of Loyola." Whatever their destination, the Jesuits were from their beginning unique.

That first generation under Loyola's zealous leadership rode full gallop into their new assignments: convert the heathen, reconvert Protestant Europe. Francis Xavier leaped from India to Southeast Asia to Japan, a country that had never before heard the Christian message. More than any others, the Society of Jesus stemmed, and sometimes reversed, the tide of Protestantism in France, the Low Countries, and Central Europe. When Ignatius died in 1556, his order was nearly 1,000 strong and had dispatched its apostles to four continents.

No mission in that first generation proved more decisive than the band of Jesuits assigned to the Council of Trent. Only thirty-one council fathers led by three papal legates were present for the opening ceremonies of the council. None of them could have guessed that their modest beginning would lead to the most important council between Nicea (325) and Vatican II (1962–1965). Under the influence of the Jesuits, Trent developed into a powerful weapon of the Counter Reformation. Two suave, intelligent, and highly influential members of the society—Diego Laynez and Alfonso Salmeron—guided the agenda more and more toward "the correct churchly attitude" of the followers of Loyola.

The council fathers met in three main sessions: 1545–1547, 1551–1552, and 1562–1563. Throughout the sessions, the Italians were strongly represented. Other areas, notably France, were significantly underrepresented. Compared to other councils, Trent was never well attended. During the second series of sessions a number of Protestants were present, but nothing came of it. From start to finish the council reflected the new militant stance of Rome.

The Shape of Modern Catholicism

Everything the Protestant Reformation stood for was vigorously—one could almost say violently—rejected at Trent. The Protestant Reformers emphasized justification by *faith alone*. The council insisted that Christian people must perform good works lest they become lazy and indifferent.

Luther, Calvin, and Grebel stressed salvation by *grace alone*; the council emphasized grace and human cooperation with God to avoid, in Loyola's terms, "the poison that destroys freedom." "Pray as though everything depended on God alone;" Ignatius advised, "but act as though it depended on you alone whether you will be saved."

The Protestants taught the religious authority of *Scripture alone*. The council insisted on the supreme teaching office of the Roman Church—popes and bishops—as the essential interpreters of the Bible.

Thus, the Council of Trent guaranteed that modern Roman Catholicism would be governed by the collaboration between God and man. The pope remained, the seven sacraments remained, the sacrifice of the mass remained. Saints, confessions, indulgences remained. The council's work was essentially medieval, only the anger was new.

After four centuries, we can look back to the Reformation age and see that the religious unity of western Christendom was permanently shattered. Men and women in Loyola's lifetime did not see that truth. The fact dawned upon Europe slowly.

At first Luther's followers thought him so obviously right that the Catholic church would inevitably adopt his ideas. Others thought him so obviously wrong that sooner or later he would be burned as a heretic and his movement wither away. After all, the past was strewn with the corpses of heretical bodies. The point is both parties—Catholic and Protestant—thought that they represented the true, catholic Church of Christ and their enemies a false version of it. That was the spirit of Trent.

Ideological Warfare

As time went on, however, the thinking of ordinary men reached, almost imperceptibly, a second stage. The uneasy, half-conscious conviction grew that the conflict had reached a stalemate. Catholicism could not crush the new heresy, and Protestantism could not overthrow Rome. In this second stage men had no real emotional or intellectual acceptance of a stalemate, only a bitter admission of the fact.

The vast majority of people were still convinced that religious truth was identifiable. Truth stood on one side, error on the other. Error meant not only individual damnation, but infection of others and destruction of society. Resistance of these dreadful evils took the form of inquisitions, civil wars, and persecutions.

In this ideological warfare, Calvinists and Jesuits led the charge. Each embodied a militant organization calling for loyalty above and beyond national and political ties. At this stage almost no one could imagine that truth could lie on both sides of the battlefield or that both parties could peacefully coexist in the same state or even on the same continent.

The third stage of religious toleration based upon the full acceptance of religious diversity within a nation appeared before 1600 only in hints, in the attitudes of mystics, Christian humanists like Erasmus, radical Protestants like the Anabaptists, and practical politicians like Queen Elizabeth of England. Feeble as it was, this whisper was the voice of the future. No company of Christians resisted it more doggedly than the Jesuits.

The Jesuits, the Inquisition, and Catholic Mysticism

Robert D. Linder

In the following essay, scholar Robert D. Linder examines a full range of Catholic responses to the Protestant revolt, from the establishment of the Jesuits, to the revival of the Inquisition, to the revival of Catholic mysticism. According to Linder, the Jesuits had three primary goals: education, rebuttal of Protestant influence, and new missionary activities. The new Catholic Inquisition, established in 1542, was most active in Italy and Spain, and it was effective in stifling Protestant sympathies. The most prominent figure of the new Catholic mysticism was Teresa of Avila in Spain, who believed that mysticism could stimulate practical reforms in society.

The founder and leader of [the Jesuit] order was one of the most dramatic and powerful figures in Christian history, Ignatius of Loyola. Loyola is often taken as the embodiment of the Catholic Reformation.

Loyola had been a professional soldier, but a serious wound cut short his military career. While recovering, he had time to think about his rough-and-tumble past and his future. During this period of sober reflection Loyola read a number of books about the saints. He was challenged by their holiness and their achievements as 'soldiers of Christ'. Finally, he decided that, like the knights of old, he would dedicate his weapons and armour to God and take up the cross of Christ. He waited on God, to know what he should do.

Excerpted from "Rome Responds," by Robert D. Linder, from *Eerdmans Handbook to the History of the Church*, edited by Tim Dowley. Copyright 1977 by Lion Publishing plc. Used by permission of Lion Publishing plc.

Loyola's period of waiting for God's guidance was immensely important and has been compared to Luther's monastic experience. But whereas Luther finally found his peace by rejecting the traditions of the medieval church in favour of the biblical basics of primitive Christianity, Loyola finally found his peace by rededicating himself to the conventions of the medieval church. Loyola emerged from his convalescence a curious mixture of soldier, mystic and monk. He wrote up his own spiritual pilgrimage and circulated it as a book entitled *The Spiritual Exercises*. The book, with its powerful appeal to the imagination and its great emphasis on obedience to Christ and his church (meaning the church of Rome) provided the cornerstone for the new ascetic order which Loyola founded.

After many initial setbacks and discouragements, Loyola finally gathered about him a small group of young men wholly dedicated to serving Christ through the church of Rome. As the new order took shape, it bore the indelible stamp of its founder. The Jesuits were to become a new spiritual élite, at the disposal of the pope to use in whatever way he thought appropriate for spreading the 'true faith' and defending the 'true church'. Absolute, unquestioning, military-style obedience became the hallmark of the new society. The famous Jesuit dictum was that every member of the society would obey the pope and the general of the order as unquestioningly 'as a corpse'.

The Vows of the New Order

After some hesitation, Paul III gave papal approval to the Society of Jesus in 1540. The constitution of the new order insisted on a fourth vow in addition to the traditional ones of poverty, chastity and obedience: a special oath of absolute obedience to the pope. The purpose of the society was to propagate the faith by every means at the order's disposal. The approach taken was that 'the end justifies the means'. Recruits for the Jesuits were to reflect Loyola's spirituality, and stress on military-style organization and obedience. They were to be of robust health, handsome in appearance, intelligent and eloquent in speech. No one of bad character or with even the slightest hint of unorthodox belief was admitted.

The growth of the Jesuit order was extraordinarily rapid. When Loyola died in 1556, there were members of the society in Japan, Brazil, Ethiopia and the coast of central Africa, as well as in nearly every country in Europe. Many had reached high positions in the church. Two served as the pope's ambassadors in Poland and Ireland respectively. A number were professors in the largest and best universities in Europe. By 1556 the half-dozen original followers of Loyola had grown to more than 1,500.

Jesuit Goals

The Jesuits' work centred on three main tasks: education, counteracting the Protestants, and missionary expansion in new areas.

The Jesuits provided high-quality education and by this means upgraded the training of Catholic believers as well as winning the opinion-makers of society for the Roman church. Their schools soon became famous for high standards and attainments. Many individuals from the élite were won to Roman Catholicism by this means. Children were given special attention. Before long the now-familiar Jesuit saying was coined: 'Give me a child until he is seven, and he will remain a Catholic the rest of his life.'

Counter-reform was a second major Jesuit preoccupation in the second half of the sixteenth century and throughout the seventeenth century. In France, in what is today Belgium, in southern Germany, and most noticeably in eastern Europe, the Jesuits led the counter-attack against the Protestants. Using literally almost any means at their disposal, they recaptured large areas for the church of Rome. They earned a reputation as 'the feared and formidable stormtroops of the Counter Reformation'. Only in England did their onslaught fail.

The third task at which the Jesuits excelled was missionary activity in new lands. Increasingly, Jesuit priests travelled in the ships of Spain and Portugal as they sailed the seven seas in search of new colonies and new riches. Jesuit missionaries travelled to America, Africa and Asia in search of converts. As they went, they helped counterbalance the greedy imperialism of the European merchants and soldiers. They also produced scholarly accounts of the history and geography of the new places they visited. But most of all they left their converts with a fanatical brand of Catholicism and produced devout, tough Catholics, on their own model.

Missionary Activity

The Jesuits played a leading role in the conversion of Brazil and Paraguay. They were not as successful in Africa, where native peoples often resisted their efforts. The greatest stories of Jesuit heroism come from Asia. There, the incredibly courageous Francis Xavier (1506–52) towered above all the rest as the 'apostle to the Indies and to Japan'.

Xavier was born into the Portuguese nobility and was one of the original members of the Society of Jesus. Loyola early recognized that this handsome, bright and cheerful young man would make a powerful servant of God. He became the most widely-acclaimed Jesuit missionary of all time. He was appointed the pope's ambassador and sent to evangelize the East Indies in 1542. He spent three years there, followed by preaching and baptizing in present-day Malaysia, Vietnam and Japan. His most remarkable mission was in Japan where he established a Christian community which has survived to this day, despite numerous periods of severe persecution. Xavier died of a fever when he was only forty-six years old, while he was attempting to take the Christian message to China.

The Jesuits, together with the Dominicans, Franciscans and Augustinians, led the church of Rome in a new period of rapid overseas expansion between 1550 and 1650. By this means nearly all of Mexico, Central America and South America, along with a large part of the population of the Philippines and smaller numbers of people in Africa, India, the East Indies and the Far East, became adherents of the church of Rome.

Revival of the Inquisition

The Jesuits were most active in the border areas of Europe and in the newly-discovered lands overseas. In the traditionally Roman Catholic countries such as Italy, Spain and France, the Inquisition became the major instrument of the Catholic Reformation. The Inquisition, or the Supreme Sacred Congregation of the Holy Office, as it was officially called, was not an invention of the sixteenth century. The so-called Roman Inquisition begun in 1542 was child and grandchild of the medieval and Spanish Inquisitions which had gone before it in the thirteenth and fifteenth centuries respectively.

The rejuvenation of the Inquisition as a means of reform and counter-reform was largely the work of Cardinal Caraffa. Originally a theological moderate, Caraffa became increasingly conservative as the Protestant Reformation progressed. By 1542, he was an outspoken critic of those who sought reconciliation with the Protestants and, instead, advocated battling against them with the weapons of coercion, censorship and propaganda. It was at his urging that the new Roman Inquisition was established. It was 'Roman' because it was to be controlled by the papacy from Rome.

Caraffa was one of the six cardinals appointed as Inquisitors General. In this capacity, and later as pope, he supported the Inquisition as the most effective means of dealing with heretics. Caraffa and his fellow inquisitors regarded heretics as traitors against God, and the foulest of criminals. It was for their own good, and for the good of the church, that they had to be sought out and dealt with by the Inquisition. If the Holy Office could not return these benighted individuals to the church, then they must be eradicated before they contaminated other immortal souls with their spiritual disease. Thus, they were removed from the body of Christian society in much the same way that surgeons remove cancer tissue from the human body in order to save a person's life.

The Inquisition commonly used terror and torture to obtain confessions. If the death penalty was required, the convicted heretic was handed over to the civil authorities for execution, since canon law forbade churchmen to shed blood.

The Inquisition was used widely and effectively in Italy, except in Venice. In Spain, it was fused with the older Spanish Inquisition and produced substantial results. In France, it was modified and kept under quite close control by the French monarchs. It was not widely used in Germany, where there was no inquisitorial tradition. In England, common law excluded the practice. It was most effective where the population was still largely Roman Catholic. With wide popular support, it became a major deterrent to the further spread of the Protestant faith.

Books Prohibited

Associated with the concept of coercion by the Inquisition was the idea of a list of prohibited books. Actually, the practice of maintaining a catalogue of heretical and dangerous books was an old one. It had been used in the Middle Ages with varying degrees of success. In the early sixteenth century, several theological faculties and the Holy Office itself circulated lists of books pronounced unfit for the eyes of the faithful. The first real papal 'index' of prohibited books was issued by Pope Paul IV in 1559. It was extensive, naming books, parts of books, authors and printers.

The last major session of the Council of Trent issued the most authoritative index of prohibited books of the period. Their list, the so-called *Tridentine Index*, was handed over to Pope Pius IV (1559–65) to enforce. He published this *Index* in 1564 and called on true Christians everywhere to observe it. In effect, it censored nearly three-quarters of all the books that were being printed in Europe at the time. Almost the only books allowed were Catholic devotional literature and the Latin *Vulgate* Bible. The pope also appointed a Congregation of the Index to update the list periodically. The practice of keeping up the *Index* lasted until 1966, when it was finally abolished. Both in the sixteenth century, and in the centuries following, it was largely a failure.

Mystics in Spain

One expression of the Catholic Reformation which was not particularly welcomed by the church of Rome was the revival of Catholic mysticism in Spain. Mysticism makes the institutional church nervous because, carried to its logical conclusion, it does away with the need for the priesthood and the sacraments. The mystic emphasizes personal religion and his or her direct relationship to God. The ultimate goal of the mystic is to lose himself or herself in the essence of God. The Christian mystic usually stresses the personal reality of Christ and seeks personal union with God through the Son. Often this ultimate union comes in a blinding flash of supreme ecstasy. In short, Christian mysticism is contemplative, personal and usually practical. Such was the case with Teresa of Avila (1515–82), the best-known of the sixteenth-century Spanish mystics.

Teresa and her devoted follower, John of the Cross, revitalized a large part of the spiritual life of Spain through their practical mysticism. Teresa was a Carmelite nun who searched for the life of perfection. Ill-health caused her great anguish and threatened her career as a nun. Finally, in the 1550s, while in a period of intense prayer, she experienced the first of her many heavenly visions. She knew ecstasy and saw visions of hell and of the Holy Spirit. She wrote of her mystical experiences but did not stress them, because she recognized their dangers as well as their value.

Spurred on by her personal relationship with God, Teresa became the great reformer of the Carmelite Order. She travelled all over Spain founding new religious houses and introducing spiritual life into old ones. She proved that mysticism could stimulate practical reform. Because she and John of the Cross spread Catholic mysticism throughout the country, many of the faithful experienced spiritual satisfaction. This filled a void which in other parts of Europe formed the basis for the spread of Protestantism, with its emphasis on a personal, biblical faith. The reform of the Spanish monasteries and convents begun under Teresa also helped to head off the criticism of those religious houses in other parts of Europe which made the Protestant case for reform so compelling.

Europe Divided

The intensity and scope of the Catholic Reformation helped set the stage for the wars of religion which broke out in many parts of Europe following the failure of the Lutherans and Roman Catholics to achieve reconciliation at Regensburg in 1541. Major fighting between the Lutheran princes and the imperial forces in the 1540s and early 1550s finally came to an end with the compromise Peace of Augsburg in 1555. The Augsburg agreement provided for the coexistence of Lutheran and Roman Catholic expressions of Christianity in Germany on the basis of 'whose the rule, his the religion'. That is, the prince could decide the faith of his subjects.

In France, a series of civil wars involving both religious and political considerations raged intermittently from 1562 to 1598 The conflict was basically between the Huguenots (Calvinist Protestants) and the Roman Catholics, with political issues often complicating the picture. Finally, a third force appeared when the *politiques* (politically-inspired) announced that it was immaterial which religion dominated France. All that mattered was the political well-being of the nation.

After such devastation, and with all parties on the point of total exhaustion, a compromise was reached by partitioning the country. This settlement, expressed in the royal Edict of Nantes in 1598, gave the Huguenots religious freedom and political control of certain parts of the country, while Roman Catholicism remained the official religion of the realm and retained by far the larger portion of the nation. . . .

The Thirty Years' War

The last of the so-called wars of religion was the Thirty Years' War, 1618–48. This conflict began as a basically religious struggle with political overtones, and ended as a basically political struggle with religious overtones—heralding the modern era.

The build-up of tension between Protestants and Catholics in Germany in the period from the Peace of Augsburg in 1555 to the outbreak of the Thirty Years' War in 1618 reflects in part the vitality of the Catholic Reformation in that area. When the Jesuit-educated Ferdinand II became Emperor and king of Bohemia, growing religious tensions came to a head. Anti-Protestant religious violence broke out in 1618, and the Bohemian nobles, mostly Protestants, appealed to the Emperor for protection and a guarantee of their religious liberties. Receiving no satisfaction, they rose in revolt.

The war began as a conflict between the Calvinists and the Catholics. Calvinism had not been recognized as a legal religion in the Empire in the treaty of Augsburg in 1555. This posed a continuing problem for those German princes who became Calvinists after 1555. The situation became even more complicated when in 1618 the Bohemian nobles declared their king, Ferdinand II, deposed, and offered the crown to the Calvinist ruler of the Palatinate, one of the major German states. His acceptance of the crown of Bohemia touched off fighting between Calvinists and Catholics all over Germany. Finally, the German Lutherans, Danes, Swedes and even the French became involved in the warfare in Germany.

The war dragged on sporadically for nearly thirty years. Finally, a peace was hammered out between the belligerents in a series of conferences held in the German province of Westphalia in the years 1643–48. The resultant agreements are known, together, as the Peace of Westphalia.

The war left Germany culturally, politically, economically and physically devastated. Only the principality of Brandenburg escaped major destruction. But the peace signalled the end of the religious wars in Europe. Ironically, the treaty in essence provided for a return to the religious situation of 1529, when certain German princes and representatives of various imperial free cities made their first famous 'protestation' on behalf of the Lutheran faith at the Diet of Speyer. All the bloodshed and misery had brought the religious settlement full circle in that tormented land. In 1648, the religious lines were in general drawn much as they were in 1529—and much as they remain to this day.

Results of the Catholic Reformation

What then were the results of the response of Rome to the Protestant Reformation? Out of the rubble of the medieval church arose a new Roman Catholic piety and a better-defined Roman Catholic orthodoxy. The Council of Trent and the leadership of reform-minded popes provided a solid basis for this new piety and renewed orthodoxy. The beliefs of the church of Rome were better understood, even by the rank and file. Differences between Roman orthodoxy and Protestant doctrine now stood out more clearly to the average Catholic priest. To be sure, the Catholic Reformation retained a great many non-apostolic, medieval practices and beliefs.

Roman Catholic missionary expansion overseas in this period was fuelled as a response to the Protestant Reformation. Partly in order to make up for the loss of large areas of Europe, the rejuvenated church turned its attention to the newly-discovered lands overseas as a means of recouping its fortunes. Thanks mainly to the Jesuits and other monastic missionaries, many people in other parts of the world embraced the Roman faith during this period. Even today large numbers of people in the Americas, Africa, India, Japan and Sri Lanka (Ceylon) owe their affiliation to the Roman church to the Catholic Reformation.

The political and cultural consequences of the Catholic Reformation were far-reaching. The resurgence of the church of Rome in countries such as Germany and France kept them from becoming Protestant in the same way as England, Scotland and Sweden. The political development of France and Germany over the years has reflected these religious divisions. The Catholic Reformation also helped Italy and Spain to retain their particular Catholic religious and cultural identities. Most important, the success of the Catholic Reformation in stopping the spread of the Protestant faith meant that Europe developed from that time without a shared cultural base. Once again, the irony is striking. The success of the Catholic response to the Protestant Reformation led to a final end to the cultural and religious unity of medieval Europe.

Catholic Piety in the Sixteenth Century

Eugene F. Rice Jr.

In this concise overview of the Catholic Counter-Reformation, Eugene F. Rice Jr., former professor of history at Columbia University, argues that the most significant development of the Counter-Reformation may not be the Jesuits or the decrees of the Council of Trent, but rather a new form of Catholic piety growing out of new devotional practices. This new approach to the individual's engagement with God involved deep emotion and mystical enthusiasm. This new piety also involved, according to Rice, a reaffirmation and intensification of such traditional devotional practices as devotion to the Virgin Mary, appeals for the intercession of the saints, and prayers for the dead.

While Protestant revolutionaries founded and ordered new churches and sects, Catholic reformers repaired the fabric of the old Church. Already before 1517, . . . the reformation of abuses preoccupied dedicated clerics and laymen in every country of Europe. Their efforts to reform the church gathered momentum after 1517, and became in the 1530's a vast movement of spiritual, moral, and ecclesiastical renewal, independent of Protestantism and not necessarily directed against it. This movement is appropriately called the Catholic Reformation. It was an increasingly successful effort, at every level of the hierarchy—papacy, cardinalate, diocese, parish, and monastery—to correct ecclesiastical

Excerpted from *The Foundations of Early Modern Europe, 1460–1559, Second Edition*, by Eugene F. Rice Jr. and Anthony Grafton. Copyright ©1994, 1970 by W.W. Norton & Company, Inc. Reprinted by permission of W.W. Norton & Company, Inc.

abuses within the traditional sacramental and institutional framework of the Church. Catholic reformation culminated in mid-century in the decrees of the Council of Trent concerned with the correction of abuses. Although Catholic sovereigns enforced the decrees at the local level with more deliberation than speed, much progress was made in rationalizing Church government and jurisdiction, eliminating the chaos in ecclesiastical appointments, and improving the discipline and education of priests and monks. Such reforms made possible the revitalization of the Church which is so striking a fact of the later sixteenth century.

The Struggle Against Protestantism

Intertwined with the reforming impulse of sixteenth-century Catholicism were policies and practices which took their origin from the need to repel Protestant attack, and in due course, to counterattack and recover the ground steadily being lost to Protestantism between the beginning of the Lutheran revolt and 1560. This long, and in the end remarkably successful, struggle against Protestantism is appropriately called the Counter-Reformation. It was fought on many fronts and with a variety of weapons. As Protestant ideas spread, the need to protect the faithful against heretical proselytizing and propaganda became ever more urgent. Local authorities tightened censorship; and to guide them the papacy began to issue more elaborate indexes of prohibited books. In 1542, in order more effectively to discover heretics and to try and judge them, the pope established the Roman Inquisition, which successfully rooted out every trace of Protestantism in Italy. A lively concern to bolster the doctrinal reliability of clergy and laity and to convert Protestants in Europe and heathens overseas encouraged the foundation and proliferation of new orders. The most famous was the Jesuit order, founded by the great Spanish soldier-mystic St. Ignatius of Loyola (1491–1556) and officially approved by Pope Paul III in 1540 in a bull beginning with the stirring words, *Regimini militantis ecclesiae* ("For the order of the church militant"). The best-known paragraph in Loyola's *Spiritual Exercises* (written 1522–1542) catches perfectly the commitment, passion, and discipline of mid-century Catholic militancy: "To arrive at complete certainty, this is the attitude of mind we should maintain: I will believe that the white object I see is black if that should be the decision of the hierarchical Church, for I believe that linking Christ our Lord the Bridegroom and His Bride the Church, there is one and the same Spirit, ruling and guiding us for our souls' good. For our Holy Mother the Church is guided and ruled by the same Spirit, the Lord who gave the Ten Commandments."

But the most important and interesting development in sixteenth-century Catholicism was neither the reform of abuses within the Church nor the Church's successful effort to stem the spread of Protestantism; it was rather the emergence during the decades before the end of the Council of Trent of the doctrine and style of piety that have stamped Roman Catholicism in modern times.

Opposing Systems of Doctrine

The medieval Church was more ecumenical, more genially encompassing, more permissive doctrinally, than either the sixteenth-century Protestant churches or the post-Trentine Catholic Church. There was more room in it for doctrinal maneuver. More possibilities existed for disagreement and debate among the orthodox. Most of the doctrines propounded in Calvin's *Institutes* and all of the doctrines embodied in the decrees and canons of the Council of Trent had coexisted peacefully in the Middle Ages. Intellectual clerics could and did debate them, question them, believe them, and defend them. In a word, all the bits and pieces that were to make up the sixteenth-century theologies of Protestantism and Catholicism were in solution in medieval thought. What so dramatically happened during the age of the Reformation is that they crystallized into two distinct and opposed systems, each more exclusive, more consistent, and more rigid than the medieval theological tradition from which they both derived. First, Protestants built up a systematic theology based on Luther's three *solae:* faith, grace, and Scripture. Inevitably, Catholics felt the need to redefine and reorganize Catholic doctrine in response to this challenge. This was the task and accomplishment of the Council of Trent.

The council sat in three sessions. The first lasted from 1545 to 1547; the second met in 1551–1552; the third, in 1562–1563. The dogmatic decrees of the first and second sessions left no doubt about what Catholicism was, and little subtlety was required to distinguish it from Protestantism. Protestants admitted only one authority—Scripture. The fathers at Trent reestablished two—Scripture and tradition. Moreover, they declared the Latin Vulgate translation to be an authentic text of the Bible, and they stressed the exclusive

The Jesuit Practice of Mental Prayer

While many interpretations of the "militant" Jesuit order focus on how it differed from Protestantism, its founder, Ignatius of Loyola, also exerted a profound influence on modes of spiritual experience. In this excerpt, Catholic scholar John Patrick Donnelly explains the Jesuit practice of mental prayer and its widespread influence.

The *Exercises* [of Ignatius of Loyola] also teach several methods of mental prayer. The most fundamental sort of meditation involves the application of memory and reasoning powers to various religious truths, followed by efforts to employ the emotions and issuing in practical resolutions for personal reform. Another method is the reconstruction by the imagination of incidents from the Gospels, followed by resolutions drawn from the example of Christ. Another method consists in taking a standard prayer, the Lord's Prayer, for instance, and reflecting prayerfully on it phrase by phrase for an hour. Loyola includes a system of examining the conscience to be used daily for the rest of the exercitant's life. There is a general examination of the day, plus a specific or particular examination on a single virtue that is being cultivated or a single sinful inclination that is being attacked. Exercitants keep notebooks in which they track their daily progress. The general desire for reform of life is thereby given specific focus as one problem area after another is brought under control. It is easy to dismiss such methods as

right of Holy Mother Church "to judge of the true sense and interpretation of the holy Scriptures." Protestants asserted that men were justified by faith alone, without the works of the law; in a masterly exposition, the fathers at Trent decreed that men were saved by faith in combination with good works. The decrees and canons concerning the sacraments sharply distinguished the Catholic interpretation from the views of Lutherans, Zwinglians, and Calvinists. The last session of the council redefined and reaffirmed almost every belief and practice that Catholic humanists like Erasmus had considered superstitious half a century before: the making of

mere bookkeeping, but as A.G. Dickens has observed: "The craving of a troubled but order-seeking century was a craving for precise guidance, and this Loyola offered."

Loyola's teaching on mental prayer made clearer and more precise those methods which were spreading in the late Middle Ages. The *Exercises*, more than any other single source, added to the rise of systematic meditation that became characteristic of reforming Catholicism in the sixteenth and seventeenth centuries. After Loyola's death an hour's meditation became obligatory for Jesuits, and many other religious orders, even monastic orders with rather different traditions, took up the practice. The new Tridentine seminaries taught these methods of prayer to their students. St. Francis de Sales adapted meditation for lay men and women. The *Spiritual Exercises* itself became a great all-time best-seller with nearly five thousand editions, and it has been translated into over twenty languages. Several treatises and manuals of meditation, today remembered only by specialists, outsold Shakespeare and Descartes in the seventeenth century. The growth of systematic mental prayer probably contributed more to real religious reform among Catholics than did the reform legislation of the Council of Trent.

John Patrick Donnelly, SJ, "For the Greater Glory of God: St. Ignatius Loyola," in *Leaders of the Reformation*, ed. Richard L. DeMolen, Selinsgrove: Susquehanna UP, 1984.

vows, the belief in purgatory, the invocation of saints, the veneration of relics, and the giving of indulgences. On November 13, 1564, the pope summed up the Catholic faith as taught at Trent in the Creed of Pope Pius IV.

Emotion and Mysticism in Catholic Piety

Growing differences in their devotional practices and styles of piety and feeling created a psychological gap between Catholics and Protestants even wider than the doctrinal gap so precisely defined by Calvin and the Trent fathers. An unusually heated emotionalism is the most noticeable characteristic of Catholic piety by the mid-century. Contemporary religious paintings suggest the ideal attitudes of worship: copious weeping, distorted features, extravagant gestures, eyes turned up dramatically to heaven. A medieval literary genre, the poem of tearful contrition, was revived and enjoyed a great vogue. The purpose of such verses was to describe, for example, the remorseful tears of St. Peter after he had denied Christ, or those of St. Mary Magdalene deploring her early life, in order to provoke the tears of the faithful and freshen their faith and piety. To encourage the spectator to relive the sufferings of Christ on the Cross or the torments of the martyrs, the Church asked its artists to picture these holy agonies in gruesome detail: St. Agatha with her breasts being torn away, St. Dorothy branded, St. Fidelis scourged, St. Edward with his throat cut. A revival of the late medieval preoccupation with death is another aspect of this holy enthusiasm. Representations of skulls are regularly found on tombstones after Trent. Epitaphs take on a more somber tone than they had had during the fifteenth-century Renaissance. On the tomb of a cardinal who died in 1451 in Rome was inscribed, "Why fear death, which brings us rest?" but a typical epitaph of the later sixteenth century reads: "My turn yesterday, yours today."

At the heart of Catholic religious emotion was mysticism. No other period, except possibly the fourteenth century, has produced so abundant a crop of attractive visionaries as the age of the Council of Trent. One reason for this development is the harmony between the dogmatic decrees of Trent and the assumptions of mysticism. The mystic assumes that man, with the aid of God's grace, can gradually perfect himself and briefly see God face to face. Mysticism—how unlike classical Protestantism—is optimistic about God and about man. With its emphasis on planned and ordered meditation, spiritual exercises, and a rigorous training of the will, sixteenth-century mysticism admirably complemented a theology built on an affirmation of the freedom of the will, man's ability to cooperate in his own salvation, and the efficacy of charity and good works. It answered too the need of devout men and women for a more personal, warmer piety and a more direct relation between God and man. Protestantism met this need by eliminating hierarchical and sacramental intermediaries between God and man; Trentine mysticism offered an ascending ladder of contemplation and perfection on whose upper rungs men experienced brief moments of ineffaceable sweetness and joy.

Reaffirmation of Traditional Practices

Perhaps the most striking characteristic of the new Catholic piety was its stress on just those elements in the traditional inheritance of Christian devotion which were rejected or minimized by Protestants. Protestants minimized the religious significance of the Virgin Mary and the saints. In late sixteenth-century Catholicism, on the other hand, devotion to the Virgin gained a popularity it had enjoyed at no time since the thirteenth century. The doctrine of the Immaculate Conception of Mary, vigorously attacked by late medieval and Renaissance Dominican theologians as a popular superstition, was now officially defended in Rome. New and related devotions appeared: of the Holy Family, of St. Joseph (a figure of ribald fun in the Middle Ages), of the Child Jesus. Correspondingly, increased attention was paid to the saints, and especially to St. Peter. At St. Peter's in Rome, frescoes painted during this period show him walking on the waters, raising the dead, healing sick people with his shadow, meeting Christ at the gates of Rome, vanquishing the magician Simon Magus, all episodes designed to illustrate and defend the primacy of the papal see. Protestants denied the existence of purgatory. Catholics multiplied confraternities to pray for the dead. In the *Spiritual Exercises* Loyola urged his readers to speak with particular approval of religious orders, of virginity and celibacy, of the relics of the saints, "showing reverence for them and praying to the saints themselves," of pilgrimages, indulgences, jubilees, Crusade bulls, fasting and abstinence in Lent, and the lighting of candles in churches. The iconography of the Last Supper changed, reflecting the renewed emphasis on the doctrine of the Real Presence. The normal medieval and Renaissance depiction of the Last Supper (Leonardo da Vinci's is a good example) shows Christ and the apostles at the moment when Christ says, "One of you shall betray me." After the middle of the sixteenth century, painters chose the moment when Christ says, "This is my body," that is, the institution of the Eucharist. Protestants, finally, had rejected much of the sensuousness and beauty of the medieval liturgy and of earlier church decoration. The Trentine Church did everything possible to make the Catholic service as splendid as possible. A vivid symbol of the growing differences in feeling, taste, and habits between Protestants and Catholics is the contrast between the whitewashed inside walls of the Grossmünster in Zurich and the interior of the Jesuit church in Rome—theatrical, brilliantly painted and gilded, filled with magnificent frescoes and sculptures, sounding with the serpentine polyphony of Palestrina and the massed brasses of Gabrieli.

By 1560 the religious unity of Europe had been irreparably shattered. A vigorous Catholic church, a Lutheran church, Zwinglian and Calvinist churches, an Anglican church, and a variety of sects competed for men's minds and loyalties. For the first time in many centuries, problems of religious choice and conversion became of major concern for ordinary men and women.

Chapter 5

The Legacy of the Reformation

Turning | Points

IN WORLD HISTORY

The Rise of Individualism, Tolerance, and Popular Education

Harold J. Grimm

Harold J. Grimm, noted scholar and professor of history at Ohio State University, argues here that the Reformers promoted, both directly and indirectly, such modern values as individualism, tolerance, and popular education. While individualism was not a direct part of the Protestant agenda, it was an indirect result of the Protestant stress on individual conscience. In the same way, tolerance was not a direct objective of Protestantism, but it was an outgrowth of the fact that the various rival religious systems were not going to disappear. As Grimm notes, the push for popular education was a significant part of the Protestant agenda, for the Reformers wanted children to be able to read the Bible for themselves.

The Reformation Era, the period between 1500 and 1650, was above all else an age of religious faith, when what people believed had a significant bearing upon political, economic, and social theories and upon literary and artistic expression. That is not to say that other than religious motives were not at times decisive, for secular interests were present throughout the period, as in earlier centuries. It was not until the end of the era, however, that these secular interests began to take precedence over the religious.

Much has been written concerning the question whether the Reformation was medieval or modern. The fact that it

Excerpted from *The Reformation Era 1500–1650*, 2nd ed. by Harold J. Grimm. Copyright ©1973 by Harold J. Grimm. Reprinted by permission of Prentice-Hall, Inc., Upper Saddle River, NJ.

contained so many elements of both, that it was a period in which the domination of society by the Church and feudalism gave way to a secularization of society and the triumph of the territorial state, bespeaks its significance in the development of our western civilization. This secularization of society, which had its largest roots in the medieval urban centers, attained its first widely accepted cultural expression in the Italian Renaissance. Although its leaders did not question the authority of the medieval Church, they criticized medieval scholastic methods, laid greater emphasis upon the development of personality, and paid greater attention to man and nature and the sensual enjoyment of the things of this world.

Although the early Protestant reformers stressed man's corruption through Adam's fall and were essentially inimical to the humanist belief in man's ability to solve his own problems, they continued to emphasize man's individuality, his personal relation to God, and his responsibility to his neighbor. Luther's bold statement at Worms, to the effect that he would retract his religious views only if he were proved to be in error, did much to further individuality, even though such a thought was furthest from his mind. His *The Freedom of the Christian Man* was not a manifesto in behalf of religious freedom from authority but of the freedom of his conscience, for both Protestants and Catholics still believed that there was only one truth. By the end of the era, however, there was considerable toleration of the religious views of dissenters and some outright skepticism. The rulers of the secularized European states were now more concerned with the maintenance of law and order and the outward conformity to their state churches than with the theological views of their subjects. Religious dissenters were accordingly frequently discriminated against and exiled, but they were no longer executed for their religious beliefs.

Political Thought of the Reformers

Nonetheless, the teachings of the Reformers and their followers had a considerable influence upon the development of modern political, economic, and social thought. It is a historical axiom that opposition to the state develops among the minorities whose interests are not furthered by the established order. Throughout the Reformation Era, from the Peasants Revolt to the Puritan Revolution, the most radical political theories did not evolve from the necessity of logic but grew out of the demands of dissatisfied minorities. In most cases, their religious and political views coincided. Therefore they drew their political, economic, and social theories from religious sources, particularly the Bible.

Although Luther and Calvin both dared to challenge the authority of Catholicism, they did so with the assistance of their respective states and taught allegiance to those states by reference to the Pauline injunctions to obey established governments as divinely established institutions. Nevertheless, their revolutionary religious views were often accompanied by revolutionary political conceptions.

Although Luther's political, economic, and social views remained medieval in many respects, he made a number of important positive contributions to the development of modern political and social thought. He taught that the state, like the church, was divinely established and therefore not necessarily subservient to the church; that the church was an invisible communion of the faithful, not a "perfect society" that should dominate the state; that the state did not have the right to determine spiritual matters but only to carry out the decisions of the church with respect to them; and that the state was the only recognized social institution, the smallest unit of which was the family. But the ruler, like any other individual, was obligated to serve both God and man in his calling, the same as a miller or a maid. This service included the maintenance of peace and provision for the general welfare of all classes, as commanded by God in the Bible.

Religious Freedom and Conscience

According to Luther, the individual Christian had gained religious freedom through faith; yet his love of God bound him to serve his neighbor. Moreover, if his conscience, which was free, conflicted with the commands of the state, he must suffer punishment rather than obey the state. This theory of passive disobedience did not imply either complete obedience, on the one hand, or the right of the individual to resist the government, on the other. Yet Luther demonstrated by his own bold actions and words that the citizen had the right to criticize the government and finally admitted that the imperial estates had the right to resist the emperor by force if he acted contrary to the laws of the land.

Calvin's political views were not unlike those of Luther with respect to the origin and nature of the state. Differences appeared, however, because of Calvin's emphasis upon predestination, the majesty of God as the only true king, and church and state as a new Israel. Moreover, his doctrines were put into practice in different circumstances from those that prevailed in Lutheran lands. Because his state of Geneva was a republic, he, for example, laid greater emphasis upon man's political duties. He himself actively participated in the affairs of his community.

According to Calvin the state should be Christian. Therefore it should further Christianity by supporting the church in carrying out its administrative, disciplinary, and doctrinal functions; maintain correct doctrine and worship; suppress heresy by force; and regulate society according to the Word of God as interpreted by the clergy. But like Luther, he maintained that the Christian owed obedience to all rulers, even to tyrants, and that there was no defense against the tyrant except in prayer and flight. Both reformers agreed, however, that one should obey God rather than man. In the event that a ruler demanded what was contrary to the Word of God, passive disobedience was obligatory. Yet Calvin went further than Luther in clarifying the right of resistance. Like Bucer before him, he believed that a ruler who violated the laws of God, nature, and man could be resisted by duly constituted "inferior magistrates," such as the plebeian tribunals of ancient Rome.

The form of government, as we have seen, did not greatly concern Calvin, although he felt that a monarchy detracted from the glory of God and a democracy tended toward anarchy. He believed that an aristocracy of the godly would be inclined to permit God to be the real sovereign of the state.

He was so certain that the meaning of the Word of God was unequivocal and demonstrable that he believed that every honest ruler could readily comprehend it and apply it to political exigencies. . . .

Religious Toleration

The Reformation, as an age of faith, was also an age of religious persecution in general. The rise of Protestantism did not of itself assure the end of trials and punishment for heresy, for Protestants, like Catholics, believed that they were in possession of the sole, objective truth; that heresy would lead to the damnation of the individual and the corruption of society as a whole; and that the persecution of heretics was pleasing to God and beneficial to society. Although Luther maintained that force should not be used in matters of faith, he later permitted religious persecution in effect by making heresy virtually identical with blasphemy. Calvin, by stressing the majesty of God, made heresy an insult to God and one of the greatest of crimes. He went further than the Catholics by making heresy itself, not a relapse into heresy, punishable by death.

One of the most important differences between Catholics and Protestants with respect to persecution lay in the fact that the latter discarded canon law and substituted for it the Bible and Roman law. In time, however, it became evident that the Bible was too uncertain a guide to persecution, and the Justinian Code of the Roman law, which provided the death penalty for the denial of the Trinity and a repetition of baptism, gradually lost its popularity. Because the Protestants relied primarily upon the Roman law, it is easy to see why the chief heresies punished by them in the sixteenth century were anti-trinitarianism and Anabaptism and why the Anabaptists insisted that they did not believe in rebaptizing but only in adult baptism.

Doubts About Persecution

Although the Protestants held theories concerning persecution that were in the main similar to those of the Catholics, they contributed more to the theory of religious liberty. In the first place, the presence of a large number of creeds tended to raise among Protestants the question whether any one was absolutely right in every respect, especially when ethics came to be considered a test for the validity of the creeds. In the second place, there was a growing tendency among Protestants to reduce the essentials of Christianity to a common denominator, to a few basic doctrines common to

The Revolutionary Implications of Luther's Theology

The Protestant movement associated with Luther had a lasting impact on the major political and religious institutions of Europe, and that impact, as noted by scholar Charles G. Nauert Jr., had its roots in the basic premises of Luther's theology. Luther aimed at a restoration of the true church, as Nauert observes, but his theological conclusions justified the "total repudiation of the authority of the church" in sixteenth-century Europe.

True Christian reformation involved first and foremost not mere tinkering with the details of Church ceremonies but a drastic abandonment of false doctrine and a return to the true doctrine of the New Testament. Luther's conclusions about the fundamental errors of the Church in doctrine meant that in the long run, quite unlike Erasmus or even Savonarola, he was able to justify to himself and to others a total repudiation of the authority of the Church hierarchy and to conclude that Scripture alone, not the traditions and authoritative definitions of a perverted hierarchy, was the sole source of authority for Christians. Hence unlike the humanists or even such a rebellious spirit as Savonarola, he could defy the institutional Church when it tried to silence him. Justification by faith alone, the priesthood of all believers, and the sole authority of Scripture: these were the three foundations on which Luther based his eventual rejection of the old Church and his creation of his own Evangelical (i.e., Gospel-based) religion.

Charles G. Nauert Jr., *The Age of Renaissance and Reformation*. Lanham, MD: University Press of America, 1981, pp. 139–40.

all the Christian creeds. In the third place, many Protestants began to feel that, because men were predestined to salvation, persecution could not produce the desired results.

The growth of religious toleration was furthered largely by (1) the sectarian theory of the church, (2) favorable political conditions, and (3) the growing number of liberal and rational thinkers. The sectarians from the outset maintained that a church existed only where believers covenanted to walk in the ways of Christ. Therefore they could not accept the theory of a state church. . . .

Protestantism, greatly divided yet firm in its religious convictions, was gradually influenced by the arguments of the liberal and rational religious thinkers but did not sacrifice the fundamentals of Christianity. The broad tolerance of Erasmus found a few courageous defenders in the age of persecution. Probably the greatest plea for religious toleration was made by Sebastian Castellio, the Erasmian who joined Calvin in Geneva, only to break with him over the question of the divine inspiration of the Song of Songs in the Old Testament. In his *Concerning Heretics* and subsequent writings, prompted by the execution of Servetus, Castellio drew a distinction between essentials and nonessentials in Christianity, including among the latter the doctrines of the Trinity, predestination, and the location of Christ's body. He argued that only a belief in the clear scriptural statements concerning the way of salvation should be made mandatory. Reason, through which God continued to reveal the plan of salvation, must correct what we learn by sensual perception and revelation. Reason and ethical considerations show how wrong it is for Christians to persecute their fellow believers. . . .

So far had religious toleration progressed by the end of the sixteenth century that punishment of heresy with death gradually disappeared. In England only two persons were compelled to die for their faith in the seventeenth century, and on the Continent the usual punishment was banishment or imprisonment. The struggle for religious liberty was thereafter furthered mostly by Englishmen who were simultaneously carrying the torch for greater personal freedom in the political and economic as well as the religious spheres. In these circumstances Milton could eloquently defend the toleration of the sects as long as they did not deny what he considered the essentials of Christianity, and Roger Williams could advance his belief that each individual should be allowed to believe and act according to the dictates of his own conscience. But Williams believed that only the select few could belong to the true Christian Church. It remained for John Locke to formulate the most potent theories for religious toleration and liberty, and for men of later centuries to carry them into practice.

The Extension of Popular Education

The Reformation, both Protestant and Catholic, also greatly influenced education. Inherited scholastic methods and content were retained; but they were gradually modified by the humanism of the Renaissance, the theology and pedagogy of the reformers, and, eventually, the development of rational, scientific thought.

Probably the most significant influence of Protestantism was its extension of education to a much larger segment of the population. Luther insisted that all the cities, towns, and villages of Germany should establish schools supported by public funds and compel the children to attend. He thus gave the first great impetus to free, compulsory education for all children, for he wished to provide them all not only with religious instruction but also with an appreciation of culture. Melanchthon, called the *praeceptor Germaniae*, or teacher of Germany, helped the civil authorities of Saxony establish schools, suggested the division of the children into classes, and wrote a number of widely used textbooks. The schools of Wittenberg, Strassburg, and Geneva served as models for the many Protestant educators who came into contact with them.

In England the dissolution of the monasteries and the suppression of chantries and chantry schools led Henry VIII to order the clergy to instruct the young; but the king did little to support schools. Edward VI, however, endowed about thirty grammar schools. By the end of the seventeenth century, nearly five hundred new schools had been founded in

England. The so-called public schools of Eton, Winchester, and Westminster were supported by private or royal endowments and were attended only by the sons of the nobles, the gentry, and the wealthy townsmen. Scotland, by a law of 1641, provided free elementary education for all children. But education was first made compulsory as well as universal and free in the American colonies. Two laws of the General Court of Massachusetts, passed in 1642 and 1647, finally incorporated those provisions that had been recommended by many educators since the days of Luther and served as models for the other colonies.

In the Catholic countries, education remained in the hands of the Church and by the end of the sixteenth century was advanced most rapidly by the Jesuits. In their schools, less emphasis was placed upon flogging than upon the stimulation of ambition and love of learning and discipline. They were usually subsidized by the state as well as the Church and private endowments and were soon opened to outsiders.

Changing Subject Matter

The fact that Protestant governments began to take over the responsibility of educating children did not at first notably alter the contents and purposes of education, for the chief subjects remained religion and the classics. The main changes made by the educators of the sixteenth century were concerned with method, that is, improving the teaching of the old subjects—religion, reading, writing, Latin, Greek, and, in some schools, Hebrew. The entire approach remained literary. History and science were studied only as by-products, the former of the study of Livy, the latter of Pliny. Yet a few bold spirits demanded the enlargement of the scope of education. Rabelais wanted schools to teach morals, physical well-being, and science; Montaigne advocated the study of modern languages; Bacon complained of the lack of laboratories for the study of science; Milton suggested such practical subjects as geography, navigation, engineering, law, politics, music, and the natural sciences; and the Jesuits demanded a more thorough study of history and scholastic philosophy. . . .

Advancement of Learning

Despite the tardiness of the educators of the period in accepting new pedagogical theories and adapting themselves to new scientific discoveries and the practical needs of their day, they did much to arouse an interest in learning and to prepare the way for the great achievements of later centuries. When the religious controversies receded and the lines dividing the various bodies of Christendom were well defined, the secularization of education followed rapidly and greater attention was given to secular interests.

Not the least of the consequences of the rise of Protestantism was the stimulus given to the publishing of books and the accumulation of manuscripts and books by libraries. Throughout the sixteenth century, Germany was the greatest producer of books, and the fair at Frankfurt was the greatest center for their distribution. These books reflected the predominant religious interests of the age.

Democratic Values and the Reformation

Carter Lindberg

Professor Carter Lindberg of the school of theology at Boston University claims that the Reformation "introduced into western culture the problem of pluralism—religious, social, and cultural." While the first Protestants were as intolerant to each other as they were to Catholics (and vice versa), eventually they realized that the religious divisions were more or less permanent, resulting in an attitude of tolerance. Another legacy of the Reformation, according to Lindberg, is the political theory of resistance to tyranny which was developed by French Protestants as a logical outgrowth of Luther's thinking on individual conscience. While the reformers would not have endorsed democracy *per se*, the Protestant emphasis on the individual's direct relationship to God, without intermediaries, worked to empower individuals to make religious decisions for themselves, which in turn contributed to what Lindberg calls a democratic philosophy.

The competitiveness of the [Catholic and Protestant] churches led to a kind of siege mentality. Protestant theologians became so involved in constructing theological systems to protect their churches and to wall off alternatives that the late sixteenth and early seventeenth centuries came to be known as the period of Protestant orthodoxy or Protestant scholasticism. Both Lutherans and Calvinists de-

veloped theories of verbal and plenary inspiration to safe-
guard the sole authority of Scripture against the Roman
Catholic use of tradition on the one hand and the dissidents'
use of experience and "inner light" on the other hand. The
Reformers' original understanding of faith as trust and confidence in God's promise shifted in the heat of battle to understanding faith in terms of intellectual assent to correct
doctrine. The resulting highly rationalized schemata of salvation are exemplified by the chart of election and reprobation drawn up by the Elizabethan Puritan, William Perkins
(1558–1602), and the strict Calvinism formulated at the
synod of Dort (1618–19) in the Netherlands. The latter is
sometimes referred to as the "Tulip synod" because its decrees may be arranged to spell the flower for which Holland
is famed: *T*otal depravity, *U*nconditional election, *L*imited
atonement, *I*rresistible grace, *P*erseverance of the saints.

A rationalistic and creed-bound Protestantism and Catholicism contributed politically to the developments of the consolidation of the early modern state and its concomitant impo-
sition of social discipline, and intellectually to the rationalism,
Deism, and Pietism that fed the Enlightenment of the eigh-
teenth and nineteenth centuries. The medieval aspiration for
a Christian society, the *corpus Christianum*, fragmented into the
aspirations of the different confessional groups. Without a
unitary sacred ideal for the integration of society and without
the means and will to enforce a particular confessional ideal
for all Europe, toleration became a path to social peace and the
eventual secularization of society. The displacement of a uni-
fied sacred society by confessional communities also had psychological and ethical consequences. [As R. Po-Chia Hsia has
argued:]

> Translated in psychological terms, it meant the internalization
> of discipline, based on decorum and piety, and the suppression,
> or at least, the redirection of violence and anger.... Described
> variously as "the civilizing process," or "social disciplining,"
> the transformation of social norms expressed itself also in the
> spread of bourgeois values, epitomized by the emphasis on
> learning and self-quest, and by the simultaneous praise of fam-
> ily life and more rigid definition of its sexual boundaries.

Responses to Pluralism

The Reformations introduced into western culture the problem of pluralism—religious, social, and cultural. Since the modern world is still struggling with this legacy in its classrooms and courtrooms, and on its streets and battlefields, it should not be surprising that the people of the sixteenth century found it exceedingly difficult to live with alternative and competing commitments. This was compounded by a universal fear of anarchy and social disorder. The first response by all parties was to compel conformity. But religious commitments are not easily swayed by laws and force. In some cases Protestant triumphalism contributed to the development of a "chosen nation" syndrome. England's overcoming of the threats of the Spanish Armada (1588) and the failure of the recusant (English Catholic rejection of the Anglican church) conspiracy to blow up the Houses of Parliament and the king (the Gunpowder Plot, 1605) were interpreted in terms of God's election and blessing of the nation. This messianic sense of being a chosen nation was carried into the new world and contributed to the nascent identity of the United States as a "city set on a hill" with a "manifest destiny," characteristics which continue to exert political influence.

Another response to political pluralism was to assert the rights of the individual conscience. In various ways, Luther's statement to the emperor at the diet of Worms in 1521 has had political echoes ever since: "My conscience is captive to the Word of God. I cannot and will not retract anything, for it is neither safe nor right to go against conscience. I cannot do otherwise, here I stand, may God help me, Amen." Later Luther was equally adamant in defending the freedom of faith against both the theological right (the pope) and left (Karlstadt and Müntzer): "I will constrain no man by force, for faith must come freely without compulsion." Passive resistance was not confined to Protestants but was common to all those who differed on religion with their rulers, such as Catholics in Elizabethan England.

If a ruling authority is in the wrong, Luther supported conscientious objection. "What if a prince is in the wrong?

Are his people to follow him then too? Answer: No, for it is
no one's duty to do wrong; we must obey God (who desires
the right) rather than men [Acts 5: 29]." Soon Lutheran ju-
rists and theologians were developing constitutional and
theological arguments for the resistance of lesser magistrates
to the emperor's coercion of the faith of his subjects. Protestant political resistance was first defended in the Lutheran
Magdeburg confession (1550–1) which in turn directly influenced French Calvinist political thought. Huguenot arguments for a constitutionalism that limited royal power and
defended individual conscience were advanced by François
Hotman's *Franco-Gallia* (1573), Theodore Beza's *Right of
Magistrates* (1574), and Philippe du Plessis-Mornay's more
radical *Vindication Against Tyrants* (1579) which authorized
individual rebellion on the explicitly religious grounds that
God may "raise up new liberators" outside the constitutional
framework. In England, John Poynet's *A Short Treatise of
Politic Power* (1556), the first break with the English conception of passive obedience, was also influenced by Luther and
the Magdeburg confession. The authority of kings became
relative before God, the King of kings. Protestant arguments
for resistance to tyranny continued to ferment political
change in the eighteenth-century American and French revolutions. [As Robert Kingdon contends,] these arguments
"provided significant ingredients of the constitutionalism
that was such an important part of those ideologies. Traces
of these sixteenth-century ideas even survive into the twentieth century. They were used in the midcentury struggle
against modern totalitarianisms. They are with us still."
That Luther's theological exposition of the duty of political
resistance to unjust government is not merely of historical
interest is seen in its use in the Norwegian and German resistance to Nazism. In the lapidary phrase of Luther and
later of Dietrich Bonhoeffer: "If the coachdriver is drunk, we
have to put a spoke in the wheel."

A Democratic Ethos

But the Reformation legacy to politics was not merely
rooted in the defense of conscience against compulsion.

Many of the doctrinal positions of the Reformation contributed to the rise of a democratic ethos. This point should
not be taken anachronistically, for the Renaissance had reinforced centuries of political thought which viewed "democracy" as undisciplined and unprincipled mob rule subject to
self-serving demagogues. Nevertheless, Luther's translation
of the Bible and his emphasis upon universal education to fa-
cilitate reading it, a path followed by other Reformers as
well, was a step toward depriving the elite of exclusive control over words as well the Word. The doctrine of the
priesthood of all the baptized proclaimed that the ordained
priest or minister is distinguished from all other Christians
only by office. For Luther the church is no longer a hierarchical institution but a community of believers in which "no
one is for himself, but extends himself among others in
love." Thus he translated *ecclesia* not as "church" but as
"community," "congregation," and "assembly." And his 1523
pamphlet, *The Right and Power of a Christian Congregation or
Community to Judge All Teaching and to Call, Appoint, and Dismiss Teachers, Established and Proved from Scripture*, has been
viewed as "a 'whopping endorsement' of *communal* equality
and autonomy" [Steven Ozment]. The Calvinist idea of the
church as a covenanted community contributed to the idea
of social contract. These anti-hierarchical, leveling processes
were corrosive of political as well as ecclesiastical structures.
In the words of William Tyndale: "As good is the prayer of
a cobbler as of a cardinal, and of a butcher as of a bishop; and
the blessing of a baker that knoweth the truth is as good as
the blessing of our most holy father the pope." Religious
egalitarianism could lead to social and political egalitarianism. Politically, the Reformers' goal was the social experience of communion. As [Scottish reformer] John Knox declared: "Take from us the freedom of assemblies and [you]
take from us the evangel."

The Political and Cultural Consequences of the Reformation

Hans J. Hillerbrand

The most fundamental political consequence of the Reformation is the separation of church and state; no longer does
the church attempt to control the state. The state began to
assume a separate stature and take on responsibilities previously handled by the church. This was one phase of the
increasing secularization of European societies. Hans J.
Hillerbrand, professor of religion at Duke University,
notes that the words tolerance and religious freedom were
not really part of the sixteenth century vocabulary. Still,
through the Protestant concept of vocation—that each individual has a calling from God—along with the concept of
education for all, Protestants contributed to the further
secularization of society and a growing individualism.

'And all the king's horses and all the king's men. . . .' One
thinks of this trivial rhyme when reflecting on the Reformation, for its most spectacular consequence undoubtedly was
the division of Western Christendom. To be sure, there had
been schisms before: the eminent one between East and
West, the modest one between the Bohemian and the
Roman Church, the pathetic one between the rival factions
of Rome and Avignon in the 14th century. But these divisions (not to speak of those created by the heretical splinter
groups of the Middle Ages) had hardly entered the consciousness of Western man. At the dawn of the 16th century

Excerpted from *Christendom Divided*, by Hans J. Hillerbrand. Copyright ©1971 by
Corpus Instrumentorum Inc. Used by permission of Westminster John Knox Press.

the Church was one, bedazzling in its complexity and confusing in its structure, yet one in faith. There was no doubt about allegiance to this Church, holy, catholic, and apostolic. And even those who were uneasy about it, as for example the humanists, still remained loyal. But at the twilight of the century everything was different: the unity of Western Christendom had vanished and had become a wistful dream. Christendom in the West was divided—indeed not only into two factions, but into four, even five: Catholics on the one hand, and Lutherans, Calvinists, Anglicans, and Anabaptists on the other. The coexistence of these rival Churches was an uneasy one, since each claimed stubbornly the sole possession of Christian truth and denounced its rivals with vehemence and self-confidence. As a matter of fact, the mutual denunciations between Protestants were hardly less pronounced than those between Catholics and Protestants.

One Religion per Country

To what extent this diversity of the Christian Church was a nagging or perplexing awareness on the part of the 16th-century man is difficult to say. Within the borders of a country only one Church was officially recognized and, accordingly, a kind of pragmatic, if artificial, uniformity existed. Only France, the Low Countries, Poland, Germany, and England experienced religious diversity, though often of a most bitter kind, and thus evidenced the division of Christian truth in blunt and spectacular fashion. One must keep in mind that whatever ecclesiastical uniformity existed was maintained by an external force, namely, the political authorities. Once this factor was removed (by the self-limitation of the authorities), the full impact of the religious diversity was bound to be felt in a dramatic way. Even in the 16th century, however, the empirical division of Christendom lessened the Christian claims for truth.

On the face of things the division in the West entailed a weakening of the Catholic Church, since the new Protestant churches grew on soil vacated by Catholicism. A glance at the map of Europe in 1600 might convey the conclusion that the Catholic losses were tolerable. Indeed, in the end the desertion from Catholic ranks was less than had been hoped by some and feared by others: Germany, at one time on the verge of embracing the new faith completely, retained a Catholic majority, especially in the South and Northwest; Poland, Hungary, and France, at one time likewise on the way toward Protestantism, eventually declared for the Catholic faith; Italy, Spain, and Ireland escaped the religious turmoil altogether.

To minimize the Catholic losses would be, however, a superficial conclusion. The most populous countries, even as the most powerful ones, were (with the exception of France) Protestant. The political scales increasingly tipped in favor of Protestant Europe—England, Sweden, Prussia were the countries that were to dominate the future world of European diplomacy and politics.

If, as has been noted, the signal consequence of the Reformation was the division of Western Christendom, the significance of the division in Protestant ranks requires further comment. Neither historically nor theologically was there ever a single Reformation; there were several—certainly no less than five, perhaps more. The Protestant Reformation was never a monolithic phenomenon, but always a house divided against itself. . . .

Division in the Ranks

None of the new Protestant bodies, once they had established themselves, was truly 'catholic' in the sense that diverse or heterogeneous points of view were subsumed within them. Catholicism, on the other hand, possessed the ability to do precisely that. Moreover, it had the 'escape valve' of monasticism, which allowed those dissatisfied with the standard ecclesiastical practices to go their own way and yet remain within the Church. Such possibility did not exist in any of the Protestant churches, where a break was necessary to assert a different religious or theological position. Also, the mood of separation unmistakably was in the air, and prompted many to leave whatever ecclesiastical body they happened to be associated with (Catholic or Protestant) and venture to start a new one.

Once the ties with Rome had been cut and a new Church had been created—the cases of England, Geneva, and Saxony show that this could be done with greater or lesser dependence on traditional forms—the Protestants found themselves confronted with the need to undertake a pedagogical effort of major proportions. The task was to educate the people. . . .

Clerical and Popular Ignorance

In the first few years of the Reformation considerable exuberance had prevailed for things religious; but this had slowly faded, rather like the evening sun. The Lord's Prayer, the Apostles' Creed, and the Decalogue were the mainstays of the instruction—hardly sufficient, one suspects, to express the fullness of the Protestant faith. The visitation records indicate that the Decalogue was as much a mystery as the Trinity for the common people and that the simple recitation of the Apostles' Creed was connected with unsurpassable difficulties—all this the fateful legacy from Catholic days. Nor was the clergy generally better. The famous visitation of the clergy of Gloucester by Bishop Hooper in 1551 revealed appalling clerical ignorance. The men of the cloth hardly knew the basic affirmations of the faith, not to speak of the specific Protestant affirmations. If theological insight was thus restricted, it is not surprising that the ministerial incumbents in England found no reason to protest the ecclesiastical changes of 1547, 1553, or 1558, no matter how theologically incisive. Increasingly, an effort was also made to convey the specific emphases of the particular tradition. While the details of this effort belong to a subsequent epoch of Christian history, its systematic and conscientious pursuit created a distinct confessional identity. The early decades of the Reformation had brought a confessional self-consciousness, though not always a concomitant identity. The new confessional identity entailed a deeper theological understanding, a sharper denunciation of the opponent and a distinct liturgical life.

Obviously, a causal relationship existed between clerical incompetence and popular ignorance. Only as ministerial standards rose in the second half of the 16th century did the general situation improve. More and more Protestant ministers received a university education and attained the formal competence to function as teachers. Still, the lower clergy, such as the village vicar or pastor, continued to find themselves in a difficult economic position with few, if any, financial attractions. Such had been the case before the Reformation, though now the married clergy had significantly larger economic needs. In the 16th century the ministerial profession possessed little social dignity. . . .

From every indication, the picture differed little among Catholics or Protestants. Both were heirs to the same situation, which must not be attributed to any Catholic shortcomings: the fact that even in Protestant regions the problem persisted into the second half of the century should quickly dispel such a notion. To be sure, the Catholic Church had stressed the liturgical life and shown itself slow to undertake the vast catechetical effort, once the invention of printing had made this feasible. But the twin problems of illiteracy and religious apathy were no respecters of ecclesiastical tradition.

Both Catholics and Protestants thus emerged from the Reformation era with a gigantic educational task—to dispel religious ignorance and to further spirituality. The task of dispelling religious ignorance enjoyed an advantage and labored under a handicap, the former because of the increasing stress on public education and widespread literacy, the latter because of the religious apathy that followed the intense preoccupation with religion during the Reformation.

The Political Dimension of Reformation

To talk about the significance of the Reformation is, to quote the proverb, to step boldly 'where even angels fear to tread.' Even sophisticated canons of historical research cannot convincingly demonstrate the inevitable generalizations, and an element of doubt will always linger on. The question is whether ideas, specifically religious ideas, can influence political, economic, social or cultural behavior—and if they did so in the 16th century. . . .

Politically, the eminent significance of the Reformation was the comprehensive repudiation of ecclesiastical control over the state. The perennial struggle between *imperium* and *sacerdotium*, between political and ecclesiastical authority, so graphically evidenced by Pope Boniface VIII's bull *Unam Sanctam*, was resolved in favor of the former. One might see this as the culmination of a trend extending over the later Middle Ages. But more was at stake, if for no other reason than that the new relationship received a theological rationalization on the part of Protestant divines. Indeed, some of the Protestant political theorists, such as Stephen Gardiner in England, took an opposite position, insisting that the authority of the ruler embraced ecclesiastical matters as well. The most dramatic reversal of the relationship between Church and state occurred in England, where the King's new title 'Supreme Head of the Church' was a spectacular symbol for the change. Later in the century Thomas Erastus wrote his *Explicatio gravissimae quaestionis* [Explication of Most Serious Questions] to argue for the complete submission of ecclesiastical affairs under political authority. Indeed, even Catholic practice often conformed to Protestant theory. Little difference existed between Catholic and Protestant countries, a fact partially explained by the importance of the ruler in rejecting or introducing the new faith.

The acquisition of certain ecclesiastical authority on the part of government was only one of several developments that grew out of the religious turbulence of the 16th century. The state was autonomous, not under the jurisdiction of the Church, and at the same time it exercised educational and charitable functions. This meant that the state assumed a direct moral stature which it had theretofore lacked. In a way, it was a matter of taking over responsibilities previously carried out by the Church through endowments and monasteries, perhaps a case of a bad conscience.

A New Kind of State

The Reformation provided the theoretical justification for this, whether as an ex post facto *piéce justificative* or as a revolutionary innovation need not be of concern here. The fact itself proved to be of immense significance. A new kind of state made its appearance as a consequence of the Reformation. No longer did it wrestle with the Church, for it had acquired the power and prerogatives desired. While the state was still far from secular—religious affairs were important and in all countries an 'established' Church existed—religion was only one facet of many, not unlike trade and commerce.

Even as the proper care of ecclesiastical affairs was seen as the responsibility of the ruler, so loyalty and obedience on the part of the subjects were thought to be an expression of piety, as Stephen Gardiner's tract on *Vera Oboedientia* [True Obedience] so tellingly argued. Religion was seen as an immensely cohesive factor in society, its moral handmaid (with the cost to the state very modest). All this can be viewed as the continuation of principles long established, though a new element entered the picture on account of the delineation of the right to rebellion. Among the Calvinists in France and the Low Countries a full-fledged theory of resistance was developed, precipitated by the concrete circumstances which they faced at mid-century. Bitter persecution and an ambiguous constitutional situation made this development almost inevitable, and once the new theories had been propounded they could not be retrieved. . . .

Otherwise, the changes in the political realm were few. Religious dissent, if publicly expressed, continued to be unthinkable and was suppressed with varying degrees of sternness or ruthlessness. Neither tolerance nor religious freedom was an entry in the vocabulary of 16th-century man, though generally only the Anabaptists experienced fire and sword, and they suffered the double liability of being suspected revolutionaries and blasphemers. Otherwise, confiscation of property, compulsory emigration, or imprisonment was the more normal legal procedure. Whether these constituted a dramatic advance over previous practice is dubious. All countries, Catholic and Protestant alike, clung to the notion that religious uniformity was indispensable to the tranquility of a political commonwealth. And despite the direct or indirect changes resulting from the Protestant Reformation, the notion of the 'Christian commonwealth' continued. Even the secularized functions assumed by the state, such as education, for example, did not lose their religious ornamentation.

The Idea of Vocation

With respect to the economic and social dimensions of society, the Protestant Reformation was indirectly revolutionary and directly conservative. Luther's concept of 'vocation,' which held that all professions and endeavors, no matter how lowly and mundane, had a spiritual blessing, was of immense significance. It made the work of the butcher and baker, if performed in the proper spirit, God-pleasing and thereby undoubtedly released creative and stimulating forces. Of course, there had always been butchers and bakers, and even if one accepts the impact of Luther's notion, one may be entitled to an expression of doubt if sausages and bread were made any tastier, cheaper, or faster by Protestants as the result of this new ethos. Probably not. The difference lies in the fact that this secularization of man's 'vocation' redirected some of the talent that previously had wound up in the ministerial profession and made some men become teachers, lawyers, or doctors who might have turned to the Church in an earlier age. In the early 18th century the English physico-theologian William Derham was to calculate how much manpower had been lost to European society through the monasteries. His point was naïve, but well taken. Instead of disappearing behind the walls of the monasteries, men in Protestant lands strove to live their religious faith in the classroom or the court chamber. To use a modern term, they 'secularized' the Gospel. The impact, while beyond verification, must have been substantial.

The Market Place

On the more explicit level of economic and social considerations, however, the reformers were conservative. Though they differed over what were the mandates of the Gospel for the economic and social realms, they were concerned to explicate these mandates and, moreover, basically express their distrust of the market place. Rather like their scholastic predecessors, the reformers pondered endlessly such problems as the just price, the legitimacy of taking interest, or poverty. They propounded new notions (Calvin, for example, rejected the economic dogma of the Middle Ages that money was sterile), but they sought to influence society by hammering in the rigoristic ethical concepts of the Gospel rather than by offering innovations in economic theory. If Luther and Calvin had had their way, economic life would have continued as before.

The plain fact was that commerce and trade were not any more receptive to Protestant counsel than they had been to Catholic. Indeed, new empirical developments, such as the supplies of silver and spices from the New World, the rise of the chartered trading companies, the geographic discoveries, and increased population, increasingly cast their spell over the economic activities of the 16th century. Actually, little spectacular economic innovation can be discerned in Europe until the early 17th century—and at that time Protestantism, including Calvinism, was playing a different role in the affairs of society. . . .

The Impact on Culture and Education

With respect to the cultural consequences of the Reformation, the conclusions come more easily since the evidence is more clear cut. Still, a caveat is necessary: whatever consequences can be discerned were indirect ramifications of religious emphases rather than a cultural concern as such. And they were derived from the nature of the Protestant message, which was as demanding as it was simple. Thus, people had to be able to read in order to comprehend for themselves the meaning of Scripture. If the Church was to be a dynamic community of all the faithful, literate men and women were necessary. The consequences of such premises were many. The Scriptures and pamphlets in the vernacular were emphasized, a fact which aided the emergence of vernacular literature in the various countries. By way of contrast one may recall that the humanists had written primarily in Latin.

The concern for public education, first propounded by Luther in 1524, was a corollary. The intent was not so much to further secular education or the liberal arts, but to train informed Christians. Religion and education worked harmoniously together. At the beginning of the religious controversy the Reformation had seemed hostile to education. This was the way Erasmus felt. As late as 1528 he bewailed the matter in a letter: 'Wherever the Lutheran teaching has come to rule, learning is perishing.' In part Erasmus's word of gloom grew out of his yearning for tranquility, which he saw as the indispensable prerequisite for learning. But there was also the seeming anti-intellectualism of the Reformation. Had not Luther's proclamation been a blunt and comprehensive repudiation of traditional learning? Had the reformers not charged that the universities were teaching abominable error, and that the study of Aristotle was despicable? Luther had asserted that the learned theologians and academicians were in error and that it was given to simple and unlearned men to understand the Gospel. Such emphases helped rally the unlearned but literate segments of society behind Luther's cause. And as time passed it became obvious that these emphases entailed considerable pedagogical demands and that, in the final analysis, the lines between the Reformation and education were positive.

Education prior to the Reformation was characterized not so much by quantity as quality; it was, moreover, undertaken by the Church. The reformers argued that the responsibility should be in the hands of the secular authorities. Luther argued the case in his 1524 tract *To the Councillors of all German Cities That They Establish and Maintain Christian Schools*, and this was the way it worked out practically. The confiscated ecclesiastical property of the Catholic Church provided the financial basis for the educational effort, even as in England the chantry endowments funded education.

Educational Innovations

The contribution of the Reformation to the notion of public education was thus twofold. It consisted in the demand, perpetually put forward, that schools be established and, secondly, in the transfer of educational responsibility from the Church to the state. This did not mean, however, that the

Church abdicated its educational involvement. The ties between Church and school remained strong and the Peace of Westphalia of 1648 explicitly stated that schools were 'annexum religionis.' Often the Protestant parson took care of the heavenly alphabet and the worldly one as well.

The reformers echoed the goals of the humanists concerning the content of education. They stressed the study of languages (Latin for clarity of thought, Greek and Hebrew for understanding Scripture) and advocated textual criticism and literary analysis. At the same time they emphasized the value of historical studies. The primary motivation was to provide the basis for theological understanding (along lines congenial to Protestant thought), with the training of teachers, lawyers, and doctors as a corollary concern. Protestant learning enjoyed the advantage of not being unduly restricted by the weight of tradition. It was able to explore new avenues. Above all, scholarly endeavor in Protestant lands could be pursued (in the later part of the 16th and then in the 17th century) without undue ecclesiastical interference or restriction. That the Nuremberg reformer Andreas Osiander contributed a preface to Copernicus's famous work on *The Revolutions of the Heavenly Bodies*, in which he defended the scientist's right to offer hypotheses, is worthy of note in this connection. In part this attitude finds its explanation in the self-confidence of Protestantism, in part by the Protestant conviction that any pursuit of truth would confirm rather than deny religious truth. Even more important, however, may have been a kind of pragmatic self-limitation. Protestantism, after all, was a divided house, and nowhere possessed the universal stature of Catholicism. The condemnation of Galileo by the Saxon consistory would have looked rather foolish and would have been rather ineffectual. In other words, the very division of Protestantism made for its relative congeniality to scientific endeavor. . . .

A New Ethos

That there were cultural consequences of the Reformation would seem to need little verification. The difficult question pertains to their extent and significance. What can be said is that the Reformation instilled a new ethos into society—the notion of direct, personal responsibility; the concept of personal (and corporate) election; the postulates of discipline, of autonomy of the secular powers. To say this, however, is neither to suggest that such notions were absent before the Reformation nor to argue that the fact of their propagation alone proves their practical influence. Marriage is here a good case in point: one of the emphatic assertions of the reformers had been that marriage was as acceptable a state in the sight of God as celibacy. Marriage was made religiously respectable. Whether these pronouncements, such as those found in Luther's tract *On Marital Life*, made any practical difference, however, is a different question. One suspects that people after the Reformation married for much the same reasons as others had before.

The question of the broad cultural consequences of the Reformation is, in the final analysis, the question of the role of ideas in the affairs of men. Religious ideas were present in the 16th century, forceful, daring, revolutionary ideas, though we do well to remind ourselves that in such interaction of religious ideas and society, the former rarely appeared in pristine form. But they made their impact within the Protestant churches, probably also within the broader realm of society, and thereby may have done their share to help transform Western civilization.

Appendix

Excerpts from Original Documents Pertaining to the Reformation

Document 1: Erasmus Attacks Abuses Within the Catholic Church

Desiderius Erasmus was one of the leading figures of Christian human-ism, a movement promoting educational and moral reform which pre-ceded and influenced the Reformation. Known throughout Europe for his scholarly endeavors, Erasmus became well known with the publication of Praise of Folly *in 1509. In this wide-ranging work of satire, Erasmus takes on the persona of Dame Folly, who claims to be proud of her many followers, including many inside the Catholic Church. In passages like the following Erasmus clearly shares the Protestant indignation over super-stition and corruption in the church, and he attacks those who are proud of their "good works." Later in his career, though, Erasmus was drawn into public disagreement with Martin Luther, and he stayed loyal to the Catholic Church.*

Then what shall I say about those who happily delude themselves with false pardons for their sins? They calculate the time to be spent in Purgatory down to the year, month, day, and hour as if it were a container that could be measured accurately with a mathematical formula. There are also those who think there is nothing they can-not obtain by relying on the magical prayers and charms thought up by some charlatan for the sake of his soul or for profit. . . .

I can see some businessman, soldier, or judge taking one small coin from all his money and thinking that it will be proper expia-tion for all his perjury, lust, drunkenness, fighting, murder, fraud, lying, and treachery. After doing this he thinks that he can start a new round of sinning with a clean slate. . . .

The life of Christians everywhere abounds with such nonsense. The priests allow and even encourage such things. They know that it brings in much profit. . . .

Those who are the closest to [the theologians] in happiness are generally called "the religious" or "monks," both of which are de-ceiving names, since for the most part they stay as far away from religion as possible and frequent every sort of place. I cannot, how-ever, see how any life could be more gloomy than the life of these monks if I [Folly] did not assist them in many ways. Though most people detest these men so much that accidentally meeting one is considered to be bad luck, the monks themselves believe that they are magnificent creatures. One of their chief beliefs is that to be illiterate is to be of a high state of sanctity, and so they make sure that they are not able to read. Another is that when braying out their gospels in church they are making themselves very pleasing and satisfying to God, when in fact they are uttering these psalms as a matter of repetition rather than from their hearts. Indeed, some of these men make a good living through their uncleanliness and beggary by bellowing their petitions for food from door to door; there is not an inn, an announcement board, or a ship into which they are not accessible, here having a great advantage over other common beggars. According to them, though, they are setting an apostolic example for us by their filthiness, their ignorance, their bawdiness, and their insolence. . . .

Our popes, cardinals, and bishops have, for a long while now, diligently followed the example of the state and the practices of the princes, and have come near to beating these noblemen at their own game. . . .

As to the Supreme Pontiffs, if they would recall that they take the place of Christ and would attempt to imitate His poverty, tasks, doctrines, crosses, and disregard of safety; if they were even to contemplate the meaning of the name Pope—that is, Father—or of the title of Most Holy, then they would become the most humble and mortified of men. How many would then be willing to spend all their wealth and efforts in order to procure this position? If someone were foolish enough to procure it in this manner, would they further be willing to defend their position by the shedding of blood, by the use of poison, or by any other necessary means? Oh, how wisdom would upset their nefarious plans if it were to inflict them! Wisdom, did I say? Nay! Even a grain of salt, that salt spoken of by Christ, would be sufficient to upset their plans. It would lose them all their wealth, their honor, their belongings, their powers won by victories, their offices, dispensations, tributes, and indulgences. They would lose a great many horses, mules, and carts. And finally, they would lose a great many pleasures. (See how I have comprehended in a few words many marketsful, a great harvest, a wide ocean of goods.) These forfeitures would be replaced by vigils, fasts sorrows, prayers, sermons, education, weariness, and a thousand other bothersome tasks of the sort. We should also mention that a great many copyists, notaries, lobbyists, promoters, secretaries, muleteers, grooms, bankers, and pimps—I was about to add something more tender, though rougher on the ears, I am afraid—would be out of jobs. In other words, that large group of men that burdens—I beg your pardon, I meant to say adorns—the Holy Roman See would be done away with and would have to, as a result, resort to begging as a means of making a living. Those who are even worse, those very princes of the Church and guiding lights of the world, would become nothing more than a staff and a wallet.

Desiderius Erasmus, *The Praise of Folly* in *The Essential Erasmus*, ed. and tr. John P. Dolan, New York: Mentor, 1964, pp. 129–57 passim.

Document 2: Luther's Insight on Justification by Faith

In the following brief excerpt, Luther describes how and when he came to his insight about the meaning of Christian faith and righteousness. This new understanding of faith had enormous implications for many of the practices and rituals of the Catholic Church, including five of the seven sacraments, which Luther then began to condemn. This doctrine of justification by faith alone became a cornerstone of all subsequent Protestant theology.

Here, in my case, you may also see how hard it is to struggle out of and emerge from errors which have been confirmed by the example of the whole world and have by long habit become a part of nature, as it were. How true is the proverb, "It is hard to give up the accustomed," and, "Custom is second nature." How truly Augustine says, "If one does not resist custom, it becomes a necessity." I had then already read and taught the sacred Scriptures most diligently privately and publicly for seven years, so that I knew them nearly all by memory. I had also acquired the beginning of the knowledge of Christ and faith in him, i.e., not by works but by faith in Christ are we made righteous and saved. Finally, regarding that of which I speak, I had already defended the proposition publicly that the pope is not the head of the church by divine right. Nevertheless, I did not draw the conclusion, namely, that the pope must be of the devil. For what is not of God must of necessity be of the devil.

So absorbed was I, as I have said, by the example and the title of the holy church as well as my own habit, that I conceded human right to the pope, which nevertheless, unless it is founded on divine authority, is a diabolical lie. For we obey parents and magistrates not because they themselves command it, but because it is God's will, I Peter 3 [2:13]. For that reason I can bear with a less hateful spirit those who cling too pertinaciously to the papacy, particularly those who have not read the sacred Scriptures, or also the profane, since I, who read the sacred Scriptures most diligently so many years, still clung to it so tenaciously.

In the year 1519, Leo X, as I have said, sent the Rose with Karl von Miltitz, who urged me profusely to be reconciled with the pope. . . . Therefore he begged me to seek the things which made for peace. He would put forth every effort to have the pope do the same. I also promised everything abundantly. Whatever I could do with a good conscience with respect to the truth, I would do most promptly. I, too, desired and was eager for peace. Having been drawn into these disturbances by force and driven by necessity, I had done all I did: the guilt was not mine. . . .

Meanwhile, I had already during that year [1519] returned to interpret the Psalter anew. I had confidence in the fact that I was more skilful, after I had lectured in the university on St. Paul's epistles to the Romans, to the Galatians, and the one to the Hebrews. I had indeed been captivated with an extraordinary ardor for understanding Paul in the Epistle to the Romans. But up till then it was not the cold blood about the heart, but a single word in Chapter 1 [:17], "In it the righteousness of God is revealed," that had stood in my way. For I hated that word "righteousness of God," which, according to the use and custom of all the teachers, I had been taught to understand philosophically regarding the formal or active righteousness, as they called it, with which God is righteous and punishes the unrighteous sinner.

Though I lived as a monk without reproach, I felt that I was a sinner before God with an extremely disturbed conscience. I could not believe that he was placated by my satisfaction. I did not love, yes, I hated the righteous God who punishes sinners, and secretly, if not blasphemously, certainly murmuring greatly, I was angry with God, and said, "As if, indeed, it is not enough, that miserable sinners, eternally lost through original sin, are crushed by every kind of calamity by the law of the decalogue, without having God add pain to pain by the gospel and also by the gospel threatening us with his righteousness and wrath!" Thus I raged with a fierce and troubled conscience. Nevertheless, I beat importunately upon Paul at that place, most ardently desiring to know what St. Paul wanted.

At last, by the mercy of God, meditating day and night, I gave heed to the context of the words, namely, "In it the righteousness of God is revealed, as it is written, 'He who through faith is righteous shall live.'" There I began to understand that the righteousness of God is that by which the righteous lives by a gift of God, namely by faith. And this is the meaning: the righteousness of God is revealed by the gospel, namely, the passive righteousness with which merciful God justifies us by faith, as it is written, "He who through faith is righteous shall live." Here I felt that I was altogether born again and had entered paradise itself through open gates. There a totally other face of the entire Scripture showed itself to me. Thereupon I ran through the Scriptures from memory. I also found in other terms an analogy, as, the work of God, that is, what God does in us, the power of God, with which he makes us strong, the wisdom of God, with which he makes us wise, the strength of God, the salvation of God, the glory of God.

And I extolled my sweetest word with a love as great as the hatred with which I had before hated the word "righteousness of God." Thus that place in Paul was for me truly the gate to paradise.

John Dillenberger, ed., *Martin Luther: Selections from his Writings.* Garden City, NY: Doubleday, 1961, pp. 8–12.

Document 3: Luther's Appeal to the Ruling Class in Germany

During a six month period in 1520, Luther composed three of his most influential Reformation treatises. The first of these, excerpted here, was An Appeal to the Ruling Class, *an appeal for the German nobility to back the reform movement and to institute specific church reforms. In his* Appeal, *Luther promotes such fundamental Protestant ideas as the priesthood of all believers and the authority of Scripture over the authority of the Pope.*

To call popes, bishops, priests, monks and nuns the religious class, but princes, lords, artisans and farm-workers the secular class is a specious device invented by certain time-servers; but no one ought to be frightened by it, and for good season. For all Christians whatsoever really and truly belong to the religious class, and there is no difference among them except insofar as they do different work. That is St. Paul's meaning in I Corinthians 12 [:12 f.], when he says: "We are all one body, yet each member hath his own work for serving others." This applies to us all, because we have one baptism, one gospel, one faith, and are all equally Christian. For baptism, gospel, and faith alone make men religious and create a Christian people. When a pope or bishop anoints, grants tonsures, ordains, consecrates, dresses differently from laymen, he may make a hypocrite of a man, or an anointed image, but never a Christian or a spiritually-minded man. The fact is that our baptism consecrates us all without exception and makes us all priests. As St. Peter says, I Pet. 2 [:9], "You are a royal priesthood and a realm of priests," and Revelation, "Thou hast made us priests and kings by Thy blood" [Rev. 5:9 f.]. If we ourselves as Christians did not receive a higher consecration than that given by pope or bishop, then no one would be made priest even by consecration at the hands of pope or bishop. . . .

The Romanists profess to be the only interpreters of Scripture, even though they never learn anything contained in it their lives long. They claim authority for themselves alone, juggle . . . words shamelessly before our eyes, saying that the pope cannot err as to the faith, whether he be bad or good, although they cannot quote a single letter of Scripture to support their claim. . . .

Therefore it is a wicked, base invention, for which they cannot adduce a tittle of evidence in support, to aver that it is the function of the pope alone to interpret Scripture or to confirm any particular interpretation. And if they claim that St. Peter received authority when he was given the keys—well, it is plain enough that the keys were not given to St. Peter only, but to the whole Christian community. . . .

Romanists have no Scriptural basis for their contention that the pope alone has the right to summon or sanction a council. This is their own ruling, and valid only as long as it is not harmful to Christian well-being or contrary to God's laws. If, however, the pope is in the wrong, this ruling becomes invalid, because it is harmful to Christian well-being not to punish him through a council. . . .

Therefore, when need requires it, and the pope is acting harmfully to Christian well-being, let anyone who is a true member of the Christian community as a whole take steps as early as possible to bring about a genuinely free council. No one is so able to do this as the secular authorities, especially since they are also fellow Christians, fellow priests, similarly religious, and of similar authority in all respects. They should exercise their office and do their work without let or hindrance where it is necessary or advantageous to do so, for God has given them authority over everyone. Surely it would be an unnatural proceeding, if fire were to break out in a town, if everyone should stand still and let it burn on and on, simply because no one had the mayor's authority, or perhaps because it began at the mayor's residence. In such a case, is it not the duty of each citizen to stir up the rest and call upon them for help? Much more ought it to be the case in the spiritual city of Christ, were a fire of offence to break out, whether in the pope's regime or anywhere else. . . .

It is empty talk when the Romanists boast of possessing an authority such as cannot properly be contested. No one in Christendom has authority to do evil or to forbid evil from being resisted. The church has no authority except to promote the greater good. Hence, if the pope should exercise his authority to prevent a free council, and so hinder the reform of the church, we ought to pay no regard to him and his authority. If he should excommunicate and fulminate, that ought to be despised as the proceedings of a foolish man. Trusting in God's protection, we ought to excommunicate him in return and manage as best we can; for this authority of his would be presumptuous and empty. He does not possess it, and he would fall an easy victim to a passage of Scripture; for Paul says to the Corinthians, "For God gave us authority, not to cast down Christendom, but to build it up" [II Cor. 10:8]. Who would pretend to ignore this text? Only the power of the devil and the Antichrist attempting to arrest whatever serves the reform of Christendom. Wherefore, we must resist that power with life and limb, and might and main. . . .

And now, I hope that I have [allayed] these false and deceptive terrors, though the Romanists have long used them to make us diffident and of a fearful conscience. It is obvious to all that they, like us, are subject to the authority of the state, that they have no warrant to expound Scripture arbitrarily and without special knowledge. They are not empowered to prohibit a council or, according to their pleasure, to determine its decisions in advance, to bind it and to rob it of freedom. But if they do so, I hope I have shown that of a truth they belong to the community of Antichrist and the devil, and have nothing in common with Christ except the name.

Lewis W. Spitz, ed., *The Protestant Reformation.* Englewood Cliffs, NJ: Prentice-Hall, Inc., 1966, pp. 53–59.

Document 4: Luther's Exposition of Christian Liberty

Luther's Treatise on Christian Liberty, *published in 1520, contains his detailed thinking on the idea of justification by faith alone, as well as consideration of the implications of this for Christian life.*

An easy thing has Christian faith seemed to many, and not a few have counted it simply as one of the Christian virtues; which they do because they have never proved it by experiment nor ever tasted the power of its virtue. For to write well about it or fully to understand what has rightly been written of it is impossible for those who have never tasted its spirit when oppressed by tribulations.

Once, however, a man has tasted of it no matter how little, he can never have enough of writing, speaking, thinking and hearing about it. For it is a living "well of water springing up into everlasting life," as Christ calls it (John 4.14). But I, though I cannot boast of an abundance of faith and know how small my supply is, yet hope to have attained to some drop of it, assailed as I have been by many and various temptations; and I think I can speak of it with more substance, if not more elegance, than have earlier discourses by some men of letters and remarkably subtle disputants who cannot even understand their own writings.

In order to open an easier road for the unlearned (whom alone I serve), I shall begin with the following two propositions about the liberty and servitude of the spirit.

> A Christian man is the most entirely free lord of all, subject to none.
>
> A Christian man is the most entirely dutiful servant of all, subject to everybody.

Although these sentences may seem to be in conflict, yet if they were to be found in agreement they would serve our purpose fairly. They are both sayings of Paul himself: "For though I be free from all men, yet have I made myself servant unto all" (1 Cor. 9.19), and "Owe no man anything, but to love one another" (Rom. 13.8). Love by its nature is ready to serve and obey him who is loved. So Christ, too, though lord of all, was born of woman, was born under the law, at once free and slave, at the same time "in the form of God" and "in the form of a servant" (Phil. 2.6–7).

Let us start further back and more simply. Man has a twofold nature, spiritual and corporal. After the spiritual, called the soul, he is termed spiritual, inner or new man; after the corporal, called the flesh, he is termed carnal, outward or old man. . . . It is because of this diversity that Scripture says contradictory things of the same men; for these two men struggle inside the same man as long as "the flesh lusteth against the Spirit and the Spirit against the flesh" (Gal. 5.17).

First we consider the inner man: in what manner does a man become just, free and truly Christian—that is, spiritual, new and inner? It is clear that no external thing, by whatever name it may be called, can in any way conduce to Christian righteousness or liberty, any more than it can lead the way to unrighteousness or bondage. This can be shown by a simple argument. What can it profit the soul if the body is well, free and active, if it eats, drinks and does as it likes, since in these respects even the most impious slaves of vice may stand very well? On the other hand, what harm can the soul take from illness, imprisonment, hunger, thirst, or any external discomfort, since in these respects even the most godly men—free men in the purity of their conscience—may be afflicted? None of these things touches the liberty or servitude of the soul. Thus it will profit nothing if the body be adorned with holy garments in the manner of priests, or live in holy places or occupy itself with holy offices, or pray, fast, abstain from certain foods, and do whatever labor can be done by the body and in the body. A far other thing is needed for the righteousness and liberty of the soul, since the works I have rehearsed might be observed by any sinner, and their pursuit produces nothing but hypocrites. By the same token, it will not harm the soul if the body be dressed plainly, live in unconsecrated places, eat and drink as others do, do not pray aloud, and leave out everything which, as I have said, can be done by hypocrites.

To clear the ground completely: even contemplation, meditation, and everything the soul can do are of no avail. One thing, and one thing only, is necessary for the Christian life, righteousness and liberty. It is the most Holy Word of God, the gospel of Christ, as He says (John 11.25): "I am the resurrection and the life: he that believeth in me, though he were dead, yet shall he live"; or again (John 8.36): "if the Son therefore shall make you free, ye shall be free indeed"; and (Matt. 4.4): "Man shall not live by bread alone, but by every word which proceedeth out of the mouth of God." Therefore let us accept it as certain and firmly established that the soul may lack all things except the Word of God, without which, in turn, there is no help for it at all. . . .

You may ask, "What then is the Word of God, and how shall it be used, since there are so many words of God?" I answer: the apostle explains in Rom. 1 that it is the gospel of God concerning His Son who was made flesh, suffered, rose again from the dead, and was glorified through the spirit that sanctifies. To have preached Christ is to have fed the soul, to have made it righteous and free, to have saved it—provided the soul believed in the preaching. For faith alone is the saving and efficacious use of the Word of God. "If thou shalt confess the Lord Jesus with thy mouth, and shalt believe in thine heart that God hath raised him from the dead, thou shalt be saved" (Rom. 10.9). . . .

To say it plainly: a Christian man finds his faith sufficient for all purposes and has no need of works to be justified; if he has no need of works, he has none of the law; if he does not need the law, assuredly he is free of the law and it is true that "the law is not made for a righteous man" (1 Tim. 1.9). Therefore this is that Christian liberty: our faith, which does not lead us to idleness or wickedness but frees man from the need of the law and of works for his justification and salvation. . . .

Not only are we the freest kings of all, but we are also priests for all time, which is much better than any kingship. Our priesthood fits us to appear before God, to pray for others, and to teach one another the things that are God's. This constitutes priesthood, and these functions cannot be granted to any unbeliever. If we believe in Him, Christ has thus made us not only His brethren, coheirs, and fellow kings, but also His fellow priests, ready in the spirit of faith to come boldly before God and to cry, "Abba, Father," to pray for one another, and to do all things which we see represented by the visible and corporeal office of priests. . . .

The question arises, "If all who are in the Church are priests, by what name are those whom now we call priests distinguished from laymen?" To this I answer that an injury was done to those words—priest, cleric, spiritual person, ecclesiastic—when they were transferred from the totality of Christians to those few who are now by false usage called churchmen. For Holy Scripture makes no such distinction, except that it gives the names of ministers, servants or stewards to those who now boast the names of popes, bishops and lords, and who in the ministry of the Word should serve the rest by teaching them the faith of Christ and the freedom of believers.

G.R. Elton, ed. and tr., *Renaissance and Reformation: 1300–1648*, 3rd ed., New York: Macmillan, 1976, pp. 176–81.

Document 5: Henry VIII of England Defends Catholicism

After Luther's book The Babylonian Captivity of the Church *became known in England, King Henry VIII launched a vehement attack on Luther in the form of his* Assertion of the Seven Sacraments *in 1521. Included here are excerpts from Henry's "Dedicatory Epistle to the Pope" and from John Clark's "Oration," also dedicated to the Pope. For his effort, King Henry was awarded an additional title, Defender of the Faith.*

The Dedicatory Epistle

Most Holy Father: I most humbly commend myself to you, and devoutly kiss your blessed feet. Whereas we believe that no duty is more incumbent on a Catholic sovereign than to preserve and increase the Christian faith and religion and the proofs thereof, and to transmit them preserved thus inviolate to posterity, by his example in preventing them from being destroyed by any assailant of the faith or in any wise impaired, so when we learned that the pest of Martin Luther's heresy had appeared in Germany and was raging everywhere, without let or hindrance, to such an extent that many, infected with its poison, were falling away, especially those whose furious hatred rather than their zeal for Christian truth had prepared them to believe all its subtleties and lies, we were so deeply grieved at this heinous crime of the German nation (for whom we have no light regard), and for the sake of the Holy Apostolic See, that we bent all our thoughts and energies on uprooting in every possible way, this cockle, this heresy from the Lord's flock. When we perceived that this deadly venom had advanced so far and had seized upon the weak and ill-disposed minds of so many that it could not easily be overcome by a single effort, we deemed that nothing could be more efficient in destroying the contagion than to declare these errors worthy of condemnation, after they had been examined by a convocation of learned and scholarly men from all parts of our realm.

The Oration of John Clark

Most Holy Father:

What great troubles have been stirred up, by the pernicious opinions of Martin Luther; which of late years first sprung out of the lurking holes of the Hussite heresy, in the school of Wittenberg in Germany; from thence spreading themselves over most parts of the Christian world; how many unthinking souls they have deceived, and how many admirers and adherents they have met with; because these are all things very well known; and because, in this place, a medium is more requisite, than prolixity; I care not for relating. Truly, although many of Luther's works are most impiously by his libels, spread abroad in the world: Yet none of them seems more execrable, more venomous, and more pernicious to mankind, than that, entitled, *The Babylonian Captivity of the Church;* in refuting which, many grave and learned men have diligently laboured.

My most serene and invincible Prince, Henry VIII, King of England, France and Ireland, and most affectionate son of your Holiness, and of the sacred Roman Church, hath written a book against this work of Luther's, which he has dedicated to Your Holiness; and hath commanded me to offer, and deliver the same; which I here present.

Hans J. Hillerbrand, ed. *The Reformation: A Narrative History Related by Contemporary Observers and Participants.* New York: Harper & Row, 1964, pp. 310–311.

Document 6: Luther's Response to Henry VIII

Immediately after Henry VIII published his attack on Luther, Luther responded with an open letter to Henry and all his critics, published in 1522. Henry responded right away with another open letter "The Answer of King Henry VIII . . . unto the letter of Martin Luther." This debate, undertaken in print, foreshadowed later similar arguments between Erasmus and Luther and between Sir Thomas More and William Tyndale.

Our Lord Jesus Christ has smitten the whole realm of papal abomination with blindness and madness. For three years now, the mad giants have been struggling against Luther and they still do not grasp what my fight with them is all about. It seems, in vain have I published so many writings which testify openly that I seek to demonstrate that Scripture should count as the exclusive authority, as is right and fair; that human contrivances and doctrines should be given up as evil scandals or, at least, that once their poison is extracted (that is, the power to enforce them and to make them obligatory for the conscience), they should be regarded as a matter for free investigation just as any other calamity or plague in the world. Because they fail to understand this, they quote against me exclusively man-made laws, glosses on the writings of the fathers and from the history of old customs, in short: precisely what I reject and what I am contesting. . . . Thus, they study and teach until they turn grey—right to their grave—with endless labour and at great cost, the miserable men. They themselves cannot do anything else with their teaching; it is the only way they can dispute. And that is the reason why it happens that, if I always cry: 'Gospel! Gospel! Gospel!' they can only answer: 'Fathers! Fathers! Custom! Custom! Decretals! Decretals!' If then I answer that customs, fathers and decretals have often erred, that reform must be based upon sounder foundation because Christ cannot err, then they are silent like the fishes.

Hans J. Hillerbrand, ed., *The Reformation: A Narrative History Related by Contemporary Observers and Participants*. New York: Harper & Row, 1964, p. 313.

Document 7: Zwingli's Basic Protestant Premises

Ulrich Zwingli, sometimes called "third man" of the Reformation, began pressing for reform of church abuses in Switzerland about the same time that Luther came to prominence. When Zwingli became pastor of the church in Zurich in 1519, he initiated a broad reform movement based on Protestant premises he held in common with Luther. His views are summarized in his Sixty-Seven Articles, which were presented for open debate in Zurich in 1523.

1. Those who say that the Gospel is nothing without the confirmation of the Church err and blaspheme God.

2. The sum of the Gospel is that our Lord, Jesus Christ, God's dear Son, has revealed to us the will of His Father and by His innocence has redeemed us from death and has reconciled God.

7. He is the salvation and head of all believers who are his body.

8. Hence, all those who live in this head are members and sons of God, and this is the Church, the communion of the saints, the bride of Christ, the Catholic Church.

9. Consequently the so-called ecclesiastical pomp, holy days, estates, titles and laws are sheer foolishness because they do not agree with Christ, the Head.

13. One who is redeemed by him learns clearly and purely the Word of God and by his spirit is drawn to him and transformed into him.

17. On the Pope: Christ is the one eternal high priest, therefore those who vaunt themselves as high priests oppose the honor and power of Christ.

18. On the Mass: Christ who gave himself once and for all upon the cross is a sacrifice and victim making satisfaction in eternity for the sins of all the faithful. Hence the Mass is not a sacrifice, but a commemoration of the sacrifice made once and for all upon the cross and is, as it were, a sign of our redemption in Christ.

19. On the intercession of the saints: Christ is the only mediator.

20. God gives us everything in the name of Christ. Hence we need no other intercessors.

22. Of good works: Since Christ is our righteousness, our works are good only insofar as they are of Christ.

24. On dietary laws and clothes: Since a Christian is not bound to works which God has not enjoined, any food may be eaten at any time and special permits to eat cheese and butter are an imposture.

26. God's disapproval of hypocrisy does away with cowls, vestments, and tonsures.

29. On clerical marriage: The clergy sin, if discovering that God has denied them the gift of chastity, they do not marry.

31. On the ban: No private individual can impose the ban, but only the Church in conjunction with the minister.

33. On unjust gain: Unjust gains, if they cannot be duly restored, should not be given to temples, cloisters, monks, priests, and nuns but to the needy.

36. The temporal authority arrogated by priests belongs to the civil government.

37. Whom all Christians are obligated to obey.

38. Provided they do nothing against God.

40. Magistrates may take the lives of those guilty of public offense.

42. If magistrates go against the rule of Christ they may be deposed.

43. That kingdom is best and soundest which is from God and in God.

44. Concerning prayers: Since the true worshippers worship God in spirit and in truth.

46. Singing or rather bawling in churches without piety and for gain is done simply to be seen and recompensed by men.

49. Concerning offense: There is no greater offense than that marriage should be forbidden to priests but they are allowed to have concubines or harlots and are taxed on this account.

51. Absolution: to attribute absolution to a creature is to deprive God of His glory.

52. Consequently, confession to a priest or a neighbor is not for remission of sins but for counseling.

53. Works of satisfaction imposed by a priest are a human device, except excommunication.

54. To ascribe to works of satisfaction what Christ has done is to condemn God.

55. He who declines to remit any sin to a penitent stands not in the place of God or Peter but of the devil.

56. He who remits any sin for money is a confederate of Simon Magus and Baalam and a legate of the devil.

57. On purgatory: Scripture knows of no purgatory beyond this life.

58. The judgment of the dead is known only to God.

61. On the priesthood: With regard to the [*indelible*] character of the priest, lately claimed, Scripture knows nothing.

64. On the reform of abuse: Those who confess their errors may be left to die in peace and thereafter their revenues may be redistributed.

65. Those who do not, are not to be molested with violence unless they so carry themselves that the magistrates must step in for the public peace.

66. Let the clergy erect the cross of Christ and not money boxes. The ax is laid to the root of the tree.

67. I am willing to discuss tithes, infant baptism, and confirmation.

Roland Bainton ed., *The Age of the Reformation*. Malabar, FL: Robert E. Krieger Publishing, 1984, pp. 123–125.

Document 8: Zwingli Compares his Efforts to Luther's

By 1523, Luther's impact on Europe was such that Zwingli, the influential Reformation leader in Switzerland, had to deal with the accusation of being a "Lutheran," which is his topic in the following excerpt. Zwingli died in 1531 in a battle against Catholic forces in Switzerland.

The high and mighty of this world have begun to persecute and hate Christ's teaching under the presence of the name of Luther. They call all of Christ's teaching 'Lutheran', no matter who on earth proclaims it. Even if one never read about Luther and is faithful solely to the Word of God, he would yet be scolded to be a 'Lutheran'. This is now my fate. I began to preach the Gospel of Christ in 1516, long before anyone in our region had ever heard of Luther. I never went into the pulpit without taking the words read the same morning in the mass as the Gospel and interpreting them according to biblical Scripture. . . . When I began to preach in Zürich in 1519 I announced that, God willing, I would proclaim the Gospel according to Matthew, without human speculation. From this I would neither move nor change. Early that year no one here among us knew anything about Luther, except that he had published something concerning indulgence. This taught me little, since I knew all along that indulgences were a deception and farce. . . . Therefore Luther's writings helped me little at that time in my preaching on Matthew. Those who were eager for the Word of God flocked together so unceasingly that I was amazed. I ask the enemies of Christ's teachings, 'Who called me then a Lutheran?' When Luther's booklet on the *Lord's Prayer* was published, after I had already interpreted it in my exposition of Matthew, I knew well that many pious people would suspect that I had written the booklet and published it in Luther's name. Who could accuse me of being a Lutheran? Why did not the Roman cardinals and delegates living in Zürich at that time, who hated me and tried to bribe me with money, call me a Lutheran until they had declared Luther to be a heretic? This is my testimony and all here can testify to it. . . .

Who called me to proclaim the Gospel and to interpret an entire Gospel? Was it Luther? Why, I began to preach in this fashion long before I ever heard of Luther. For this reason I began some ten years ago to study Greek in order to learn Christ's teaching in the original language. I leave it to others to judge how well I comprehended it. At any rate, Luther did not teach me anything. Two years after I concerned myself solely with biblical writings, his name was still unknown to me. The papists none the less burden me and others maliciously with such names and say, 'You must be a Lutheran, for you preach the way Luther writes.' I answer them, 'I preach the way Paul writes. Why do you not also call me a follower of Paul? Indeed, I proclaim the word of Christ. Why do you not call me a Christian?' They are full of malice. Luther is, as I gather, an admirable warrior for God, who earnestly searches the Scriptures, as has not been the case on earth for a thousand years. (I do not mind if the papists consider me a heretic with him.) Not since the papacy has been in existence has his manly, courageous mind, with which he attacked the Roman Pope, had an equal. Who did such deed? God or Luther? Ask Luther himself. I know that he will say, God. Why then do you ascribe the teachings of other men to Luther when he himself ascribes everything to God? . . .

I do not wish to bear Luther's name, for I have read little of his teaching and have often purposely desisted from reading his books in order to conciliate the papists. What I have read of his writings (concerning the doctrines, teachings, views, and meaning of the Scripture—his later writings I have not read) is altogether so well discussed and based on the Word of God that nobody can repudiate it. I also know that in some respects he yields to the weak, but would on principle act differently. Here I do not agree with him. Not that he says too much; rather he does not say enough. . . .

Therefore, let us not change the honourable name of Christ into the name of Luther. For Luther did not die for us, but teaches us to recognize him from whom alone we have all salvation. . . . Yet, I will bear no name than that of my Captain Christ. I am his soldier. He will give me titles and reward according to his good pleasure. I hope that everyone understands why I do not want to be called Lutheran even though I esteem Luther as much as any other living person. I testify before God and all men that I never wrote a single letter to him nor he to me. . . . I did not refrain from this because I was fearful, but because I wanted to show how uniform is the Spirit of God. Though far distant from each other, we still unanimously proclaim the teaching of Christ without any explicit agreement.

Hans J. Hillerbrand, ed., *The Reformation: A Narrative History Related by Contemporary Observers and Participants*. New York: Harper & Row, 1964, pp. 125–27.

Document 9: A Radical Protestant Encourages Another

While radical Protestant groups took their inspiration from the teachings of Luther and Zwingli, they rejected the partnership of church and state endorsed by most Protestants. The largest groups of these radicals were

called Anabaptists because of their common rejection of infant baptism.
Some radical Protestants, usually called Spiritualists, went even farther
than the Anabaptists in their complete rejection of a physical church on
earth, arguing that the lot of true Christians is to wander and suffer. Se-
bastian Franck represents this view; he rejects Luther and Zwingli, as
well as the Church Fathers, and he contends that only the few true be-
lievers can understand the hidden wisdom of God. What follows are ex-
cerpts from a letter written by Franck to an Anabaptist friend in 1531.

To be brief, my dear brother Campanus, that I may say it in summary fashion and openly and be understood by thee, I maintain
against all ecclesiastical authorities that all outward things and ceremonies, which were customary in the church of the apostles, have
been done away with and are not to be reinstituted, although many
without authorization or calling undertake to restore on their own
the degenerated sacraments.

For the church will remain scattered among the heathen until
the end of the world. Indeed, only the Advent of Christ will at last
destroy and make away with Antichrist and his church. He will
gather together dispersed and ever fugitive Israel from the four
places of the world. Therefore, it is my opinion that nothing of
these churches should be reinstituted which were once held in
great esteem in the church.

These are the things which the aforementioned wolves, the doctors of unwisdom, apes of the apostles and antichrists, have vigorously propagated. And they who understood the truth of these
things—their writings and instructions were suppressed by these as
godless heresies and nonsense; and in their place in esteem come
foolish Ambrose, Augustine, Jerome, Gregory—of whom not even
one knew the Lord, so help me God, nor was sent by God to teach.
But rather all were the apostles of Antichrist and are that still. I am
a liar if all their own books don't prove as much, which never hold
together and are far different from and unlike the apostles'. There
is not a one of them, so far as can be seen from the books they have
left, who appears to have been a Christian, unless it be that they, at
last, felt differently in their hearts, being taught by God with something else and repented of their lost labor. For they teach nothing
properly that concerns Christian faith. Yea, they have not known
nor taught what God is [or] law, gospel, faith, baptism, Supper, true
righteousness, Scripture, the church, and its law.

They mix the New Testament with the Old, as also today their
descendants do. And when they have nothing with which to defend
their purposes, they run at once to the empty quiver, that is, to the

Old Testament, and from it prove [the legitimacy of] war, oath, government, power of magistracy, tithes, priesthood; and praise everything and ascribe this all forcibly to Christ without his will. And just as the popes have derived all this from it, so also many of those who would have themselves be called Evangelicals hold that they have nobly escaped the snare of the pope and the devil and have nevertheless achieved, with great effort and sweat, nothing more than that they have exchanged and confounded the priesthood of the pope with the Mosaic kingdom!

But this remains a firm sentence: If the priesthood cannot be reestablished out of the old law, neither can [Christian] government and outward government be established according to the law of Moses. Yet the Evangelicals at court are now fashioning for the princes another [rule] and nicely press the sword into their hands and, as the proverb has it, pour oil into the fire.

George Huntsdon Williams and Angel M. Mercal, eds., *Spiritual and Anabaptist Writers: Documents Illustrative of the Radical Reformation.* Philadelphia: Westminster Press, 1957, pp. 147–60 passim.

Document 10: Calvin Defends Protestantism to the King of France

France remained Catholic throughout the Reformation era, and the outspoken French Protestant John Calvin remained in exile in Geneva, Switzerland. There he composed the first edition of his Institutes of Christian Religion *in 1536 as a statement of doctrine for Protestants. In his Prefatory Address to King Francis of France, Calvin reiterates many Protestant themes, emphasizing the willingness of Protestants to die for their beliefs, and he attempts to refute some of the common charges leveled at the Protestant movement.*

Examine briefly, most mighty King, all the parts of our case, and think us the most wicked of wicked men, unless you clearly find that "we toil and suffer reproach because we have our hope set on the living God" [I Tim. 4:10]; because we believe that "this is eternal life: to know the only true God, and Jesus Christ whom he has sent" [John 17:3 p.]. For the sake of this hope some of us are shackled with irons, some beaten with rods, some led about as laughingstocks, some proscribed, some most savagely tortured, some forced to flee. All of us are oppressed by poverty, cursed with dire execrations, wounded by slanders, and treated in most shameful ways.

Now look at our adversaries (I speak of the order of priests, at whose nod and will the others are hostile toward us), and consider with me for a moment what zeal motivates them. They readily allow themselves and others to ignore, neglect, and despise the true religion, which has been handed down in the Scriptures, and which ought to have had a recognized place among all men. They think it of no concern what belief anyone holds or does not hold regarding God and Christ, if only he submit his mind with implicit faith (as they call it) to the judgment of the church. The sight of God's glory defiled with manifest blasphemies does not much trouble them, provided no one raises a finger against the primacy of the Apostolic See and against the authority of Holy Mother Church. Why, therefore, do they fight with such ferocity and bitterness for the Mass, purgatory, pilgrimages, and bides of that sort, denying that there can be true godliness without a most explicit faith, so to speak, in such things, even though they prove nothing of them from God's Word? Why? unless for them "their God is the belly" [Phil. 3:19]; their kitchen their religion! If these are taken away, they believe that they will not be Christians, not even men! For, even though some glut themselves sumptuously while others gnaw upon meager crusts, still all live out of the same pot, a pot that without this fuel would not only grow cold but freeze through and through. Consequently, the one most concerned about his belly proves the sharpest contender for his faith. In fine, all men strive to one goal: to keep either their rule intact or their belly full. No one gives the slightest indication of sincere zeal.

Despite this, they do not cease to assail our doctrine and to reproach and defame it with names that render it hated or suspect. They call it "new" and "of recent birth." They reproach it as "doubtful and uncertain." They ask what miracles have confirmed it. They inquire whether it is right for it to prevail against the agreement of so many holy fathers and against most ancient custom. They urge us to acknowledge that it is schismatic because it wages war against the church, or that the church was lifeless during the many centuries in which no such thing was heard. Finally, they say that there is no need of many arguments, for one can judge by its fruits what it is, seeing that it has engendered such a heap of sects, so many seditious tumults, such great licentiousness. Indeed, it is very easy for them to revile a forsaken cause before the credulous and ignorant multitude. But if we too might speak in our turn, this bitterness which they licentiously and with impunity spew at us from swollen cheeks would subside.

First, by calling it "new" they do great wrong to God, whose Sacred Word does not deserve to be accused of novelty. Indeed, I do not at all doubt that it is new to them, since to them both Christ himself and his gospel are new. But he who knows that this preaching of Paul is ancient, that "Jesus Christ died for our sins and rose again for our justification" [Rom. 4:25 p.], will find nothing new among us.

That it has lain long unknown and buried is the fault of man's impiety. Now when it is restored to us by God's goodness, its claim to antiquity ought to be admitted at least by right of recovery.

The same ignorance leads them to regard it as doubtful and uncertain. This is precisely what the Lord complains of through his prophet, that "the ox knew its owner, and the ass its master's crib; but his own people did not know him" [Isa. 1:3 p.]. But however they may jest about its uncertainty, if they had to seal their doctrine in their own blood, and at the expense of their own life, one could see how much it would mean to them. Quite the opposite is our assurance, which fears neither the terrors of death nor even God's judgment seat.

In demanding miracles of us, they act dishonestly. For we are not forging some new gospel, but are retaining that very gospel whose truth all the miracles that Jesus Christ and his disciples ever wrought serve to confirm. . . .

Our controversy turns on these hinges: first, they contend that the form of the church is always apparent and observable. Secondly, they set this form in the see of the Roman Church and its hierarchy. We, on the contrary, affirm that the church can exist without any visible appearance, and that its appearance is not contained within that outward magnificence which they foolishly admire. Rather, it has quite another mark: namely, the pure preaching of God's Word and the lawful administration of the sacraments. They rage if the church cannot always be pointed to with the finger. . . .

Lastly, they do not act with sufficient candor when they invidiously recount how many disturbances, tumults, and contentions the preaching of our doctrine has drawn along with it, and what fruits it now produces among many. The blame for these evils is unjustly laid upon it, when this ought to have been imputed to Satan's malice. Here is, as it were, a certain characteristic of the divine Word, that it never comes forth while Satan is at rest and sleeping. This is the surest and most trustworthy mark to distinguish it from lying doctrines, which readily present themselves, are received with attentive ears by all, and are listened to by an applauding world. Thus for some centuries during which everything was submerged in deep darkness, almost all mortals were the sport and jest of this lord of the world, . . . Satan lay idle and luxuriated in deep repose. For what else had he to do but jest and sport, in tranquil and peaceable possession of his kingdom? Yet when the light shining from on high in a measure shattered his darkness, when that "strong man" had troubled and assailed his kingdom, he began to shake off his accustomed drowsiness and to take up arms. And first, indeed, he stirred up men to action that thereby he might violently oppress the dawning truth. And when this profited him nothing, he turned to stratagems: he aroused disagreements and dogmatic contentions through his catabaptists and other monstrous rascals in order to obscure and at last extinguish the truth. And now he persists in besieging it with both engines. With the violent hands of men he tries to uproot that true seed, and seeks (as much as lies in his power) to choke it with his weeds, to prevent it from growing and bearing fruit. But all that is in vain, if we heed the Lord our monitor, who long since laid open Satan's wiles before us, that he might not catch us unawares; and armed us with defenses firm enough against all his devices. . . .

But I return to you, O King. May you be not at all moved by those vain accusations with which our adversaries are trying to inspire terror in you: that by this new gospel (for so they call it) men strive and seek only after the opportunity for seditions and impunity for all crimes. "For our God is not author of division, but of peace" [I Cor. 14:33 p.]; and the Son of God is not "the minister of sin" [Gal. 2:17], for he has come to "destroy the devil's works" [I John 3:8].

And we are unjustly charged, too, with intentions of such a sort that we have never given the least suspicion of them. We are, I suppose, contriving the overthrow of kingdoms—we, from whom not one seditious word was ever heard; we, whose life when we lived under you was always acknowledged to be quiet and simple; we, who do not cease to pray for the full prosperity of yourself and your kingdom, although we are now fugitives from home! We are, I suppose, wildly chasing after wanton vices! Even though in our moral actions many things are blameworthy, nothing deserves such great reproach as this. And we have not, by God's grace, profited so little by the gospel that our life may not be for these disparagers an example of chastity, generosity, mercy, continence, patience, modesty, and all other virtues. It is perfectly clear that we fear and worship God in very truth since we seek, not only in our life but in our death, that his name be hallowed [cf. Phil. 1:20]. And hatred itself has been compelled to bear witness to the innocence and civic uprightness of some of us upon whom the punishment of death was inflicted for that one thing which ought to have occasioned extraordinary praise.

John Calvin, *Institutes of the Christian Religion*, ed. John T. McNeill, Philadelphia: Westminster Press, 1960, pp. 13–30 passim.

Document 11: The Geneva Confession of Faith

The Geneva Confession of Faith, written by William Farel and John Calvin in 1536, served as a kind of pledge of allegiance to the Protestant church in Geneva. As such, it provides a concise summary of the Calvinist version of Protestant beliefs, and it begins with the fundamental premise of sola scriptura, *or the Bible as the authority for all Christian teaching. The following excerpt contains the first part of this confession of faith.*

CONFESSION OF FAITH
*which all the citizens and inhabitants of Geneva
and the subjects of the country must promise to
keep and hold
(1536)*

1. THE WORD OF GOD

First we affirm that we desire to follow Scripture alone as rule of faith and religion, without mixing it with any other thing which might be devised by the opinion of men apart from the Word of God, and without wishing to accept for our spiritual government any other doctrine than what is conveyed to us by the same Word without addition or diminution, according to the command of our Lord.

2. ONE ONLY GOD

Following, then, the lines laid down in the Holy Scriptures, we acknowledge that there is one only God, Whom we are both to worship and serve, and in *Whom* we are to put all our confidence and hope; having this assurance, that in Him alone is contained all wisdom, power, justice, goodness and pity. And since He is spirit, He is to be served in spirit and in truth. Therefore we think it an abomination to put our confidence or hope in any created thing; to worship anything else than Him, whether angels or any other creatures; and to recognize any other Saviour of our souls than Him alone, whether saints or men living upon earth; and likewise to offer the service which ought to be rendered to Him in external ceremonies or carnal observances, as if He took pleasure in such things; or to make an image to represent His divinity or any other image for adoration.

3. THE LAW OF GOD ALIKE FOR ALL

Because there is one only Lord and Master who has dominion over our consciences, and because His will is the only principle of all justice, we confess all our life ought to be ruled in accordance with the commandments of His holy law in which is contained all perfection of justice, and that we ought to have no other rule of good and just living, nor invent other good works to supplement it than those which are there contained, as follows: Exodus 20: "I am the Lord thy God, who brought thee," and so on.

4. NATURAL MAN

We acknowledge man by nature to be blind, darkened in understanding, and full of corruption and perversity of heart, so that of himself he has no power to be able to comprehend the true knowledge of God as is proper, [nor] to apply himself to good works. But on the contrary, if he is left by God to what he is by nature, he is only able to live in ignorance and to be abandoned to all iniquity. Hence he has need to be illumined by God, so that he come to the right knowledge of his salvation, and thus . . . be redirected in his affections and reformed to the obedience of the righteousness of God.

5. MAN BY HIMSELF LOST

Since man is naturally (as has been said) deprived and destitute in himself of all the light of God and of all righteousness, we acknowledge that by himself he can only expect the wrath and malediction of God, and hence that he must look outside himself for the means of his salvation.

6. SALVATION IN JESUS

We confess that it is Jesus Christ who is given to us by the Father, in order that in Him we should recover all of which in ourselves we are deficient. Now all that Jesus Christ has done and suffered for our redemption we veritably hold without any doubt, as it is contained in the Creed which is recited in the Church, that is to say: "I believe in God the Father Almighty," and so on.

7. RIGHTEOUSNESS IN JESUS

Therefore we acknowledge the things which are consequently given to us by God in Jesus Christ: first, that being in our own nature enemies of God and subjects of His wrath and judgment, we are reconciled with Him and received again in grace through the intercession of Jesus Christ, so that by His righteousness and guiltlessness we have remission of our sins, and by the shedding of His blood we are cleansed from all our stains.

8. REGENERATION IN JESUS

Second, we acknowledge that by His Spirit we are regenerated into a new spiritual nature. That is to say that the evil desires of our flesh are mortified by grace, so that they rule us no longer. On the contrary, our will is rendered conformable to God's will, to follow in His way and to seek what is pleasing to Him. Therefore we are by Him delivered from the servitude of sin, under whose power we were of ourselves held captive, and by this deliverance we are made capable and able to do good works and not otherwise.

9. REMISSION OF SINS ALWAYS NECESSARY FOR THE FAITHFUL

Finally, we acknowledge that this regeneration is so effected in us that, until we slough off this mortal body, there remains always in us much imperfection and infirmity, so that we always remain poor and wretched sinners in the presence of God. And, however much we ought day by day to increase and grow in God's righteousness, there will never be plenitude or perfection while we live here. Thus we always have need of the mercy of God to obtain the remission of our faults and offences. And so we ought always to look for our righteousness in Jesus Christ and not at all in ourselves, and in Him be confident and assured, putting no faith in our works.

10. ALL OUR GOOD IN THE GRACE OF GOD

In order that all glory and praise be rendered to God (as is His due), and that we be able to have true peace and rest of conscience, we understand and confess that we receive all benefits from God, as said above, by His clemency and pity, without any consideration of our worthiness or the merit of our works, to which is due no other retribution than eternal confusion. None the less our Saviour in His goodness, having received us into the communion of His son Jesus, regards the works that we have done in faith as pleasing and agreeable; not that they merit it at all, but because, not imputing any of the imperfection that is there, He acknowledges in them nothing but what proceeds from His Spirit.

11. FAITH

We confess that the entrance which we have to the great treasures and riches of the goodness of God that is vouchsafed to us is by faith; inasmuch as, in certain confidence and assurance of heart, we believe in the promises of the gospel, and receive Jesus Christ as He is offered to us by the Father and described to us by the Word of God.

12. INVOCATION OF GOD ONLY AND INTERCESSION OF CHRIST

As we have declared that we have confidence and hope for salvation and all good only in God through Jesus Christ, so we confess that we ought to invoke Him in all necessities in the name of Jesus Christ, who is our mediator and advocate with Him and has access to Him. Likewise we ought to acknowledge that all good things come from Him alone, and to give thanks to Him for them. On the other hand, we reject the intercession of the saints as a superstition invented by men contrary to Scripture, for the reason that it proceeds from mistrust of the sufficiency of the intercession of Jesus Christ.

13. PRAYER INTELLIGIBLE

Moreover since prayer is nothing but hypocrisy and fantasy unless it proceed from the interior affections of the heart, we believe that all prayers ought to be made with clear understanding. And for this reason, we hold the prayer of our Lord to show fittingly what we ought to ask of Him: "Our Father which art in heaven, . . . but deliver us from evil. Amen."

14. SACRAMENTS

We believe that the sacraments which our Lord has ordained in His Church are to be regarded as exercises of faith for us, both for fortifying and confirming it in the promises of God and for witnessing before men. Of them there are in the Christian Church only two which are instituted by the authority of our Saviour; baptism and the supper of our Lord; for what is held within the realm of the pope concerning seven sacraments, we condemn as fable and lie.

15. BAPTISM

Baptism is an external sign by which our Lord testifies that He desires to receive us for His children, as members of His Son Jesus. Hence in it there is represented to us the cleansing from sin which we have in the blood of Jesus Christ, the mortification of our flesh which we have by His death that we may live in Him by His Spirit. Now since our children belong to such an alliance with our Lord, we are certain that the external sign is rightly applied to them.

16. THE HOLY SUPPER

The supper of our Lord is a sign by which under bread and wine He represents the true spiritual communion which we have in His body and blood. And we acknowledge that according to His ordinance it ought to be distributed in the company of the faithful, in order that all those who wish to have Jesus for their life be partakers of it. Inasmuch as the mass of the pope was a reprobate and diabolical ordinance subverting the mystery of the holy supper, we declare that it is execrable to us, an idolatry condemned by God; for so much is it itself regarded as a sacrifice for the redemption of souls that the bread is in it taken and adored as God. Besides there are other execrable blasphemies and superstitions implied here, and the abuse of the Word of God which is taken in vain without profit or edification.

17. HUMAN TRADITIONS

The ordinances that are necessary for the internal discipline of the Church, and [that] belong solely to the maintenance of peace, honesty and good order in the assembly of Christians, we do not hold to be human traditions at all, inasmuch as they are comprised under the general command of Paul, where he desires that all be done among them decently and in order. But all laws and regulations made binding on conscience which obliged the faithful to things not commanded by God, or [which] establish another service of God than which he demands, thus tending to destroy Christian liberty, we condemn as perverse doctrines of Satan, in view of our Lord's declaration that He is honored in vain by doctrines that are the commandment of men. It is in this estimation that we hold pilgrimages, monasteries, distinctions of foods, prohibition of marriage, confessions and other like things.

Lewis W. Spitz, ed., *The Protestant Reformation*. Englewood Cliffs, NJ: Prentice-Hall, Inc., 1966, pp. 114–20.

Document 12: Calvin on Justification by Faith

John Calvin was in full agreement with Luther on the centrality of justification by faith as the cornerstone of the Protestant movement, as is evidenced by this excerpt from Calvin's Reply to Sadoleto *in 1540.*

You, in the first place, touch upon justification by faith, the first and keenest subject of controversy between us. Is this a knotty and useless question? Wherever the knowledge of it is taken away, the glory of Christ is extinguished, religion abolished, the church destroyed, and the hope of salvation utterly overthrown. That doctrine, then, though of the highest moment, we maintain that you have nefariously effaced from the memory of men. Our books are filled with convincing proofs of this fact, and the gross ignorance of this doctrine, which even still continues in all your churches, declares that our complaint is by no means ill-founded. But you very maliciously stir up prejudice against us, alleging that by attributing everything to faith, we leave no room for works. . . .

First, we bid a man begin by examining himself, and this not in a superficial and perfunctory manner, but to cite his conscience before the tribunal of God, and when sufficiently convinced of his iniquity, to reflect on the strictness of the sentence pronounced upon all sinners. Thus confounded and amazed at his misery, he is prostrated and humbled before God; and, casting away all self-confidence, groans as if given up to final perdition. Then we show that the only haven of safety is in the mercy of God, as manifested in Christ, in whom every part of our salvation is complete. As all mankind are, in the sight of God, lost sinners, we hold that Christ is their only right-eousness, since, by His obedience, He has wiped off our transgres-sions; by His sacrifice, appeased the divine anger; by His blood, washed away our sins; by His cross, borne our curse; and by His death, made satisfaction for us. We maintain that in this way man is reconciled in Christ to God the Father, by no merit of his own, by no value of works, but by gratuitous mercy. When we embrace Christ by faith, and come, as it were, into communion with Him, this we term, after the manner of Scripture, *the righteousness of faith.*

What have you here, Sadoleto, to bite or carp at? Is it that we leave no room for works? Assuredly we do deny that in justifying a man they are worth one single straw. For Scripture everywhere cries aloud, that all are lost; and every man's own conscience bit-terly accuses him. The same Scripture teaches that no hope is left but in the mere goodness of God, by which sin is pardoned, and righteousness imputed to us. It declares both to be gratuitous, and finally concludes that a man is justified without works. . . .

Hans J. Hillerbrand, ed., *The Protestant Reformation.* New York: Walker and Company, 1968, pp. 161–62.

Document 13: Calvin's Doctrine of Predestination

John Calvin is usually associated with the doctrine of predestination, the idea that God has designated some people for heaven and some for hell, from before birth. Predestination is a logical outcome of Calvin's empha-sis on the power and sovereignty of God, and it is not really at the center of his theology. Still, in later editions of the Institutes, *Calvin continu-ally enlarged his discussion of predestination, showing the topic to have been a preoccupation of sorts.*

Human curiosity renders the discussion of predestination, already somewhat difficult of itself, very confusing and even dangerous. No restraints can hold it back from wandering in forbidden by-paths and thrusting upward to the heights. If allowed, it will leave no secret to God that it will not search out and unravel. Since we see so many on all sides rushing into this audacity and impudence, among them certain men not otherwise bad, they should in due season be reminded of the measure of their duty in this regard.

First, then, let them remember that when they inquire into pre-destination they are penetrating the sacred precincts of divine wisdom. If anyone with carefree assurance breaks into this place, he will not succeed in satisfying his curiosity and he will enter a labyrinth from which he can find no exit. For it is not right for man unrestrainedly to search out things that the Lord has willed to be hid in himself, and to unfold from eternity itself the sublimest wisdom, which he would have us revere but not understand that through this also he should fill us with wonder. He has set forth by his Word the secrets of his will that he has decided to reveal to us. These he decided to reveal in so far as he foresaw that they would concern us and benefit us.

Doctrine of predestination to be sought in Scripture only

"We have entered the pathway of faith," says Augustine, "let us hold steadfastly to it. It leads us to the King's chamber, in which are hid all treasures of knowledge and wisdom. For the Lord Christ himself did not bear a grudge against his great and most select disciples when he said: 'I have . . . many things to say to you, but you cannot bear them now' [John 16:12]. We must walk, we must advance, we must grow, that our hearts may be capable of those things which we cannot yet grasp. But if the Last Day finds us advancing, there we shall learn what we could not learn here." If this thought prevails with us, that the Word of the Lord is the sole way that can lead us in our search for all that it is lawful to hold concerning him, and is the sole light to illumine our vision of all that we should see of him, it will readily keep and restrain us from all rashness. For we shall know that the moment we exceed the bounds of the Word, our course is outside the pathway and in darkness, and that there we must repeatedly wander, slip, and stumble. Let this, therefore, first of all be before our eyes: to seek any other knowledge of predestination than what the Word of God discloses is not less insane than if one should purpose to walk in a pathless waste [cf. Job 12:24], or to see in darkness. And let us not be ashamed to be ignorant of something in this matter, wherein there is a certain learned ignorance. . . .

Predestination and foreknowledge of God

No one who wishes to be thought religious dares simply deny predestination, by which God adopts some to hope of life, and sentences others to eternal death. But our opponents, especially those who make foreknowledge its cause, envelop it in numerous petty objections. We, indeed, place both doctrines in God, but we say that subjecting one to the other is absurd.

When we attribute foreknowledge to God, we mean that all things always were, and perpetually remain, under his eyes, so that to his knowledge there is nothing future or past, but all things are present. And they are present in such a way that he not only conceives them through ideas, as we have before us those things which our minds remember, but he truly looks upon them and discerns them as things placed before him. And this foreknowledge is extended throughout the universe to every creature. We call predestination God's eternal decree, by which he compacted with himself what he willed to become of each man. For all are not created in equal condition; rather, eternal life is foreordained for some, eternal damnation for others. Therefore, as any man has been created to one or the other of these ends, we speak of him as predestined to life or to death. . . .

Foolish men contend with God in many ways, as though they held him liable to their accusations. They first ask, therefore, by what right the Lord becomes angry at his creatures who have not provoked him by any previous offense; for to devote to destruction whomever he pleases is more like the caprice of a tyrant than the lawful sentence of a judge. It therefore seems to them that men have reason to expostulate with God if they are predestined to eternal death solely by his decision, apart from their own merit. If thoughts of this sort ever occur to pious men, they will be sufficiently armed to break their force even by the one consideration that it is very wicked merely to investigate the causes of God's will. For his will is, and rightly ought to be, the cause of all things that are. For if it has any cause, something must precede it, to which it is, as it were, bound; this is unlawful to imagine. For God's will is so much the highest rule of righteousness that whatever he wills, by the very fact that he wills it, must be considered righteous. When, therefore, one asks why God has so done, we must reply: because he has willed it. But if you proceed further to ask why he so willed, you are seeking something greater and higher than God's will, which cannot be found. . . .

To overthrow predestination our opponents also raise the point that, if it stands, all carefulness and zeal for well-doing go to ruin. For who can hear, they say, that either life or death has been appointed for him by God's eternal and unchangeable decree without thinking immediately that it makes no difference how he conducts himself, since God's predestination can neither be hindered nor advanced by his effort? Thus all men will throw themselves away, and in a desperate manner rush headlong wherever lust carries them. Obviously they are not completely lying, for there are many swine that pollute the doctrine of predestination with their foul blasphemies, and by this pretext evade all admonitions and reproofs. God knows what he once for all has determined to do with us: if he has decreed salvation, he will bring us to it in his own time; if he has destined us to death, we would fight against it in vain.

But Scripture, while it requires us to consider this great mystery with so much more reverence and piety, both instructs the godly to a far different attitude and effectively refutes the criminal madness of these men. For Scripture does not speak of predestination with intent to rouse us to boldness that we may try with impious rashness to search out God's unattainable secrets. Rather, its intent is that, humbled and cast down, we may learn to tremble at his judgment and esteem his mercy. It is at this mark that believers aim.

John Calvin, *Institutes of the Christian Religion*, ed. John T. McNeill, Philadelphia: Westminster Press, 1960, pp. 922–60 passim.

Document 14: Castellio's Argument for Toleration

Like the Catholics, the Protestants persecuted and sometimes executed those they considered to be heretics. Sebastian Castellio, a Protestant professor at the University of Basel, was particularly horrified by the execution of the heretic Michael Servetus in Geneva in 1553. As a consequence, Castellio wrote Concerning Heretics Whether They Are to Be Persecuted, *from which the following passage is taken.*

Most Illustrious Prince, suppose you had told your subjects that you would come to them at some uncertain time and had commanded them to make ready to go forth clad in white garments to meet you whenever you might appear. What would you do if, on your return, you discovered that they had taken no thought for the white robes but instead were disputing among themselves concerning your person? Some were saying that you were in France, others that you were in Spain; some that you would come on a horse, others in a chariot; some were asserting that you would appear with a great equipage, others that you would be unattended. Would this please you?

Suppose further that the controversy was being conducted not merely by words but by blows and swords, and that one group wounded and killed the others who did not agree with them. "He will come on a horse," one would say.

"No, in a chariot," another would retort.

"You lie."

"You're the liar. Take that." He punches him.

"And take that in the belly." The other stabs.

Would you, O Prince, commend such citizens? Suppose, however, that some did their duty and followed your command to prepare the white robes, but the others oppressed them on that account and put them to death. Would you not rigorously destroy such scoundrels?

But what if these homicides claimed to have done all this in your name and in accord with your command, even though you had previously expressly forbidden it? Would you not consider that such outrageous conduct deserved to be punished without mercy? Now I beg you, most Illustrious Prince, to be kind enough to hear why I say these things.

Christ is the Prince of this world who on His departure from the earth foretold to men that He would return some day at an uncertain hour, and He commanded them to prepare white robes for His coming; that is to say, that they should live together in a Christian manner, amicably, without controversy and contention, loving one another. But consider now, I beg you, how well we discharge our duty.

How many are there who show the slightest concern to prepare the white robe? Who is there who bends every effort to live in this world in a saintly, just and religious manner in the expectation of the coming of the Lord? For nothing is there so little concern. The true fear of God and charity are fallen and grown cold. Our life is spent in contention and in every manner of sin. . . . Men are puffed up with knowledge or with a false opinion of knowledge and look down upon others. Pride is followed by cruelty and persecution so that now scarcely anyone is able to endure another who differs at all from him. Although opinions are almost as numerous as men, nevertheless there is hardly any sect which does not condemn all others and desire to reign alone. Hence arise banishments, chains, imprisonments, stakes and gallows and this miserable rage to visit daily penalties upon those who differ from the mighty about matters hitherto unknown, for so many centuries disputed, and not yet cleared up.

If, however, there is someone who strives to prepare the white robe, that is, to live justly and innocently, then all others with one accord cry out against him if he differ from them in anything, and they confidently pronounce him a heretic on the ground that he seeks to be justified by works. Horrible crimes of which he never dreamed are attributed to him and the common people are prejudiced by slander until they consider it a crime merely to hear him speak. Hence arises such cruel rage that some are so incensed by calumny as to be infuriated when the victim is first strangled instead of being burned alive at a slow fire.

This is cruel enough, but a more capital offense is added when this conduct is justified under the robe of Christ and is defended as being in accord with His will, when Satan could not devise anything more repugnant to the nature and will of Christ!

Roland Bainton, ed., *The Age of the Reformation*. Malabar, FL: Robert E. Krieger Publishing, 1984, pp. 183–85.

Document 15: Ignatius' "Rules for Thinking with the Church"

Ignatius of Loyola's most influential work is his Spiritual Exercises, *which includes a section called "Rules for Thinking with the Church." These rules were intended to be disseminated to all Catholics, especially those who might come into contact with the Protestant heresy. For Ignatius, the key to right thinking lies in unquestioning submission to the authority of the church and its hierarchy.*

In order to think truly, as we ought, in the Church Militant, the following rules should be observed.

The first: Laying aside all private judgment, we ought to hold our minds prepared and prompt to obey in all things the true Spouse of Christ our Lord, which is our holy Mother, the hierarchical Church.

The second: To praise confession to a priest, and the reception of the Most Holy Sacrament once a year, and much better every month, and much better still every eight days, with the requisite and due conditions.

The third: To praise the frequent hearing of Mass, also chants, psalms, and prolonged prayers both in and out of church; likewise the hours ordained at fixed times for the whole divine office, and for prayer of every kind, and all canonical Hours.

The fourth: To praise greatly Religious Orders, virginity and continency, and matrimony not so much as any of these.

The fifth: To praise vows of Religion, of obedience, of poverty, of chastity, and of other works of perfection and supererogation. . . .

The Sixth: To praise the relics of saints, paying veneration to the relics, and praying to the saints; and to praise likewise stations, pilgrimages, indulgences, jubilees, cruzadas, and candles lighted in churches.

The seventh: To praise the enactments of the Church with regard to fasts and abstinences, as those of Lent, Ember days, Vigils, Fridays, and Saturdays; likewise penances, not only interior but also exterior.

The eighth: To praise the building and adornment of churches; and also images, and to venerate them according to what they represent.

The ninth: To praise in fine all the precepts of the Church, preserving a ready mind to seek reasons for defending her, and in no way impugning her.

The tenth: We ought to be more ready to approve and praise the enactments and recommendation, and also the customs of our superiors; because, although sometimes they may not be or may not have been praise-worthy, still to speak against them, whether in public discourse or before the common people, would give rise to murmurs and scandal, rather than edification; and thus the people would be irritated against their superiors, whether temporal or spiritual. . . .

The eleventh: To praise theology, positive and scholastic. . . .

The twelfth: We ought to guard against making comparisons between ourselves who are now living and the blessed who have passed away, for no slight error is committed in this. . . .

The thirteenth: To arrive at the truth in all things, we ought always to be ready to believe that what seems to us white is black, if the hierarchical Church so defines it. . . .

The fourteenth: Although it is very true that no one can be saved unless he is predestined, and has faith and grace, we must be very careful in our manner of speaking and treating of these subjects.

The fifteenth: We ought not habitually to speak much of predestination; but if sometimes mention should be made of it in any way, we must so speak that the common people may not fall into any error. . . and therewith becoming paralyzed they neglect good works conducive to their salvation, and to the spiritual profit of their souls.

The sixteenth: In the same way we must take heed lest by speaking much and with great earnestness on faith, without any distinction and explanation, occasion be given to become slothful and negligent in good works, whether before faith is formed by charity or after. . . .

Karl H. Dannenfeldt, *The Church of the Renaissance and Reformation*. St. Louis, MO: Concordia, 1970, pp. 137–39.

Document 16: Ignatius' Strategy for Combatting Protestantism

Ignatius of Loyola was painfully aware of the progress of Protestant ideas throughout Europe, and, in the following letter, he proposes some specific measures to combat the Protestant heresy to be taken by the Society of Jesus, or, Jesuits. These strategies are all educational, including the circulation of a condensed summary of Catholic theology, the multiplication of Jesuit schools, and the promotion of Catholic doctrine in pamphlet form.

Seeing the progress which the heretics have made in a short time, spreading the poison of their evil teaching throughout so many countries and peoples, and making use of the verse of the Apostle to describe their progress, 'And their speech spreadeth like a canker', it would seem that our society, having been accepted by Divine Providence among the efficacious means to repair such great damage, should be solicitous to prepare the proper steps, such as are quickly applied and can be widely adopted, thus exerting itself to the utmost of its powers to preserve what is still sound and to restore what has fallen sick of the plague of heresy, especially in the northern nations.

The heretics have made their false theology popular and presented it in a way that is within the capacity of the common people. They preach it to the people and teach it in the schools, and scatter booklets which can be bought and understood by many, and make their influence felt by means of their writings when they cannot do so by their preaching. Their success is largely due to the negligence of those who should have shown some interest; and the bad example and the ignorance of Catholics, especially the clergy, have made such ravages in the vineyard of the Lord. Hence it would seem that our Society should make use of the following means to put a stop and apply a remedy to the evils which have come upon the Church through these heretics.

In the first place, the sound theology which is taught in the universities and seeks its foundation in philosophy, and therefore requires a long time to acquire is adapted only to good and alert minds; and because the weaker ones can be confused and, if they lack foundations, collapse, it would be good to make a summary of theology to deal with topics that are important but not controversial, with great brevity. There could be more detail in matters controversial, but it should be accommodated to the present needs of the people. It should solidly prove dogmas with good arguments from Scripture, tradition, the councils, and the doctors, and refute the contrary teaching. It would not require much time to teach such a theology, since it would not go very deeply into other matters. In this way theologians could be produced in a short time who could take care of the preaching and teaching in many places. The abler students could be given higher courses which include greater detail. Those who do not succeed in these higher courses should be removed from them and put in this shorter course of theology.

The principal conclusion of this theology, in the form of a short catechism, could be taught to children, as the Christian doctrine is now taught, and likewise to the common people who are not too infected or too capable of subtleties. This could also be done with the younger students in the lower classes, where they could learn it by heart. . . .

Another excellent means for helping the Church in this trial would be to multiply the colleges and schools of the society in many lands, especially where a good attendance could be expected. There might possibly be need of a dispensation to accept colleges with a smaller number of students than our Institute demands, or else that classes be accepted without undertaking perpetual charge of a college, if there is among ours, or elsewhere, someone to teach the said theology to the students and preach sound doctrine to the people, which with the administration of the sacraments will promote their spiritual welfare.

Not only in the places where we have a residence, but even in the neighbourhood, the better among our students could be sent to teach the Christian doctrine on Sundays and feast days. Even the extern students, should there be suitable material among them, could be sent by the rector for the same service. Thus, besides the correct doctrine, they would be giving the example of a good life, and by removing every appearance of greed they will be able to refute the strongest argument of the heretics—a bad life, namely, and the ignorance of the Catholic clergy.

The heretics write a large number of booklets and pamphlets, by means of which they aim at taking away all authority from the Catholics, and especially from the society, and set up their false dogmas. It would seem expedient, therefore, that ours here also write answers in pamphlet form, short and well written, so that they can be produced without delay and bought by many. In this way the harm that is being done by the pamphlets of the heretics can be remedied and sound teaching spread. These works should be modest, but lively; they should point out the evil that is abroad and uncover the evil machinations and deceits of the adversaries. A large number of these pamphlets could be gathered into one volume. Care should be taken, however, that this be done by learned men well grounded in theology, who will adapt it to the capacity of the multitude.

With these measures it would seem that we could bring great relief to the Church, and in many places quickly apply a remedy to the beginnings of the evil before the poison has gone so deep that it will be very difficult to remove it from the heart. But we should use the same diligence in healing that the heretics are using in infecting the people. We will have the advantage over them in that we possess a solidly founded, and therefore an enduring, doctrine. . . .

Hans J. Hillerbrand, ed., *The Reformation: A Narrative History Related by Contemporary Observers and Participants*. New York: Harper & Row, 1964, pp. 446–47.

Document 17: The Index of Trent

Because of an exponential increase in the output of printing presses in the sixteenth century, authorities were hard pressed to keep control over their subjects' reading material. One result of the Catholic Council of Trent was the institution of new rules governing the prohibition and censorship of books. The so-called Index of Trent *was published in 1559.*

Rule I

All books which were condemned prior to 1515 by popes or ecumenical councils, and are not listed in this Index, are to stand condemned in the original fashion.

Rule II

Books of arch-heretics—those who after 1515 have invented or incited heresy or who have been or still are heads and leaders of heretics, such as Luther, Zwingli, Calvin, Hubmaier, Schwenckfeld, and the like—whatever their name, title or argumentation—are prohibited without exception. As far as other heretics are concerned, only those books are condemned without exception which deal *ex professo* with religion. Others will be permitted after Catholic theologians have examined and approved them by the order of bishops and inquisitors. Likewise, Catholic books written by those who subsequently fell into heresy or by those who after their lapse returned into the bosom of the Church can be permitted after approval by a theological faculty or the inquisition.

Rule III

Translations of older works, including church fathers, made by condemned authors, are permitted if they contain nothing against sound doctrine. However, translations of books of the Old Testament may be allowed by the judgment of bishops for the use of learned and pious men only. These translations are to elucidate the Vulgate so that Sacred Scripture can be understood, but they are not to be considered as a sacred text. Translations of the New Testament made by authors of the first sections in this Index are not to be used at all, since too little usefulness and too much danger attends such reading.

Rule IV

Since experience teaches that, if the reading of the Holy Bible in the vernacular is permitted generally without discrimination, more damage than advantage will result because of the boldness of men, the judgment of bishops and inquisitors is to serve as guide in this regard. Bishops and inquisitors may, in accord with the counsel of the local priest and confessor, allow Catholic translations of the Bible to be read by those of whom they realize that such reading will not lead to the detriment but to the increase of faith and piety. The permission is to be given in writing. Whoever reads or has such a translation in his possession without this permission cannot be absolved from his sins until he has turned in these Bibles.

Hans J. Hillerbrand, ed., *The Reformation: A Narrative History Related by Contemporary Observers and Participants*. New York: Harper & Row, 1964, pp. 474–75.

Document 18: Teresa of Avila Explains Her Motives

One of the most celebrated figures of sixteenth-century Catholicism is the Spanish mystic Teresa of Avila. Though Teresa was sometimes incapacitated by her meditations and mystical experiences, she was also industrious in founding new convents for her order, and she had serious concern for both the physical and spiritual well-being of her charges. One of her deepest motives to action was her aversion to the Protestant heresy.

When this convent was originally founded, for the reasons set down in the book which, as I say, I have already written, and also because of certain wonderful revelations by which the Lord showed me how well He would be served in this house, it was not my intention that there should be so much austerity in external matters, nor that it should have no regular income: on the contrary, I should have liked there to be no possibility of want. I acted, in short, like the weak and wretched woman that I am, although I did so with good intentions and not out of consideration for my own comfort.

At about this time there came to my notice the harm and havoc that were being wrought in France by these Lutherans and the way in which their unhappy sect was increasing. This troubled me very much, and, as though I could do anything, or be of any help in the matter, I wept before the Lord and entreated Him to remedy this great evil. I felt that I would have laid down a thousand lives to save a single one of all the souls that were being lost there. And, seeing that I was a woman, and a sinner, and incapable of doing all I should like in the Lord's service, and as my whole yearning was, and still is, that, as He has so many enemies and so few friends, these last should be trusty ones, I determined to do the little that was in me—namely, to follow the evangelical counsels as perfectly as I could, and to see that these few nuns who are here should do the same, confiding in the great goodness of God, Who never fails to help those who resolve to forsake everything for His sake. As they are all that I have ever painted them as being in my desires, I hoped that their virtues would more than counteract my defects, and I should thus be able to give the Lord some pleasure, and all of us, by busying ourselves in prayer for those who are defenders of the Church, and for the preachers and learned men who defend her, should do everything we could to aid this Lord of mine Who is so much oppressed by those to whom He has shown so much good that it seems as though these traitors would send Him to the Cross again and that He would have nowhere to lay His head.

Oh, my Redeemer, my heart cannot conceive this without being sorely distressed! What has become of Christians now? Must those who owe Thee most always be those who distress Thee? Those to whom Thou doest the greatest kindnesses, whom Thou dost choose for Thy friends, among whom Thou dost move, communicating Thyself to them through the Sacraments? Do they not think, *Lord of my soul*, that they have made Thee endure more than sufficient torments?

It is certain, my Lord, that in these days withdrawal from the world means no sacrifice at all. Since worldly people have so little respect for Thee, what can we expect them to have for us? Can it be that we deserve that they should treat us any better than they have treated Thee? Have we done more for them than Thou hast done that they should be friendly to us? What then? What can we expect—we who, through the goodness of the Lord, are free from that pestilential infection, and do not, like those others, belong to the devil? They have won severe punishment at his hands and their pleasures have richly earned them eternal fire. So to eternal fire they will have to go, though none the less it breaks my heart to see so many souls travelling to perdition. I would the evil were not so great and I did not see more being lost every day.

St. Teresa of Avila, *Way of Perfection*, tr. E. Allison Peers, London: Sheed and Ward, 1977, pp. 3–4.

Glossary

adiaphora: Literally, "things indifferent"; for Protestants, these are religious matters that lack definitive support in the Bible and, thus, are open to interpretation.

ad fontes: Literally, "to the sources"; one of the rallying cries of the scholarly humanist movement, involving a return to the original sources of ancient texts in their original languages.

anabaptism: The large but diverse movement of radical Protestants that broke away from both Zwingli and Luther; fundamental premises include the rejection of infant baptism and rejection of church-state cooperation.

anticlericalism: The widespread critique of ignorance and immorality among the Catholic clergy, a critique that preceded the Reformation but became an integral part of it.

church fathers: Interpreters of the Bible and Christian thought from the first centuries, not including the original apostles; St. Jerome was a major influence on the humanist scholar Erasmus, while Luther and Calvin found St. Augustine particularly illuminating.

cuius regio, eius religio: Literally, "whose region, his religion"; this principle reflected the fact that a particular denomination could not survive unless it was the religion of the ruler of that territory; most Christians believed in the principle of one religion per country.

erastianism: The view that the church should be under the control of the state.

indulgences: Writs of indulgence were originally provided to excuse repentant sinners from various acts of penance; they came to be exchanged for monetary considerations, giving the illusion that they could be "bought."

laity: All members of the church not in religious orders or part of the church hierarchy.

Pelagianism: The view that people play an active and significant role in meriting, even earning, their own salvation.

penance: For Catholics, the state of repentance in which the contrite sinner demonstrates genuine repentance through actions such as the repetition of prayers or a pilgrimage. For Protestants, penance is completed through inward repentance, without further acts.

predestination: The view that all people are destined for either heaven or hell, and individual destinies have always been known; this doctrine is a logical outcome of the ideas of divine providence and the omnipotence of God.

sacraments: The church services or rites believed to have been established by Jesus himself; Catholics extrapolated seven sacraments from the Bible; Protestants held to only two, baptism and the eucharist (observance of the last supper).

sola fides: Literally, "by faith alone"; one of the fundamental doctrines of Protestantism contending that salvation comes only through faith rather than through good works.

sola scriptura: Literally, "by Scripture alone"; the Protestant doctrine that the Bible is the supreme authority for beliefs and practices of the church.

vernacular bibles: Translations of the Bible into the spoken languages of Europe; these translations took the place of the Vulgate Bible in Protestant areas.

Vulgate Bible: The Latin translation of the Bible, largely derived from St. Jerome, and taken definitively by the Catholic Church; Erasmus pointed out many inaccurate translations in the early sixteenth century.

Chronology

ca. 1450 Johann Gutenberg introduces the use of moveable type; printing presses multiply across Europe

1453 Fall of Constantinople to the Turks; migration of many Greek-speaking scholars begins toward the West

1483 Birth of Martin Luther

1484 Birth of Ulrich Zwingli

1492 Columbus discovers America

1509 Publication of Erasmus's *Praise of Folly*; Henry VIII accedes to the throne in England; birth of John Calvin

1512 Luther lectures on the Bible at the University of Wittenberg

1513 Publication of Machiavelli's *The Prince*

1516 Publication of Thomas More's *Utopia*; publication of Erasmus's *New Testament* in Greek

1517 Luther posts his ninety-five theses on indulgences in Wittenberg

1519 Charles V elected emperor of the Holy Roman Empire (the affiliated principalities of Germany)

1520 Luther publishes his three treatises of reformation: *Address to the German Nobility*, *The Babylonian Captivity of the Church*, and *The Freedom of a Christian*; Luther publicly burns a papal bull in defiance of Rome

1521 The Diet of Worms; Luther refuses to recant any of his opinions and is excommunicated from the church

1522 Luther makes first translation of the New Testament into German

1524–1525 Peasants' Revolt in Germany is crushed by the nobility; Luther and Erasmus publicly clash in debate over the issue of free will

1525 Anabaptism becomes a prominent movement; persecution of it begins; William Tyndale makes first translation of New Testament into English; Luther marries Catherine von Bora, a former nun

1529 Split between Luther and Zwingli

1530 The Augsburg Confession of Faith

1531 Death of Zwingli in battle against Catholic forces in Switzerland

1534 The Affair of the Placards; repression of Protestants in France

1534–1535 The radical Anabaptist uprising at Münster in Germany

1536 Calvin's *Institutes of the Christian Religion* is published; he settles in Geneva, Switzerland

1540 Order of the Society of Jesus (the Jesuits) approved by the pope

1545–1547 Council of Trent, first session

1546 Death of Luther; religious fighting breaks out in Germany

1547 Death of Henry VIII in England; accession of the Protestant Edward VI

1555 The Peace of Augsburg; a truce between the pope and Lutherans securing freedom of worship for the free cities of Germany

1562–1593 Religious wars in France

1564 Death of Calvin; birth of William Shakespeare

For Further Research

Reference

Hans J. Hillerbrand et al, eds., *The Oxford Encyclopedia of the Reformation*. Oxford: Oxford University Press, 1995.

Histories of Christianity

John Bossy, *Christianity in the West: 1400–1700*. Oxford: Oxford University Press, 1985.

Tim Dowley, et al, eds., *Eerdmans' Handbook to the History of Christianity*. Grand Rapids, MI: Eerdmans, 1977.

Clyde L. Manshreck, *A History of Christianity in the World*. 2nd ed., Englewood Cliffs, NJ: Prentice-Hall, 1985.

Bruce L. Shelley, *Church History in Plain Language*. Updated 2nd ed., Dallas: Word Publishing, 1995.

Collections of Original Documents of the Reformation

Roland H. Bainton, ed., *The Age of Reformation*. Malabar, FL: Robert E. Krieger Publishing, 1984 (rpt. of 1956 ed.).

Michael G. Baylor, ed. and tr., *The Radical Reformation*. Cambridge: Cambridge University Press, 1991.

John Calvin, *Institutes of the Christian Religion*, tr. John T. McNeill. Philadelphia: Westminster Press, 1960.

John Dillenberger, ed., *Martin Luther: Selections from his Writings*. Garden City, NY: Doubleday & Company, 1961.

John P. Dolan, ed., *The Essential Erasmus*. New York: New American Library, 1964.

G.R. Elton, ed., *Renaissance and Reformation: 1300–1648*. 3rd ed. (enlarged), New York: Macmillan, 1976.

Hans J. Hillerbrand, ed. *The Protestant Reformation*. New York: Walker and Company, 1968.

———, *The Reformation: A Narrative History Related By Contemporary Observers and Participants*. New York: Harper & Row, 1964.

Martin Luther, *Three Treatises*. Philadelphia: Fortress Press, 1943.

Lewis W. Spitz, ed., *The Protestant Reformation*. Englewood Cliffs, NJ: Prentice-Hall, 1966.

George Huntsdon Williams and Angel M. Mergal, eds., *Spiritual and Anabaptist Writers: Documents Illustrative of the Radical Reformation*. Philadelphia: Westminster Press, 1957.

General Histories of the Reformation

Roland H. Bainton, *The Reformation of the Sixteenth Century*. Boston: Beacon Press, 1952.

Euan Cameron, *The European Reformation*. Oxford: Clarendon Press, 1991.

Owen Chadwick, *The Reformation*. Harmondsworth: Penguin Books, Ltd., 1964.

Karl H. Dannenfeldt, *The Church of the Renaissance and Reformation*. St. Louis: Concordia Publishing House, 1970.

A.G. Dickens, *Reformation and Society in Sixteenth-Century Europe*. London: Harcourt, Brace & World, 1966.

Harold J. Grimm, *The Reformation Era: 1500–1650*. 2nd ed., New York: Macmillan, 1973.

E. Harris Harbison, *The Age of Reformation*. Ithaca, NY: Cornell University Press, 1955.

Hans J. Hillerbrand, *The World of the Reformation*. New York: Charles Scribner's Sons, 1973.

De Lamar Jensen, *Reformation Europe: Age of Reform and Revolution*. Lexington, MA: D.C. Heath and Co., 1981.

Carter Lindberg, *The European Reformations*. Oxford: Blackwell Publishers, 1996.

J. Russell Major, *The Age of the Renaissance and Reformation*. Philadelphia: J.B. Lippincott Company, 1970.

Charles G. Nauert Jr., *The Age of Renaissance and Reformation*. Lanham, MD: University Press of America, 1981.

Steven Ozment, *The Age of Reform: 1250–1550*. New Haven, CT: Yale University Press, 1980.

Eugene F. Rice Jr., *The Foundations of Early Modern Europe: 1460–1559*. New York: W.W. Norton & Co., 1970.

Lewis W. Spitz, *The Protestant Reformation: 1517–1559*. New York: Harper & Row, 1985.

Bard Thompson, *Humanists and Reformers: A History of the Renaissance and Reformation*. Grand Rapids, MI: Eerdmans, 1996.

Social and Intellectual Contexts of the Reformation

Natalie Zemon Davis, *Society and Culture in Early Modern France.* Stanford: Stanford University Press, 1976.

Mark U. Edwards Jr., *Printing, Propaganda, and Martin Luther.* Berkeley: University of California Press, 1994.

Elizabeth L. Eisenstein, *The Printing Revolution in Early Modern Europe.* Cambridge: Cambridge University Press, 1983.

Carlo Ginzburg, *The Cheese and the Worms: The Cosmos of a Sixteenth-Century Miller.* New York: Penguin, 1982.

Joel Hurstfield, ed., *The Reformation Crisis.* London: Edward Arnold, 1965.

Sherrin Marshall, ed., *Women in Reformation and Counter-Reformation Europe: Public and Private Worlds.* Bloomington, IN: Indiana University Press, 1989.

Alister E. McGrath, *Reformation Thought: An Introduction.* 2nd ed., Oxford: Basil Blackwell, Ltd., 1993.

Steven Ozment, *Protestants: The Birth of a Revolution.* New York: Doubleday, 1991.

———, *When Fathers Ruled: Family Life in Reformation Europe.* Cambridge, MA: Harvard University Press, 1983.

The Progress of Protestantism

Claus-Peter Clasen, *Anabaptism: A Social History, 1525–1618.* Ithaca, NY: Cornell University Press, 1972.

Patrick Collinson, *The Elizabethan Puritan Movement.* Berkeley: University of California Press, 1967.

A.G. Dickens, *The English Reformation.* 2nd ed., London: B.T. Batsford, Ltd., 1989.

John T. McNeill, *The History and Character of Calvinism.* Oxford: Oxford University Press, 1954.

Andrew Pettegree, Alastair Duke, and Gillian Lewis, eds., *Calvinism in Europe 1540–1620.* Cambridge: Cambridge University Press, 1994.

George H. Williams, *The Radical Reformation.* 3rd ed. Kirksville, MO: Sixteenth Century Journal Publishers, 1992.

The Catholic Reformation

Louis Chatellier, *The Europe of the Devout: The Catholic Reformation and the Formation of a New Society.* Cambridge: Cambridge University Press, 1989.

W.W. Meissner, *Ignatius of Loyola: The Psychology of a Saint.* New Haven, CT: Yale University Press, 1992.

Michael Mullett, *The Counter-Reformation and the Catholic Reformation in Early Modern Europe.* London: Methuen, 1984.

John C. Olin, *The Catholic Reformation: Savonarola to Ignatius Loyola.* New York: Fordham University Press, 1992.

John W. O'Malley, *The First Jesuits.* Cambridge, MA: Harvard University Press, 1993.

Studies of Major Protestant Figures

Roland H. Bainton, *Here I Stand: A Life of Martin Luther.* New York: Mentor, 1957.

William J. Bouwsma, *John Calvin: A Sixteenth-Century Portrait.* New York: Oxford University Press, 1988.

Brian A. Gerrish, *Reformers in Profile: Advocates of Reform 1300–1600.* Philadelphia: Fortress, 1967.

Eric W. Gritsch, *Martin—God's Court Jester: Luther in Retrospect.* Philadelphia: Fortress, 1983.

James M. Kittelson, *Luther the Reformer: The Story of the Man and his Career.* Minneapolis: Augsburg Publishing House, 1986.

Bernhard Lohse, *Martin Luther: An Introduction to his Life and Work.* Philadelphia: Fortress, 1986.

Alister E. McGrath, *A Life of John Calvin: A Study in the Shaping of Western Culture.* Oxford: Blackwell, 1990.

T.H.L. Parker, *Calvin: An Introduction to his Thought.* Louisville, KY: Westminster/John Knox Press, 1995.

G.R. Potter, *Zwingli.* Cambridge: Cambridge University Press, 1976.

W.P. Stephens, *Zwingli: An Introduction to his Thought.* Oxford: Clarendon, 1992.

Index